UNDERSTANDING PUBLIC POLICY

UNDERSTANDING PUBLIC POLICY

THOMAS R. DYE

PRENTICE-HALL, INC., ENGLEWOOD CLIFFS, NEW JERSEY

© 1972 by Prentice-Hall, Inc., Englewood Cliffs, New Jersey

ISBN: 0-13-936187-1

Library of Congress Catalog Card Number: 71-173427

10   9   8   7   6   5   4   3

PRINTED IN THE UNITED STATES OF AMERICA

PRENTICE-HALL INTERNATIONAL, INC., LONDON
PRENTICE-HALL OF AUSTRALIA, PTY. LTD., SYDNEY
PRENTICE-HALL OF CANADA LTD., TORONTO
PRENTICE-HALL OF INDIA PRIVATE LIMITED, NEW DELHI
PRENTICE-HALL OF JAPAN, INC., TOKYO

CONTENTS

v

CHAPTER 6

POVERTY: The Search for a Rational Strategy   111

CHAPTER 7

EDUCATION: The Group Struggle   131

CHAPTER 8

URBAN AFFAIRS: Institutional Forces
and Public Policy   161

CHAPTER 9

PRIORITIES AND PRICE TAGS: An Analysis of Government Spending   185

CHAPTER 10

BUDGETS AND TAXES: Incrementalism At Work   205

CHAPTER 11

INPUTS, OUTPUTS, AND BLACK BOXES: A Systems Analysis of State Policies   231

CHAPTER 12

THE POLICY-MAKING PROCESS: Getting Inside the System   265

CHAPTER 13

POLICY IMPACT: Finding Out What Happens After a Law is Passed   291

PREFACE

If this book has a thesis, it is that political science can be "relevant" to public policy questions without abandoning its commitment to scientific inquiry; that social relevance does not require us to reject systematic analysis in favor of rhetoric, polemics, or activism; that knowledge about the forces shaping public policy and the consequences of policy decisions is socially relevant.

This volume is concerned with "who gets what" in American politics and, more important, "why" and "what difference it makes." We are concerned not only with *what* policies governments pursue, but also *why* governments pursue the policies they do, and *what* the consequences of these policies are.

Political science, like other scientific disciplines, has developed a number of concepts and models to help describe and explain political life. These models are not really competitive in the sense that any one could be judged "best." Each focuses on separate elements of politics and each helps us to understand different things about political life.

We begin with a brief description of six analytic models in political science and the potential contribution of each of them to the study of public policy. They are:

> the systems model,
> the elite-mass model,
> the group model,
> the rational model,
> the incremental model, and
> the institutional model.

We then attempt to describe and explain public policy by the use of these various analytic models. The reader is not only informed about public policy in a variety of key domestic policy areas but, more important, he is encouraged to utilize these conceptual models in political science to explain the causes and consequences of public policies in these areas. The policy areas studied are:

> civil rights,
> violence and repression,
> welfare and social security,
> antipoverty and economic opportunity,
> education,
> urban affairs and housing,
> government spending,
> budgeting and taxing,
> state and local spending and services.

Most public policies are a combination of rational planning, incrementalism, group activity, elite preferences, systematic forces, and institutional influences. Throughout this volume we employ these models, both singly and in combination, to describe and explain public policy. However, certain chapters rely more on one model than another.

Any of these policy areas might be studied profitably by employing more than one model. Frequently our selection of a particular analytic model to study a specific policy area was based as much upon pedagogical considerations as anything else. We simply wanted to demonstrate how political scientists employ analytical models. Once the reader is familiarized with the nature and uses of analytic models in political science, he may find it interesting to explore the utility of models other than the ones selected by the author in the explanation of particular policy outcomes.

Each chapter concludes with a series of propositions, which are derived from one or more analytic models, and which attempt to summarize the policies discussed. The purposes of these summaries are to suggest the kinds of policy explanations which can be derived from analytic models and to tie the policy material back to one or another of our models.

In short, this volume is not only an introduction to the study of public policy, but also an introduction to the models political scientists use to describe and explain political life.

THOMAS R. DYE
Florida State University

UNDERSTANDING PUBLIC POLICY

POLICY ANALYSIS:
the thinking man's response to demands for relevance

CHAPTER 1

POLICY ANALYSIS IN POLITICAL SCIENCE

This book is about public policy. It is concerned with what governments do, why they do it, and what difference it makes. It is also about political science and the ability of this academic discipline to describe, analyze, and explain public policy.

Public policy is whatever governments choose to do or not to do. More elaborate definitions of public policy are found in the literature, of course, but on examination they seem to boil down to the same thing. David Easton defines public policy as "the authoritative allocation of values for the whole society" [1]—but it turns out that only the government can "authoritatively" act on the "whole" society, and everything the government chooses to do or not to do results in the "allocation of values." Lasswell and Kaplan define policy as "a projected program of goals, values, and practices," and Carl Friedrich says that "It is essential for the policy concept that there be a goal, objective, or purpose." [2] These definitions imply a difference between specific

[1] David Easton, *The Political System* (New York: Alfred A. Knopf, 1953), p. 129.
[2] Harold D. Lasswell and Abraham Kaplan, *Power and Society* (New Haven: Yale University Press, 1970), p. 71: and Carl J. Friedrich, *Man and His Government* (New York: McGraw Hill, 1963), p. 70.

government actions and an overall program of action toward a given goal. The problem, however, in insisting that government actions must have *goals* in order to be labeled "policy" is that we can never be sure whether or not a particular action has a goal. We generally assume that if a government chooses to do something there must be a goal, objective, or purpose, but all we can really observe is what governments choose to do or not to do. Realistically, our notion of public policy must include *all* actions of government—and not just stated intentions of governments or government officials. Finally, we must also consider government inaction—what a government chooses not to do—as public policy. Obviously government inaction can have as great an impact on society as government action.[3]

Governments do many things: they regulate conflict within society; they organize society to carry on conflict with other societies; they distribute a great variety of symbolic rewards and material services to members of the society; and they extract money from society, most often in the form of taxes. Thus, public policies may be regulative, organizational, distributive, or extractive—or all of these things at once.

Public policies may deal with a wide variety of substantive areas —defense, foreign policies, education, welfare, police, highways, taxation, housing, social security, health, economic opportunity, urban development, inflation and recession, and so on. They may range from the vital to the trivial—from the allocation of tens of billions of dollars for an anti-ballistic missile system to the designation of an official national bird.

Public policy is not a new concern of political science: the earliest writings of political philosophers reveal an interest in the policies pursued by governments, the forces shaping these policies, and the impact of these policies on society. Yet the major focus of attention of political science has never really been on policies themselves, but rather on the institutions and structures of government and on the political behaviors and processes associated with policy making.

"Traditional" political science focused its attention primarily on the institutional structure and philosophical justification of government. This involved the study of: constitutional arrangements, such as federalism, separation of power, and judicial review; powers and duties of official bodies, such as Congress, President, and Courts; intergovernmental relations; and the organization and operation of legislative, executive, and judicial agencies. Traditional studies described the *institutions* in which public policy was formulated. But unfortunately the linkages between important institutional arrangements and the content of public policy were largely unexplored.

Modern *"behavioral"* political science focused its attention primarily on the processes and behaviors associated with government. This

[3] See Peter Bachrach and Martin Baratz, "Decisions and Non-decisions," *American Political Science Review*, Vol. 57 (September 1963), 632-42.

involved the study of the sociological and psychological bases of individual and group political behavior; the determinants of voting and other political activities; the functioning of interest groups and political parties; and the description of various processes and behaviors in the legislative executive and judicial arenas. While this approach described the *processes* by which public policy was determined, it did not deal directly with the linkages between various processes and behaviors and the content of public policy.

Today the focus of political science is shifting to *public policy*—to the *description and explanation of the causes and consequences of government activity.* This involves a description of the content of public policy; an assessment of the impact of environmental forces on the content of public policy; an analysis of the effect of various institutional arrangements and political processes on public policy; an inquiry into the consequences of various public policies for the political system; and an evaluation of the impact of public policies on society, both in terms of expected and unexpected consequences. For example: What is the impact of war and depression on the growth of government activity? What are the real priorities among defense and domestic policy needs, and what forces affect the determination of priorities? What forces operate to maintain the status quo in government's programs and policies, and what forces operate to induce change? What is the effect of economic growth on government taxing and spending? What is the effect of public opinion on laws relating to capital punishment, gun control, abortion, and civil rights? What is the impact of racial and religious group activity on the allocation of public monies to schools and colleges? How do differences in community power structures affect local policies on school desegregation? What are the consequences for ghetto blacks of laws prohibiting discrimination in the sale or rental of housing? Does greater party competition and increased voter participation bring about more liberal policies in welfare, health, or education? Will a guaranteed minimum income for all American families reduce or increase joblessness and social dependency? Can black students in ghetto schools receive a quality education through improvements in their neighborhood schools, or must they be bussed out of the ghetto environment for an equal educational opportunity? Who gains and who loses from the present distribution of tax burdens and expenditure benefits? Will reforms in governmental organizations result in any significant alleviation of urban problems—blight, pollution, congestion, crime, or fiscal crisis? What are the political consequences of establishing federally funded community action programs to fight poverty? Does it make any differences in the content of public policy whether Democrats or Republicans win control of government? Does violence bring about change in public policy, and if so, in what direction? These are the *kinds* of questions which can be dealt with in policy analysis.

WHY STUDY PUBLIC POLICY?

Why should political science devote greater attention to the study of public policy? First of all, public policy can be studied for purely *scientific reasons:* to gain an understanding of the causes and consequences of policy decisions improves our knowledge about society. Public policy can be viewed as a *dependent variable,* and we can ask what environmental forces and political system characteristics operate to shape the content of policy. Or public policy can be viewed as an *independent variable,* and we can ask what impact public policy has on the environment and the political system. By asking such questions we can improve our understanding of the linkages between environmental forces, political processes, and public policy. An understanding of these linkages contributes to the breadth, significance, reliability, and theoretical development of social science generally.

Public policy can also be studied for *professional reasons:* an understanding of the causes and consequences of public policy permits us to apply social science knowledge to the solution of practical problems. Presumably, if we know something about the forces shaping public policy and the consequences of specific policies, then we are in a better position to know how individuals, groups, or governments can act to achieve their goals. Factual knowledge is a prerequisite to prescribing for the ills of society. If certain end values are desired, then the question of what policies would best implement these ends if a factual question requiring scientific study. Likewise, if certain policies are desired, then the question of what environmental forces or political system characteristics would facilitate the development of these policies is also a factual question requiring scientific study. In other words, policy studies can produce professional advice, in terms of "if . . . , then . . ." statements, about how to achieve desired goals.

Finally, public policy can be studied for *political purposes:* to insure that the nation adopts the "right" policies to achieve the "right" goals. It is frequently argued that political science cannot be silent or impotent in the face of great social and political crises, and that political scientists have a moral obligation to advance specific public policies. An exclusive focus on institutions, processes, or behaviors, is frequently looked upon as "dry," "irrelevant," and "amoral," because it does not direct attention to the really important policy questions facing American society. Policy studies can be undertaken not only for scientific and professional purposes but also to inform political discussion, advance the level of political awareness, and improve the quality of public policy. Of course, these are very subjective purposes —Americans do not always agree on what constitutes the "right" policies or the "right" goals—but we will assume that knowledge is preferable to ignorance, even in politics.

POLICY ANALYSIS AND POLICY ADVOCACY

Whether one chooses to study public policy for scientific, professional, or political reasons, it is important to distinguish *policy analysis* from *policy advocacy*. *Explaining* the causes and conse-

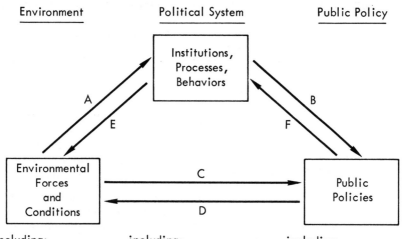

Linkage A: The effect of environmental forces and conditions on political and governmental institutions, processes, and behaviors.
Linkage B: The effect of political and governmental institutions, processes, and behaviors on public policies.
Linkage C: The effect of environmental forces and conditions on public policies.
Linkage D: The effect (feedback) of public policies on environmental forces and conditions.
Linkage E: The effect (feedback) of political and governmental institutions, processes, and behaviors on environmental forces and conditions.
Linkage F: The effect (feedback) of public policies on political and governmental institutions, processes, and behaviors.

FIG. 1-1 LINKAGES IN POLICY ANALYSIS

quences of various policies is not equivalent to prescribing what policies governments ought to pursue. Learning *why* governments do what they do and what the consequences of their actions are is not the same as saying what governments *ought* to do, or bringing about changes in what they do. Policy advocacy requires the skills of rhetoric, persuasion, organization, and activism. Policy analysis encourages scholars and students to attack critical policy issues with the tools of systematic inquiry. There is an implied assumption in policy analysis that developing scientific knowledge about the forces shaping public policy and the consequences of policy designs is itself a socially relevant activity, and that such analysis is a prerequisite to prescription, advocacy, and activism. In short, policy analysis might be labeled the "thinking man's response" to demands that social science become more "relevant" to the problems of our society.

Specifically, *policy analysis* involves:

1. *A primary concern with explanation rather than prescription.* Policy recommendations—if they are made at all—are subordinate to description and explanation. There is an implicit judgment that understanding is a prerequisite to prescription, and that understanding is best achieved through careful analysis rather than rhetoric or polemics.

2. *A rigorous search for the causes and consequences of public policies.* This search involves the use of scientific standards of inference. Sophisticated quantitative techniques may be helpful in establishing valid inferences about causes and consequences, but they are not really essential.

3. *An effort to develop and test general propositions about the causes and consequences of public policy and to accumulate reliable research findings of general relevance.* The object is to develop general theories about public policy which are reliable and which apply to different governmental agencies and different policy areas. Policy analysts clearly prefer to develop explanations which fit more than one policy decision or case study—explanations which stand up over time in a variety of settings.

Policy analysis contrasts with many of the currently popular approaches to policy questions—rhetoric, rap sessions, dialogue, confrontation, or direct action. Policy analysis offers the serious student an approach to society's problems which is both scientific and relevant. The insistence on explanation as a prerequisite to prescription, the use of scientific standards of inference, and the search for reliability and generality of knowledge, can hardly be judged "irrelevant" when these ideas are applied to important policy questions.

POLICY ANALYSIS IN ACTION—THE COLEMAN REPORT AND AMERICAN EDUCATION

One of the more interesting examples of policy analysis in recent years is the influential report on American education by James S. Coleman, *Equality of Educational Opportunity*, frequently referred to as the "Coleman Report." [4] The Coleman Report dealt primarily with the linkage between educational policy and the aspiration and achievement levels of pupils (roughly speaking, Linkage D on Figure 1-1). While Coleman's study is not without its critics,[5] it is nonetheless the most comprehensive analysis of the American public school system ever made. The Coleman Report was eighteen months in the making; it cost $2 million to produce; and it included data on 600,000 children, 60,000 teachers, and 4,000 schools. This report, and the reaction to it, can help us to understand both the problems and possibilities of systematic policy analysis.

The results of Coleman's study undermined much of the conventional wisdom about the impact of public educational policies on student learning and achievement. Prior to the study, legislators, teachers, school administrators, school board members, and the public generally, assumed that factors such as the number of pupils in the classroom, the amount of money spent on each pupil, library and laboratory facilities, teachers' salaries, the quality of the curriculum and other characteristics of the school, affected the quality of education and educational opportunity. But systematic analysis revealed that these factors had *no* significant effect on student learning or achievement. "Differences in school facilities and curriculum . . . are so little related to differences in achievement levels of students that, with few exceptions, their effects fail to appear even in a survey of this magnitude." Moreover, learning was found to be unaffected by the presence or absence of a "track system," ability grouping, guidance counseling, or other standard educational programs. Even the size of the class was found to be unrelated to learning, although educationists had asserted the importance of this factor for decades. Finally, the Coleman study reported that the quality of teaching was not a

---

[4] James S. Coleman, *Equality of Educational Opportunity* (Washington, D.C.: Government Printing Office, 1966).
[5] For reviews of the Coleman Report, see Robert A. Dentler, "Equality of Educational Opportunity: A Special Review," *The Urban Review* (December 1966); Christopher Jenks, "Education: The Racial Gap," *The New Republic* (October 1, 1966); James K. Kent, "The Coleman Report: Opening Pandora's Box," *Phi Delta Kappan* (January 1968); James S. Coleman, "Educational Dilemmas: Equal Schools or Equal Students," *The Public Interest* (Summer 1966); James S. Coleman, "Toward Open Schools," *The Public Interest* (Fall 1967); and a special issue devoted to educational opportunity of *Harvard Educational Review*, Vol. 38 (Winter 1968).

very significant factor in student achievement compared to family and peer group influences. In short, the things that "everybody knew" about education turned out not to be so!

The only factors that were found to affect a student's learning to any significant degree were his family background and the family background of his fellow students. Family background affected the child's verbal abilities and attitudes toward education, and these factors correlated very closely with scholastic achievement. Of secondary but considerable significance were the verbal abilities and attitudes toward education of the child's classmates. Peer-group influence had its greatest impact on children from lower-class families. Teaching excellence mattered very little to children from upper- and middle-class backgrounds; they learned well despite mediocre or poor teaching. Children from lower-class families were slightly more affected by teacher quality.

Coleman also found that schools serving black pupils in this nation were not physically inferior to schools serving predominately white student bodies. In the South, in fact, black schools were somewhat newer than white schools. Black teachers have about the same education and teaching experiences as white teachers, and their pay is equal. Black teachers, however, score lower than white teachers on verbal tests, and their morale was reported to be lower than that of white teachers.

Reanalyzing Coleman's data for the U.S. Civil Rights Commission, Thomas F. Pettigrew and others found that black students attending predominately black schools had lower achievement scores and lower levels of aspiration than black students *with comparable family backgrounds* who attended predominately white schools.[6] When black students attending predominately white schools were compared with black students attending predominately black schools, the average difference in levels of achievement amounted to more than *two grade levels.* On the other hand, achievement levels of white students in classes nearly half black in composition were *not* any lower than those of white students in all-white schools. Finally, special programs to raise achievement levels in predominately black schools were found to have no lasting effect.

The Coleman Report made no policy recommendations. But, like a great deal of policy research, policy recommendations can easily be implied from its conclusions. First of all, if the Coleman Report is correct, it seems pointless to simply pour more money into the present system of public education—raising per pupil expenditures, increasing teachers' salaries, lowering the number of pupils per classroom, providing better libraries and laboratories, adding educational frills,

---

[6] U.S. Commission on Civil Rights, *Racial Isolation in the Public Schools*, 2 vols. (Washington, D.C.: Government Printing Office, 1967).

or adopting any specific curricula innovations. These policies were found to have no significant impact on learning.

The findings of the Coleman Report are particularly important for Title I of the Elementary and Secondary Education Act of 1965 (see Chapter 9). This piece of Congressional legislation authorized a billion-dollar-plus per year assistance for "poverty impacted" schools. The purpose of this program was to remedy learning problems of disadvantaged children by increased spending for special remedial programs. But the Coleman Report implies that compensatory programs have little educational value. They may have symbolic value for ghetto residents, or political value for officeholders who seek to establish an image of concern for the underprivileged, but they are of little educational value for children.

The U.S. Commission on Civil Rights used the Coleman Report to buttress its policy proposals to end racial imbalance in public schools in both the North and the South. Inasmuch as money, facilities, and compensatory programs have little effect on a student learning, and inasmuch as the socioeconomic background of the student's *classmates* does affect his learning, it seemed reasonable to argue that the assignment of lower class black students to predominately middle-class white schools would be the only way to improve educational opportunities for ghetto children. Moreover, since the findings indicated that the achievement levels of middle-class white students were unaffected by blacks in the classroom (as long as blacks were less than a majority), the Commission concluded that assigning ghetto blacks to predominately white schools would not adversely affect the learning of white pupils. Hence, the Commission called for an end to neighborhood schools and the bussing of black and white children to racially balanced schools.

President Nixon's Special Assistant for Urban Affairs, Daniel P. Moynihan, declared:

> Because race is the single most inclusive (although not, of course, complete) determinant of class . . . I will argue that Coleman's data represent the most important demonstration of the absolute necessity of racial integration in education that has ever been assembled. He has shown that the achievement of lower-class students is raised when they are included in a predominately middle-class school, and that the corresponding achievement of middle-class students is not thereby lowered. The evidence is that if we are going to produce equality of educational opportunity in the United States in this generation, we must do so by sending Negro students, and other minority students as well, to majority white schools.[7]

[7] Daniel P. Moynihan, "Education and the Urban Poor," lecture delivered to the Harvard Club of New York City, February, 1967; cited by James K. Kent in "The Coleman Report: Opening Pandora's Box," p. 243.

Professor Coleman himself did not believe that integration was the only answer, despite the data, and later urged that educators continue to search for other means to increase the achievement levels of disadvantaged black children. Other commentators noted that Coleman never tested for the effects of *drastically* reduced classroom size (6-8 pupils for example), nor was the impact of teaching quality fully explored (using measures other than experience, degrees, training, etc.).[8]

The reaction of professional educators was largely one of silence. Perhaps they hoped the Coleman Report would disappear into history without significantly affecting the long-standing assumptions about the importance of money, facilities, classroom size, teacher training, and curricula. Perhaps they hoped that subsequent research would refute Coleman's findings. Daniel P. Moynihan writes:

> The whole rationale of American public education came very near to crashing down, and would have done so had there not been a seemingly general agreement to act as if the report had not occurred. But it had, and public education will not now be the same. The relations between resource input and educational output, which all school systems, all legislatures, all executives have accepted as given, appear not to be given at all. At very least what has heretofore been taken for granted must henceforth be proved. Without in any way purporting to tell mothers, school teachers, school board superintendents what *will* change educational outcomes, social science has raised profoundly important questions as to what does not.[9]

The reactions of black leaders were mixed.[10] Militant blacks were strongly offended by the Report and its implications for public policy. The findings regarding compensatory education efforts were said to deal a "death blow to all black children" in the ghetto. They reasoned that integrated education is a physical impossibility in many big city school systems with few white pupils, and it is a political impossibility in many other cities. Hence, to discredit compensatory education is to threaten the only hope for improvement in ghetto education.

A more emotional reaction was the attack on the Report as "racist" because it implied that ghetto black children could only learn by contact with middle-class white children. One commentator exclaimed: "I don't subscribe to the view that a black kid must sit next to a white kid to learn. The report is based on the myth of white supremacy."

---

[8] See footnote 2.
[9] Daniel P. Moynihan, *Maximum Feasible Misunderstanding* (New York: Free Press, 1969), p. 195.
[10] See James K. Kent, "The Coleman Report: Opening Pandora's Box," pp. 244-45.

Some educational reformers, as well as black leaders, have contended that if black ghetto residents acquired control over the schools in their community, and restructured educational programs and policies to fit their own definition of need, this would resolve the problem of student learning and achievement. They contend that black control of the schools would affect the black child's self-confidence, sense of identity, and interest in education. And indeed, the Coleman Report can be cited for partial support to this thesis: "Of all the variables measured in the survey, the attitudes of student interest in school, self-concept, and sense of environmental control show the strongest relation to achievement." [11] In part, this line of reasoning was followed in New York City's proposed school decentralization plan. Whether or not community control of ghetto schools will succeed in raising the aspiration and achievement levels of black pupils remains to be seen. In other words, this question *too* is in need of analysis.

POLICY ANALYSIS AND THE QUEST FOR "SOLUTIONS" TO AMERICA'S PROBLEMS

It is questionable that policy analysis can ever provide "solutions" to America's problems. War, ignorance, crime, ill health, poverty, racial cleavage, inequality, poor housing, pollution, congestion, and unhappy lives, have afflicted men and societies for a long time. Of course, this is no excuse for failing to work toward a society free of these maladies. But our striving for a better society should be tempered with the realization that "solutions" to these problems may be very difficult to find. There are many reasons for tempering our enthusiasm for policy analysis, some of which are illustrated in the battle over the Coleman Report.

First of all, it is easy to exaggerate the importance, both for good and for ill, of the policies of governments. It is not clear that government policies, however ingenious, could cure all or even most of society's ills. Governments are constrained by many powerful environmental forces—wealth, technology, population growth, patterns of family life, class structure, child-rearing practices, religious beliefs, and so on. These forces are not easily managed by governments, nor could they be controlled even if it seemed desirable to do so. In the final chapter of this volume we will examine policy impacts, but it is safe to say here that some of society's problems are very intractable. For example, it may be that the *only* way to insure equality of opportunity is to remove children from disadvantaged family backgrounds at a very early age, perhaps before they are six months old. The weight of social science evidence suggests that the potential for

[11] James S. Coleman, *Equality of Educational Opportunity*, p. 319.

achievement may be determined at a very young age. However, a policy of removing children from their family environment at such a young age runs contrary to our deepest feelings about family attachments. The forceable removal of children from their mothers is "unthinkable" as a governmental policy. So it may turn out that we never really provide equality of opportunity because cultural forces prevent us from pursuing an effective policy.

Second, policy analysis cannot offer "solutions" to problems when there isn't general agreement on what the problems are. The Coleman Report assumed that raising achievement levels (measures of verbal and quantitative abilities) and raising aspiration levels (the desire to achieve by society's standards) were the "problems" to which our efforts should be directed. But others have contended that such achievement and aspiration levels are really middle- or upper-class white norms, and that the education of black ghetto children should be adapted toward totally different goals. Some have argued that the educational system should *not* be organized to facilitate the entry of children into middle-class society; instead they have urged that the policies of ghetto schools be to prepare children for life in the ghetto. In other words, there is no real agreement on what societal values should be implemented in educational policy. Policy analysis is not capable of resolving value conflicts. At best it can advise on how to achieve a certain set of end values; it cannot determine what those end values should be.

Third, policy analysis deals with very "subjective" topics and must rely upon "interpretation" of results. Professional researchers frequently interpret the results of their analyses differently. For example, some scholars may wish to focus on Coleman's findings that a child's attitudes towards education are the most important variable and that programs should be undertaken to improve the ghetto child's attitude toward his school. Or some may focus on the effect of placing disadvantaged black children in middle-class white schools. Obviously, quite different policy recommendations can emerge from alternative interpretations of the results of research.

There is also the problem of public attitudes toward research, particularly social science research. Social science research cannot be "value free." Even the selection of the topic for research is affected by one's values about what is "important" in society and worthy of attention. As Louis Wirth explained:

> The distinctive character of social science discourse is to be sought in the fact that every assertion, no matter how objective it may be, has ramifications extending beyond the limits of science itself. Since every assertion of a "fact" about the social world touches the interests of some individual or group, one cannot even call attention to the existence of certain "facts" without courting the objections of those whose very

raison d'etre in society rests upon a divergent interpretation of the "factual" situation period.[12]

For example, in recent years blacks have assumed that social science research findings would generally support their views of the problems confronting American society, and therefore by implication support their policy claims. But in the case of the Coleman Report the published findings tended to undermine the view that ghetto schools could be improved by channeling additional educational funds and services to them. Blacks supporting community control of ghetto schools tended to summarily reject as "false" the social science research suggesting that the removal of a child from the ghetto school environment would have greatest impact on his achievement. Many blacks also reacted negatively to the controversial Moynihan Report in 1965 which suggested that the historical experiences of blacks with slavery and segregation had weakened the structure of black families and this weakness in turn affected other conditions of life among blacks.[13] In short, disadvantaged groups as well as established elites may not always agree with the findings of policy research.

Another set of problems in systematic policy analysis centers about inherent limitations in the design of social science research. It is not really possible to conduct some forms of controlled experiments on human beings. For example, the Coleman researchers could not order middle-class white children to go to ghetto schools for several years just to see if it had an adverse impact on their achievement levels. Likewise black children could not be totally deprived of educational resources for the sake of social experimentation. Instead, social researchers must find situations in which educational deprivation has been produced "naturally" in order to make the necessary observations about the causes of such deprivation. Since we cannot control all of the factors which go into a real world situation, it is difficult to pinpoint precisely what it is that causes educational achievement or nonachievement. Moreover, even where some experimentation is permitted, human beings frequently modify their behavior simply because they know they are being observed in an experimental situation. For example, in educational research it frequently turns out that children perform well under *any* new teaching method or curricula innovation. It is difficult to know whether the improvements observed are a product of the new teaching method or curricula improvement or merely a product of the experimental situation. Finally, it should

---

[12] Louis Wirth, Preface to Karl Mannheim, *Ideology and Utopia: An Introduction to the Sociology of Knowledge* (New York: Harcourt Brace Jovanovich, 1936).

[13] Daniel P. Moynihan, *The Negro Family: The Case for National Action* (Washington, D.C.: Government Printing Office, 1965). See Rainwater and Yancy (eds.), *The Moynihan Report and the Politics of Controversy* (Cambridge: M.I.T. Press, 1967).

be noted that the people doing policy research are frequently program administrators who are interested in proving the positive "results" of their programs. It is important to separate research from policy implementation, but this is a difficult thing to do.

Perhaps the most serious reservation about policy analysis is the fact that social problems are so complex that social scientists are unable to make accurate predictions about the impact of proposed policies. *Social scientists simply do not know enough about individual and group behavior to be able to give reliable advice to policy makers.* Occasionally policy makers turn to social scientists for "solutions," but social scientists do not have any "solutions." Most of society's problems are shaped by so many variables that a simple explanation of them, or remedy for them, is rarely possible. A detailed understanding of such a complex system as human society is beyond our present capabilities. The fact that social scientists give so many contradictory recommendations is an indication of the absence of reliable scientific knowledge about social problems. While some scholars argue that no advice is better than contradictory or inaccurate advice, policy makers still must make decisions, and it is probably better that they act in the light of whatever little knowledge social science can provide than that they act in the absence of any knowledge at all. Even if social scientists cannot predict the impact of future policies, they can at least attempt to measure the impact of current and past public policies and make this knowledge available to decision makers.

It is important to recognize these limitations on policy analysis. However, it seems safe to say that reason, knowledge, and analysis are still appropriate tools in the consideration of policy questions. Policy analysis is not likely to provide "solutions" to America's problems. But we do not need to rely exclusively on "rules of thumb" or "muddling through" or "rap sessions" or "sounding off" or emotional outpourings of one kind or another in approaching policy questions. We can try systematically to describe and explain the causes and consequences of public policy in order to advance scientific understanding, to better prescribe for the ills of society, and to improve the quality of public policy.

BIBLIOGRAPHY

DROR, YEHEZKEL. *Public Policy-Making Re-examined.* San Francisco: Chandler, 1968.

JONES, CHARLES O. *An Introduction to the Study of Public Policy.* Belmont: Wadsworth, 1970.

LERNER, DANIEL and HAROLD D. LASSWELL, eds. *The Policy Sciences.* Stanford: Stanford University Press, 1960.

RANNEY, AUSTIN, ed. *Political Science and Public Policy.* Chicago: Markham, 1968.

SHARKANSKY, IRA, ed. *Policy Analysis in Political Science.* Chicago: Markham, 1970.

MODELS OF POLITICS:
some help in thinking about public policy

CHAPTER 2

MODELS FOR POLICY ANALYSIS

Over the years political science, like other scientific disciplines, has developed a number of concepts and models to help us understand political life. The purpose of these is (1) to simplify and clarify our thinking about government and politics, (2) to identify important political forces in society, (3) to communicate relevant knowledge about political life, (4) to direct inquiry into politics, and (5) to suggest explanations for political events and outcomes.

Throughout this volume we will try to see whether the concepts and models of political scientists have any utility in the study of public policy. Specifically we want to examine public policy from the perspectives of: systems theory, elite theory, group theory, rational decision-making theory, incrementalism, and institutionalism. Each of these terms identifies a major conceptual approach to politics which can be found in the literature of political science. None of these models was derived especially to study *public policy*. Yet each offers a separate way of thinking about policy, and even suggests some of the general causes and consequences of public policy.

These models are not competitive, in the sense that any one of them could be judged "best." Each one provides a *separate* focus

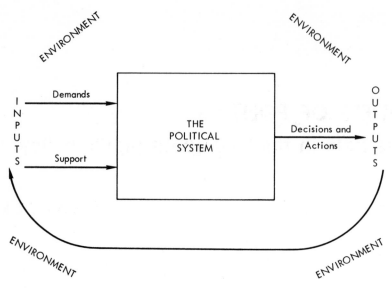

FIG. 2-1 THE SYSTEMS MODEL

on political life, and each can help us to understand *different* things about public policy. While some policies appear at first glance to lend themselves to explanation by one particular model, most policies are a combination of rational planning, incrementalism, interest group activity, elite preferences, systemic forces, and institutional influences. In later chapters these models will be employed, singularly and in combination, to describe and explain specific policies. Following is a brief description of each model, with particular attention to the separate ways in which public policy can be viewed.

SYSTEMS THEORY: POLICY AS SYSTEM OUTPUT

One way to conceive of public policy is to think of it as a response of a political system to forces brought to bear upon it from the environment.[1] Forces generated in the environment which affect the political system are viewed as *inputs*. The *environment* is any condition or circumstance defined as external to the boundaries of the political system. The political *system* is that group of interrelated structures and processes which functions authoritatively to allocate values for a society. *Outputs* of the political system are authoritative value allocations of the system, and these allocations constitute *public policy*.

[1] This conceptualization is based upon David Easton, "An Approach to the Analysis of Political Systems," *World Politics*, Vol. 9 (1957), 383-400; and Easton, *A Framework for Political Analysis* (Englewood Cliffs: Prentice-Hall, 1965).

This conceptualization of political activity and public policy can be diagramed as in Figure 2-1. This diagram is a simplified version of the idea of the political system described at great length by political scientist David Easton. The notion of a political system has been employed, either implicitly or explicitly, by many scholars who have sought to analyze the causes and consequences of public policy.

Systems theory portrays public policy as an output of the political *system*. The concept of "system" implies an identifiable set of institutions and activities in society that function to transform demands into authoritative decisions requiring the support of society. The concept of "systems" also implies that elements of the system are interrelated, that the system can respond to forces in its environment, and that it will do so in order to preserve itself. Inputs are received into the political system in the form of both demands and support. Demands occur when individuals or groups, in response to real or perceived environmental conditions, act to affect public policy. Support is rendered when individuals or groups accept the outcome of elections, obey the laws, pay their taxes, and generally conform to policy decisions. Any system absorbs a variety of demands, some of which conflict with each other. In order to transform these demands into outputs (public policies), it must arrange settlements and enforce these settlements upon the parties concerned. It is recognized that outputs (public policies) may have a modifying effect on the environment and the demands arising from it, and may also have an effect upon the character of the political system. The system preserves itself by: (1) producing reasonably satisfying outputs, (2) relying upon deeply rooted attachments to the system itself, and (3) using, or threatening to use, force.

The value of the systems model to policy analysis lies in the questions that it poses:

1. What are the significant dimensions of the environment that generate demands upon the political system?
2. What are the significant characteristics of the political system that enable it to transform demands into public policy and to preserve itself over time?
3. How do environmental inputs affect the character of the political system?
4. How do characteristics of the political system affect the content of public policy?
5. How do environmental inputs affect the content of public policy?
6. How does public policy affect, through feedback, the environment and the character of the political system?

In Chapters 11 and 12 we will examine these questions with particular reference to public policies in the American states. We will assess the impact of various environmental conditions—particularly wealth, urbanization, and education—on levels of spending, benefits, and services in education, welfare, highways, police, corrections, and finance. We will see how federal policy sometimes tries to offset the impact of environmental variables on domestic policy in the states. We will examine the impact of political system characteristics—pluralism and reformism—on levels of taxing, spending, benefits, and service, and attempt to compare the impact of these system characteristics on public policy with the impact of environmental conditions. Finally, we will investigate what goes on in the "black box" labeled "political system" and the policy impact of various elements of the political system itself, including mass opinion, elite attitudes, parties, interest groups, and bureaucratic, executive, and legislative interaction.

ELITE THEORY: POLICY AS ELITE PREFERENCE

Public policy may also be viewed as the preferences and values of a governing elite.[2] Although we often assert that public policy reflects the demands of "the people," this may express the myth rather than the reality of American democracy. Elite theory suggests that "the people" are apathetic and ill-informed about public policy, that elites actually shape mass opinion on policy questions more than masses shape elite opinion. Thus, public policy really turns out to be the preferences of elites. Public officials and administrators merely carry out the policies decided upon by the elite. Policies flow "downward" from elites to masses; they do not arise from mass demands. Elite theory can be summarized briefly as follows:

1. Society is divided into the few who have power and the many who do not. Only a small number of persons allocate values for society; the masses do not decide public policy.
2. The few who govern are not typical of the masses who are governed. Elites are drawn disproportionately from the upper socioeconomic strata of society.
3. The movement of nonelites to elite positions must be slow and continuous to maintain stability and avoid revolution. Only nonelites who have accepted the basic elite consensus can be admitted to governing circles.
4. Elites share consensus on behalf of the basic values of the social system and the preservation of the system. In America, the bases of elite consensus are the sanctity of private property, limited government, and individual liberty.
5. Public policy does not reflect demands of masses but rather the prevailing values of the elite. Changes in public policy will be incremental rather than revolutionary.
6. Active elites are subject to relatively little direct influence from apathetic masses. Elites influence masses more than masses influence elites.

[2] Elite theory is explained at length in Thomas R. Dye and Harmon Zeigler, *The Irony of Democracy* (Belmont: Wadsworth, 1970).

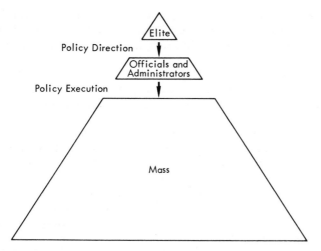

FIG. 2-2 THE ELITE MODEL

What are the implications of elite theory for policy analysis? First of all, elitism implies that public policy does not reflect demands of "the people" so much as it does the interests and values of elites. Therefore, change and innovations in public policy come about as a result of redefinitions by elites of their own values. Because of the general conservatism of elites, that is, their interest in preserving the system, change in public policy will be incremental rather than revolutionary. Public policies are frequently modified but seldom replaced. Changes in the nature of the political system occur when events threaten the system, and elites, acting on the basis of enlightened self-interest, institute reforms to preserve the system and their place in it. The values of elites may be very "public-regarding." A sense of "noblesse oblige" may permeate elite values, and the welfare of the masses may be an important element in elite decision making. Elitism does not mean that public policy will be anti-mass welfare, but only that the responsibility for mass welfare rests upon the shoulders of elites, not masses.

Second, elitism views the masses as largely passive, apathetic and ill-informed; mass sentiments are more often manipulated by elites, rather than elite values being influenced by the sentiments of masses; and for the most part, communication between elites and masses flows downward. Therefore, popular elections and party competition do not enable the masses to govern. Policy questions are seldom decided by the people through elections or through the presentation of policy alternatives by political parties. For the most part these "democratic" institutions—elections and parties—are important only for their symbolic value. They help tie the masses to the political system by giving them a role to play on election day and a political party with which they can identify. Elitism contends that the masses have at best only an indirect influence over the decision-making behavior of elites.

Elitism also asserts that elites share in a consensus about fundamental norms underlying the social system, that elites agree on the basic "rules of the game," as well as the continuation of the social system itself. The stability of the system, and even its survival, depends upon elite consensus on behalf of the fundamental values of the system, and only policy alternatives which fall within the shared consensus will be given serious consideration. Of course, elitism does not mean that elite members never disagree or never compete with each other for preeminence. It is unlikely that there ever was a society in which there was no competition among elites. But elitism implies that competition centers around a very narrow range of issues and that elites agree on more matters than they disagree.

In America elite consensus includes constitutional government, democratic procedures, majority rule, freedom of speech and press, freedom to form opposition parties and run for public office, equality of opportunity in all segments of life, the sanctity of private property, the importance of individual initiative and reward, and the legitimacy of the free enterprise, capitalist, economic system. Masses may give superficial support to democratic symbols, but they are not as consistent or reliable in their support for these values as elites.

In Chapter 3, we will examine civil rights policy largely from the perspective of elite theory. We will portray the civil rights movement as an effort of established liberal elites to insure that the benefits of the American system would be available to those blacks who accept the prevailing consensus and exhibit middle-class values. Opposition to civil rights is centered among white masses; virtually none of the progress in civil rights since World War II (Brown vs. Topeka, Civil Rights Act of 1964, Fair Housing, etc.) would have taken place if white masses rather than white elites determined public policy. Public-regarding elites were prepared to eliminate legal barriers to provide equality of opportunity under law for individual blacks. However, they were not prepared to take massive governmental action to eliminate absolute inequalities and bring black masses up to average white standards of living. Such action to eliminate inequality in society ("leveling") would violate traditional consensus regarding individual initiative and enterprise. We will contend that established liberal elites, who supported the elimination of *legal discrimination*, were not prepared to meet the demands of black masses for *absolute equality*. Moreover, in Chapter 4 we will observe that established elites reacted negatively when black masses in ghettos violated the "rules of the game" in civil disorders, riots, and violence.

GROUP THEORY: POLICY AS GROUP EQUILIBRIUM

Group theory begins with the proposition that interaction among groups is the central fact of politics.[3] Individuals with common interests ban together formally or informally to press their demands upon government. According to political scientist David Truman, an interest group is "a shared-attitude group that makes certain claims upon other groups in the society"; such a group becomes political "if and when it makes a claim through or upon any of the institutions of government."[4] Individuals are important in politics only when they act as part of, or on behalf of, group interests. The group becomes the essential bridge between the individual and his government. Politics is really the struggle among groups to influence public policy. The task of the political system is to *manage group conflict* by (1) establishing rules of the game in the group struggle, (2) arranging compromises and balancing interests, (3) enacting compromises in the form of public policy, and (4) enforcing these compromises.

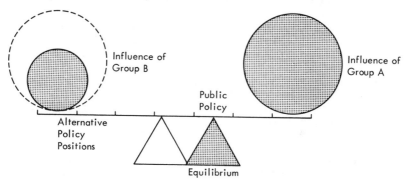

FIG. 2-3   The Group Model

According to group theorists, public policy at any given time is the equilibrium reached in the group struggle. This equilibrium is determined by the relative influence of interest groups. Changes in the relative influence of any interest groups can be expected to result in changes in public policy; policy will move in the direction desired by the groups gaining in influence, and away from the desires of groups losing influence. Political scientist Earl Latham describes public policy from the group theory viewpoint as follows:

[3] Group theory is explained at length in David B. Truman, *The Governmental Process* (New York: Knopf, 1951).
[4] *Ibid.*, p. 37.

What may be called public policy is actually the equilibrium reached in the group struggle at any given moment, and it represents a balance which the contending factions or groups constantly strive to tip in their favor. . . . The legislature referees the group struggle, ratifies the victories of the successful coalition, and records the terms of the surrenders, compromises, and conquests in the form of statutes.[5]

The influence of groups is determined by their numbers, wealth, organizational strength, leadership, access to decision makers, and internal cohesion.

Modern group theory is not very much different from the theory of "faction," described by James Madison two hundred years ago.[6] Madison believed that differences among men generated "factions," which he defined as numbers of citizens united by a common interest which is adverse to the interest of numbers of other citizens. Controlling "faction" was "the principal task of modern legislation." Madison describes the causes of faction and the major factions encountered in society:

The latent causes of faction are thus sown in the nature of man; and we see them everywhere brought into different degrees of activity, according to the different circumstances of civil society. A zeal for different opinions concerning religion, concerning government, and many other points, as well of speculation as of practice; an attachment to different leaders ambitiously contending for pre-eminence and power; or to persons of other descriptions whose fortunes have been interesting to human passions, have, in turn, divided mankind into parties, inflamed them to mutual animosity, and rendered them much more disposed to vex and oppress each other than to cooperate for their common good. So strong is this propensity of mankind to fall into mutual animosity, that where no substantial occasion presents itself, the most frivolous and fanciful distinctions have been sufficient to kindle their unfriendly passions and excite their most violent conflicts. But the most common and durable source of factions has been the various and unequal distribution of property. Those who hold and those who are without property have ever formed distinct interests in society. Those who are creditors and those who are debtors, fall under a like discrimination. A landed interest, a manufacturing interest, a mercantile interest, a moneyed interest, with many lesser interests, grow up of necessity in civilized nations, and divide them into different classes, actuated by different sentiments and views.[7]

Group theory purports to describe all meaningful political activity in terms of the group struggle. Policy makers are viewed as constantly

---

[5] Earl Latham, "The Group Basis of Politics," in Heinz Eulau, Samuel J. Eldersveld, and Morris Janowitz (eds.), *Political Behavior* (New York: Free Press, 1956), p. 239.
[6] *The Federalist*, Number 10.
[7] *Ibid.*, Modern Library Edition, pp. 55-56.

responding to group pressures—bargaining, negotiating, and compromising, among competing demands of influential groups. Politicians attempt to form a majority coalition of groups. In so doing, they have some latitude in determining what groups are to be included in the majority coalition. The larger the constituency of the politician, the greater the number of diverse interests, and the greater his latitude in selecting the groups to form a majority coalition. Thus, Congressmen have less flexibility than Senators who have larger and generally more diverse constituencies; and the President has more flexibility than Congressmen and Senators. Executive agencies are also understood in terms of the groups constitutencies.

Parties are viewed as coalitions of groups. The Democratic Party coalition from the Roosevelt era until recently was composed of labor, central city dwellers, ethnic groups, Catholics, the poor, liberal intellectuals, blacks, and Southerners. The difficulties of the Democratic Party today can be traced largely to the weakening of this group coalition—the disaffection of the South, and the group conflict between white labor and ethnic groups and blacks. The Republican coalition has consisted of rural and small town residents, the middle class, whites, Protestants, white-collar workers, and suburbanites.

The whole interest group system—the political system itself—is held together in equilibrium by several forces. First of all, there is a large, nearly universal, *latent group* in American society which supports the constitutional system and prevailing "rules of the game." This group is not always visible, but can be activated to administer overwhelming rebuke to any group which attacks the system and threatens to destroy the equilibrium.

Second, *overlapping group membership* helps to maintain the equilibrium by preventing any one group from moving too far from prevailing values. Individuals who belong to any one group also belong to other groups, and this fact moderates the demands of groups who must avoid offending their members who have other group affiliations.

Finally, the *checking and balancing resulting from group competition* also helps to maintain equilibrium in the system. No single group constitutes a majority in American society. The power of each group is checked by the power of competing groups. "Countervailing" centers of power function to check the influence of any single group and protect the individual from exploitation.

Throughout this volume we will describe group struggles over public policy. A particularly interesting example of group conflict over policy is found in the discussion of federal aid to education in Chapter 7. We will examine the role of racial and religious group conflict over federal educational policy, educational interests at the community level, and the struggle over educational opportunity for children in the nation's black ghettos.

26

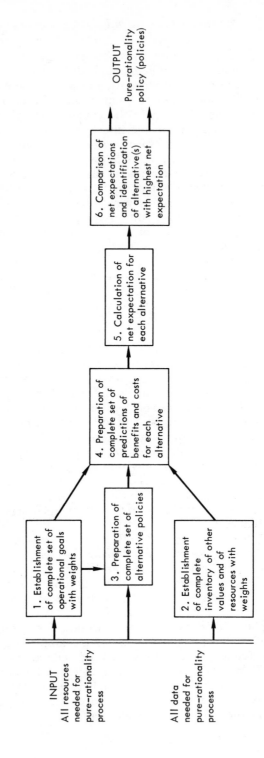

FIG. 2-4 THE RATIONAL MODEL

RATIONALISM: POLICY AS EFFICIENT GOAL ACHIEVEMENT

A rational policy is one which is correctly designed to maximize "net value achievement." [8] By "net value achievement" we mean that all relevant values of a society are known, and that any sacrifice in one or more values which is required by a policy is more than compensated for by the attainment of other values. This definition of rationality is interchangeable with the concept of efficiency—efficiency is the ratio between valued inputs and valued outputs. We can say that a policy is rational when it is most *efficient*—that is, if the ratio between the values that it achieves and the values that it sacrifices is positive and higher than any other policy alternative. One should *not* view efficiency in a narrow dollars-and-cents framework—in which basic social values are sacrificed for dollar savings. Our idea of efficiency involves the calculation of *all* social, political, and economic values sacrificed or achieved by a public policy, not just those which can be measured by quantitative symbols.

To select a rational policy, policy makers must: (1) know all of the society's value preferences and their relative weights; (2) know all of the policy alternatives available; (3) know all of the consequences of each policy alternative; (4) calculate the ratio of achieved to sacrificed societal values for each policy alternative; (5) select the most efficient policy alternative. [9] This rationality assumes that the value preferences of *society as a whole* can be known and weighted. It is not enough to know and weigh the values of *some* groups and not others. There must be a complete understanding of *societal* values. Rational policy making also requires *information* about alternative policies, the *predictive capacity* to foresee accurately the consequences of alternate policies, and the *intelligence* to calculate correctly the ratio of costs to benefits. Finally, rational policy making requires a *decision-making system* which facilitates rationality in policy formation.

Many types of rational decision models are found in the literature of economics, political science, management, administrative science, and budgeting. [10] An example of a rational approach to resource allocation policy is portrayed in Figure 2-5. This model assumes that a society has an "indifference curve" which represents the combination of values to which society is indifferent. The indifference curve slopes in a convex fashion from the upper left (a high return of Value A at the expense of lower returns on other values) to the lower right

[8] See Robert Henry Haveman, *The Economics of the Public Sector* (New York: John Wiley, 1970).

[9] See Yehezkel Dror, *Public Policy-Making Re-examined*, Part IV, "An Optional Model of Public Policy-Making" (San Francisco: Chandler, 1968).

[10] L. L. Wade and R. L. Curry, Jr., *A Logic of Public Policy: Aspects of Political Economy* (Belmont: Wadsworth, 1970).

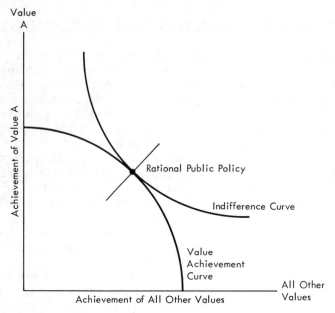

FIG. 2-5   A Rational Resource-Allocation Model

(a lower return on Value A in exchange for higher returns of other values). Any point on the curve is assumed to be equally satisfactory to society. Of course, all combinations on a higher indifference curve are preferable to those on a lower indifference curve. But we can assume that society does not have sufficient resources to achieve high levels of Value A *and* high levels of all other values. We can plot this assumption with a "value achievement curve" which represents the combination of values which it is possible for government to produce given the limitations of resources. The value achievement curve always slopes in a concave fashion from upper left (a high achievement of Value A at the sacrifice of other values) to lower right (a lower achievement of Value A but a higher achievement of other values). Any point on the curve is possible for society to achieve. A rational public policy would be determined by the intersection of society's indifference curve and its value achievement curve. This point represents the highest level of indifference (satisfaction) allowable within society's resources.

There are many barriers to such rational decision making.[11] In fact, there are so many barriers to rational decision making that it rarely takes place at all in government. Yet the model remains im-

---

[11] See Charles E. Lindblom, "The Science of Muddling Through," *Public Administration Review*, Vol. 19 (1959), 79-88; David Braybrooke and Charles E. Lindblom, *A Strategy of Decision* (New York: Free Press, 1963); Aaron Wildavsky, *The Politics of the Budgetary Process* (Boston: Little, Brown, 1964).

portant for analytic purposes because it helps to identify barriers to rationality. It assists in posing the question: Why is policy making not a more rational process? At the outset we can hypothesize several important obstacles to rational policy making:

1. There are no *societal* values which are usually agreed upon, but only the values of specific groups and individuals, many of which are conflicting.
2. The many conflicting values cannot be compared or weighted; for example, it is impossible to compare or weigh the value of individual dignity against a tax increase.
3. The environment of policy makers, particularly the power and influence system, renders it impossible for them to see or accurately weigh many societal values, particularly those values which have no active or powerful proponents.
4. Policy makers are not motivated to make decisions on the basis of societal goals, but instead try to maximize their own rewards—power, status, reelection, money, etc.
5. Policy makers are not motivated to *maximize* net goal achievement, but merely to *satisfy* demands for progress; they do not search until they find "the one best way" but halt their search when they find an alternative which "will work."
6. Large investments in existing programs and policies ("sunk costs") prevent policy makers from reconsidering alternatives foreclosed by previous decisions.
7. There are innumerable barriers to collecting all of the information required to know all possible policy alternatives and the consequences of each alternative, including the cost of information gathering, the availability of the information, and the time involved in its collection.
8. Neither the predictive capacities of the social and behavioral sciences, nor the predictive capacities of the physical and biological sciences, are sufficiently advanced to enable policy makers to understand the full range of consequences of each policy alternative.
9. Policy makers, even with the most advanced computerized analytical techniques, do not have sufficient intelligence to calculate accurately cost-benefits ratios when a large number of diverse political, social, economic, and cultural values are at stake.
10. Policy makers have personal needs, inhibitions, and inadequacies which prevent them from performing in a highly rational manner.
11. Uncertainty about the consequences of various policy alternatives compels policy makers to stick as closely as possible to previous policies to reduce the likelihood of disturbing, unanticipated consequences.
12. The segmentalized nature of policy making in large bureaucracies makes it difficult to coordinate decision making so that the input of all of the various specialists is brought to bear at the point of decision.

We cannot illustrate all of the problems of achieving rationality in public policy. In Chapters 5 and 6 we will describe the general design of alternative strategies to deal with welfare and poverty in America. We will observe how these strategies were implemented in public policy, and analyze some of the obstacles to the achievement of the goal of eliminating poverty.

INCREMENTALISM: POLICY AS VARIATIONS ON THE PAST

Incrementalism views public policy as a continuation of past government activities with only incremental modifications. Economist Charles E. Lindblom first presented the incremental model in the course of a critique of the traditional rational model of decision making.[12] According to Lindblom, decision makers do *not* annually review the whole range of existing and proposed policies, identify societal goals, research the benefits and costs of alternative policies in achieving these goals, rank-order preferences for each policy alternative in terms of the ratio of benefits to costs, and then make a selection on the basis of all relevant information. On the contrary, constraints of time, intelligence, and cost prevent policy makers from identifying the full range of policy alternatives and their consequences. Constraints of politics prevent the establishment of clear-cut societal goals and the accurate calculation of cost-benefit ratios. The incremental model recognizes the impractical nature of "rational-comprehensive" policy making, and describes a more conservative process of decision making.

Incrementalism is conservative in that existing programs, policies, and expenditures are considered as a base, and attention is concentrated on new programs and policies and on increases, decreases, or modifications of current program. Policy makers generally accept the legitimacy of established programs and tacitly agree to continue previous policies.

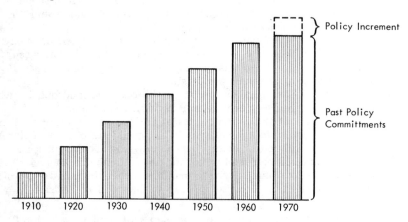

FIG. 2-6 THE INCREMENTAL MODEL

[12] Charles E. Lindblom, "The Science of Muddling Through," *Public Administration Review*, Vol. 19 (Spring 1959), 79-88.

They do this, first of all, because they do not have the time, intelligence, or money to investigate all of the alternatives to existing policy. The cost of collecting all of the information required to know the consequences of all possible policy alternatives is too great. Policy makers do not have sufficient predictive capacities, even in the age of computers, to know what all of the consequences of each alternative will be. Nor are they able to calculate cost-benefit ratios for all alternative policies when many diverse, political, social, economic, and cultural values are at stake. Thus completely "rational" policy may turn out to be "inefficient" (despite the contradiction in terms) if the time, intelligence, and cost of developing a rational policy are excessive.

Second, policy makers accept the legitimacy of previous policies because of the uncertainty about the consequences of completely new or different policies. It is safer to stick with known programs when the consequences of new programs cannot be predicted. Under conditions of uncertainty, policy makers continue past policies or programs whether or not they have proven effective.

Third, there may be heavy investments in existing programs ("sunk costs" again) which preclude any really radical change. These investments may be in money, buildings, or other hard items, or they may be in psychological dispositions, administrative practices, or organizational structure. It is accepted wisdom, for example, that organizations tend to persist over time regardless of their utility, that they develop routines which are difficult to alter and that individuals develop a personal stake in the continuation of organizations and practices which makes radical change very difficult. Hence, not all policy alternatives can be seriously considered, but only those which cause little physical, economic, organizational, and administrative dislocation.

Fourth, incrementalism is politically expedient. Agreement comes easier in policy making when the items in dispute are only increases or decreases in budgets, or modifications to existing programs. Conflict is heightened when decision making focuses on major policy shifts involving great gains or losses, or "all or nothing," "yes or no" policy decisions. Since the political tension involved in getting new programs or policies passed *every* year would be very great, past policy victories are continued into future years unless there is a substantial political realignment. Thus incrementalism is important in reducing conflict, maintaining stability, and preserving the political system itself.

The characteristics of policy makers themselves also recommend the incremental model. Rarely do human beings act to maximize all of their values; more often they act to satisfy particular demands. Men are pragmatic: they seldom search for the "one best way" but instead end their search when they find "a way that will work." This search usually begins with the familiar—that is, with policy alternatives close to current policies. Only if these alternatives appear to be unsatisfactory will the policy maker venture out toward more radical policy innovation. In most cases modification of existing programs will satisfy particular demands, and the major policy shifts required to maximize values are overlooked.

Finally, in the absence of any agreed-upon societal goals or values, it is easier for the government of a pluralist society to continue existing programs rather than engage in overall policy planning toward specific societal goals.

We will give special attention to incrementalism in our discussion to taxing and spending policy in Chapter 10. Specifically, we will examine the federal government's budgeting and appropriations processes and federal tax policy, within the context of the incremental model.

INSTITUTIONALISM: POLICY AS INSTITUTIONAL ACTIVITY

Governmental structures and institutions have long been a central focus of political science. Carl J. Friedrich, former President of both the American Political Science Association and International Political Science Association, has written:

> Modern political science is largely a critical examination of common-sense notions concerning the working of political institutions and procedures. Three axiomatic truths regarding the nature of power lie at its foundation: namely, that power ordinarily presupposes a group of human beings who can share objectives, interests, values, in other words, a community; second, therefore power presupposes objectives, interests, values, ends, which these human beings can share, fight over, or exchange; third, that all power situations contain both consent (shared objectives) and constraints (contested objectives). . . . Modern political science . . . is concerned with the instruments or techniques of political action in terms of the objectives they are supposed to serve.[13]

It is common to think of political science as the study of governmental institutions. Political activities generally center about particular governmental institutions—Congress, the Presidency, courts, states, municipalities, political parties, etc. The interests of individuals and groups, and their activities on behalf of these interests, are generally directed toward governmental institutions. Public policy is authoritatively determined, implemented, and enforced by governmental institutions.

The relationship between public policy and governmental institutions is very close. Strictly speaking, a policy does not become a *public* policy until it is adopted, implemented, and enforced by some

---

[13] Carl J. Friedrich, *Constitutional Government and Democracy* (Boston: Little, Brown, 1941), p. 593.

governmental institution. Governmental institutions give public policy three distinctive characteristics. First of all, government lends *legitimacy* to policies. Governmental policies are generally regarded as legal obligations which command the loyalty of citizens. Men may regard the policies of other groups and associations in society—corporations, churches, professional organizations, civic associations, etc.—as important and even binding. But only government policies involve legal obligations. Secondly, government policies involve *universality*. Only government policies extend to all people in a society; the policies of other groups or organizations only reach a part of the society. Finally, government monopolizes *coercion* in society—only government can legitimately imprison or kill violators of its policies. The sanctions which can be imposed by other groups or organizations in society are more limited. It is precisely this ability of government to command the loyalty of all its citizens, to enact policies governing the whole society, and to monopolize the legitimate use of force that encourages individuals and groups to work for enactment of their preferences into public policy.

Traditionally, the institutional approach in political science did *not* devote much attention to the linkages between the structure of governmental institutions and the content of public policy. Instead, institutional studies usually described specific governmental institutions—their structures, organization, duties, and functions—without systematically inquiring about the impact of institutional characteristics on policy outputs. Constitutional and legal arrangements were described in detail, as were the myriad government offices and agencies at the federal, state, and local level. Public policies were sometimes described, but seldom analyzed. The linkage between structure and policy remained largely unexamined.

Despite the narrow focus of early institutional studies in political science, the structural approach is not necessarily an unproductive one. Governmental institutions are really structured patterns of behavior of individuals and groups. By "structured" we mean these patterns of behavior tend to persist over time. These stable patterns of individual and group behavior may affect the content of public policy. Institutions may be so structured as to facilitate certain policy outcomes and to obstruct other policy outcomes. They may give advantage to certain interests in society and withhold advantage from other interests. Certain individuals and groups may enjoy greater access to government power under one set of structural characteristics than under another set. In short, the structure of governmental institutions may have important policy consequences.

The institutional approach need not be narrow or descriptive. We can ask what relationships exist between institutional arrangements and the content of public policy, and we can investigate these relationships in a comparative, systematic fashion. For example, in the area of urban affairs we can ask: Are the policies of federal agencies

The Mayor-Council Form

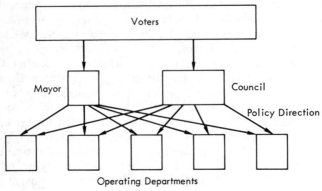

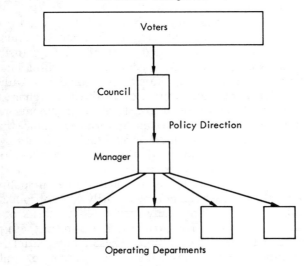

FIG. 2-7 An Institutional Model

(Congress, President, Department of Housing and Urban Development, etc.) more responsive to urban problems than the policies of state or local governments? How does the division of responsibility for urban services among federal, state, and local governments affect the content of urban policy? What is the relationship between reformed structures of city government (city managers, nonpartisan elections, at-large constituencies) and taxing and spending policies of cities? Are unreformed city governments (mayor-councils, partisan elections, and constituencies) more responsive in policy decisions to minority groups demands than reformed cities? Do consolidated metropolitan governments pursue any different policies than frag-mented municipal governments in a metropolitan area? These policy questions can be dealt with systematically and involve a focus on institutional arrangements. In Chapter 8 we shall direct ourselves to these questions about urban policy, and throughout this volume we will try to identify the policy impact of institutional arrangements.

It is important to remember that the impact of institutional ar-rangements on public policy is an empirical question which deserves investigation. Too frequently, enthusiastic reformers have asserted that a particular change in institutional structure would bring about changes in public policy without investigating the true relationship between structure and policy; they have fallen into the trap of *assuming* on the basis of a priori logic that institutional changes will bring about policy changes. We must be cautious in our assessment of the impact of structure on policy. We may discover that both struc-ture and policy are largely determined by environmental forces, and that tinkering with institutional arrangements will have little inde-pendent impact on public policy if underlying environmental forces —social, economic, and political—remain constant.

MODELS: HOW TO TELL IF THEY ARE HELPING OR NOT

A model is merely an abstraction or representation of political life. When we think of political "systems," or "elites," or "groups," or "rational decision making," or "incrementalism," or "institutions," we are abstracting from the real world in an attempt to simplify, clarify, and understand what is really important about politics. Before we begin in our study of public policy, let us set forth some general criteria for evaluating the usefulness of concepts and models:

1. Certainly the utility of a model lies in its ability to *order and simplify* political life so that we can think about it more clearly and understand the relationships we find in the real world. Yet too much simplification can lead to inaccuracies in our thinking about reality. If a concept is too narrow or identifies only superficial phenomena, we may not be able to use it to explain public policy. On the other hand, if a concept is too broad, and suggests overly complex relation-ships, it may become so complicated and unmanageable that it is not really an aid to understanding. In other words, some theories of politics may be too complex to be helpful, while others may be too simplistic.

2. A model should also *identify* the really significant aspects of public policy. It should direct attention away from irrelevant vari-ables or circumstances, and focus upon the "real" causes and "sig-nificant" consequences of public policy. Of course, what is "real," "relevant," "significant" is to some extent a function of an individual's

personal values. But we can all agree that the utility of concept is related to its ability to identify what it is that is really important about politics.

3. Generally, a model should be *congruent with reality*, that is to say, it ought to have real empirical referents. We would expect to have difficulty with a concept which identifies a process which does not really occur, or symbolizes phenomena which do not exist in the real world. On the other hand we must not be too quick to dismiss "unrealistic" concepts *if* they succeed in directing our attention to why they are unrealistic. For example, no one contends that government decision making is completely rational—public officials do not always act to maximize societal values and minimize societal costs. Yet the concept of "rational decision making" may be still useful, albeit "unrealistic," if it makes us realize how irrational government decision making really is and prompts us to inquire about why it is irrational.

4. A concept or model should also *communicate* something meaningful. If too many people disagree over the meaning of a concept, its utility in communication is diminished. For example, if no one really agrees on what constitutes an "elite," then the concept of an elite does not mean the same thing to everyone. If one defines an "elite" as democratically elected public officials who are representative of the general public, then he is communicating a different idea in using the term than one who defines an elite as an unrepresentative minority who make decisions for society based on their own interests.

5. A model should help to *direct inquiry and research* into public policy. A concept should be operational, that is, it should refer directly to real world phenomena which can be observed, measured, and verified. A concept, or a series of interrelated concepts (which we refer to as a "model"), should suggest relationships in the real world which can be tested and verified. If there is no way to prove or disprove the ideas suggested by a concept, then the concept is not really useful in developing a science of politics.

6. Finally, a model approach should *suggest an explanation* of public policy. It should suggest hypotheses about the causes and consequences of public policy—hypotheses which can be tested against real world data. A concept which merely *describes* public policy is not as useful as a concept which *explains* public policy, or at least suggests some possible explanations.

BIBLIOGRAPHY

DYE, THOMAS R. and HARMON ZEIGLER, *The Irony of Democracy*. Belmont: Wadsworth, 1970.

EASTON, DAVID, *A Framework for Political Analysis.* New York: Prentice-Hall, 1965.

TRUMAN, DAVID B., *The Governmental Process.* New York: Knopf, 1971.

WADE, L. L. and R. L. CURRY, JR., *A Logic of Public Policy: Aspects of Political Economy.* Belmont: Wadsworth, 1970.

WILDAVSKY, AARON, *The Politics of the Budgetary Process.* Boston: Little, Brown, 1964.

CIVIL RIGHTS:
elite-mass interaction

The central domestic issue of American politics over the long history of the nation has been the place of the black man in American society.[1] In describing this issue we have relied heavily on the elite model—because elite and mass attitudes toward civil rights appear to differ a great deal, and public policy appears to reflect the attitudes of *elites* rather than masses. Civil rights policy is a response of a national elite to conditions affecting a small minority of Americans, rather than a response of national leaders to majority sentiments. Policies of the national elite in civil rights have met with varying degrees of resistance from states and communities. We will contend that national policy has shaped mass opinion more than mass opinion has shaped national policy. Finally, we will argue that civil rights policy reflects elite consensus about equality of opportunity, but that civil rights policy does not reflect the demands of black masses for *absolute equality* with whites.

[1] For a full account of racial politics in America, see Thomas R. Dye, *The Politics of Equality* (New York: Bobbs-Merrill, 1971), portions of which appear in this chapter.

ELITE-MASS ATTITUDES AND CIVIL RIGHTS

White America has long harbored an ambivalence toward black America—a recognition of the evils of inequality but a reluctance to take steps to eliminte it. Gunnar Myrdal, writing in 1944, captured the essence of the American racial dilemma:

> The "American dilemma" . . . is the ever-raging conflict between, on the one hand, the valuations preserved on the general plane which we shall call the "American creed," where the American thinks, talks, and acts under the influence of high national and Christian precepts, and, on the other hand, the valuation on specific planes of individual and group living, where personal and local interests; economic, and social, and sexual jealousies; considerations of community prestige and conformity; group prejudices against particular persons or types of people; all sorts of miscellaneous wants, impulses, and habits dominate his outlook.[2]

The attitudes of white masses toward blacks in America are ambivalent. Whites agree that Negroes are discriminated against. A national opinion survey by Louis Harris revealed that 61% of whites in the nation agreed that Negroes were "discriminated against" and only 28% felt that Negroes were "not discriminated against" with 7% "not sure."[3] Even in the South a substantial number of whites agreed that Negroes were discriminated against (39% replied "discriminated against"; 47% "not discriminated against"; and 14% "not sure"). Most whites believe that blacks suffer injustices and that discrimination is wrong. Yet, even though they admit the injustices of discrimination, an overwhelming majority of whites believe that blacks are moving "too fast." "Do you feel Negroes have tried to move too fast, too slow or at about the right pace?" was:

	Total 1966	Total 1963
Too fast	70%	64%
Too slow	4%	6%
About the right pace	14%	17%
Not sure	12%	13%

Of course, this figure of 70% in 1966 was affected by the urban riots of the mid-1960s. But even in 1963, *before* the passage of the Civil

[2] Gunnar Myrdal, *An American Dilemma: The Negro Problem and Modern Democracy*, 2 vols. (New York: McGraw-Hill, 1944), Vol. I, xxi.
[3] Survey results are derived from the text and Appendix of William Brink and Louis Harris, *Black and White: A Study of U.S. Racial Attitudes Today* (New York: Simon and Schuster, 1967); with updating from William Brink and Louis Harris, "Report From Black America," *Newsweek*, June 30, 1969. The data were collected in national surveys conducted in 1963, 1966, and 1969.

Rights Act of 1964, two out of every three whites believed that blacks were moving too fast.[4]

A large majority of whites in America support legislation giving blacks equal voting rights (91%), the right to a fair jury trial (87%), nonsegregated use of buses, planes, and trains (87%), and integrated education (72%). Yet there appears to be a clear scale of white attitudes toward contacts with blacks. In general whites are willing to support laws eliminating discrimination and guaranteeing equality of opportunity. But what about compensatory efforts to overcome the effects of past discrimination and uplift the black community? Here the evidence is that most whites are not prepared to make any special effort to change the conditions of blacks. Louis Harris asked a national sample:

> Some Negroes have suggested that since Negroes have been discriminated against for one hundred years, they should be given special consideration in jobs, that they should actually be given a preference for a job opening, such as the veteran gets today in a government job. Do you agree or disagree with the idea of job preference for Negroes?[5]

Whites responded with a resounding "No!" Fully 90% of the national sample of whites opposed special consideration for blacks in jobs; only 4% favored it.

It is interesting to note the change over time in white attitudes toward blacks. In general, white Americans are much more sympathetic to Negro rights today than they were a decade or two ago. A national sample of white Americans was asked the question, "Do you think white students and Negro students should go to the same schools or separate schools?" in 1942, 1956, 1963, and 1965 (see Table 3-1). In 1942, not one American white in three approved of integrated schools. Even in the north, a majority was opposed to

TABLE 3-1   ATTITUDE CHANGE AMONG WHITES: WHITE AND NEGRO STUDENTS
SHOULD ATTEND THE SAME SCHOOLS, 1942–66

	Percentage Yes			
	1942	*1956*	*1963*	*1966*
Total whites	30	49	62	67
Northern whites	40	61	73	78
Southern whites	2	15	31	36

Source: Paul B. Sheatsley, "White Attitudes Toward the Negro," *Daedalus*, Vol. 95, No. 1 (Winter 1966).

[4] The contrast between white and black attitudes on the speed of progress of civil rights is striking. When Negroes were asked the same questions the results were as follows:

	Total 1966	*Total 1963*
Too fast	4%	3%
Too slow	43%	51%
About the right pace	35%	31%
Not sure	18%	15%

[5] Brink and Harris, *Black and White*, p. 126.

TABLE 3-2   CHANGE IN ATTITUDES OF TEXANS TOWARD INTEGRATION

Form of Integration:	*Year of Survey*				
Would you accept:	*1963*	*1964*	*1966*	*1968*	*1969*
Negroes riding in the same sections of trains and buses with you?					
Accept	49%	62%	64%	80%	75%
Reject	47	35	35	19	23
No Answer	4	3	1	1	2
Negroes eating in the same restaurant with you?					
Accept	40	54	56	73	71
Repect	57	44	42	26	28
No Answer	3	2	2	1	1
Negroes staying in the same hotel with you?					
Accept	36	49	50	66	64
Reject	60	47	48	32	34
No Answer	4	4	2	2	2
Sending your children to the same schools?					
Accept	41	52	53	69	65
Reject	55	46	45	29	32
No Answer	4	2	2	2	3
Negroes attending your church?					
Accept	46	59	54	68	68
Reject	50	38	43	30	31
No Answer	4	3	3	2	1
Negroes using the same swimming pool with you?					
Accept	19	27	29	35	39
Reject	77	69	68	60	58
No Answer	4	4	3	5	3
Negroes working side by side with you in the same kind of job?					
Accept	56	67	69	83	76
Reject	40	31	29	16	22
No Answer	4	2	2	1	2
Negroes attending the same social gathering outside your home?					
Accept	23	32	37	49	48
Reject	73	65	61	48	50
No Answer	4	3	2	3	2
Negroes attending a social gathering in your home?					
Accept	13	19	23	31	33
Reject	83	77	75	67	64
No Answer	4	4	2	2	3
Negroes living next door to you?					
Accept	23	30	29	38	41
Reject	74	67	69	59	56
No Answer	3	3	2	3	3
Having a Negro as roommate for your son or daughter at college?					
Accept	8	14	18	21	24
Reject	88	82	80	74	71
No Answer	4	4	2	5	5

Source: "The Texas Poll," Belden Associates, Dallas, Tex., September 14, 1969.

school integration, while in the south only two whites in a hundred would support integration. In 1956, two years after the historic *Brown vs. Topeka*, white attitudes had shifted markedly. Nationwide support for integration characterized about half of the white population; in the north it was the majority view, and in the south the proportion supporting integration had risen to one in in seven. By 1963, two out of every three whites believed in integrated schools, and, even more noteworthy, one out of three southern whites believed in integration. Since 1963 there has been a continuation of the upward trend in the proportion of white Americans who favor school integration. Additional survey information suggests that whites are becoming increasingly accommodating toward equal rights for blacks over time in other areas as well (see Table 3-2). But it should be noted that white opinion generally follows public policy, rather than leading it. White Americans have increasingly come to accept Negro equality, but they certainly have not pressed for integration.

There is a wide gap between the attitudes of masses and elites on the subject of the black revolution. The most hostile attitudes toward blacks are found among the less privileged, less educated whites. Low-income whites are much less willing to have contact with blacks than high-income whites, whether it is a matter of using the same public restrooms, or going to a movie or restaurant, or living next door. In fact, according to Brink and Harris survey data, only 46% of low-income whites in contrast to 78% high-income whites are prepared to believe that blacks are discriminated against. It is the affluent well-educated American who is most concerned with discrimination against blacks and who is most willing to have contact with them.

The political implication of this finding is obvious: opposition to civil rights legislation and to black advancement in education, jobs, income, housing and so on, is likely to be strongest among low-income whites. In 1968 these working-class whites formed the social basis of the Wallace-for-President movement. Within the white community, support for civil rights will continue to come from the educated, affluent American.

The black revolution has deeply divided white America. While it is true that there is a wide gulf between blacks and whites in terms of the speed of progress, the tactics of the revolution, and perhaps even the ultimate objective of the revolution, there is also a wide gulf between poor and affluent whites in their response to the Negro struggle. The better educated, more privileged whites are much more sympathetic toward black aspirations than poorly educated, low-income whites. Less privileged whites do not agree that the condition of the Negro in America is worse than the condition of whites, or that Negroes are discriminated against.[6]

[6] Brink and Harris, *Black and White*, p. 136.

	Percent Agreeing		
	All Whites	Low Income	Affluents
Negro housing is worse than white	65	46	69
Negroes are discriminated against	60	46	78
Negroes laugh a lot	56	66	49
Negroes smell different	52	61	45
Negroes have looser morals	50	56	46
Sympathize with Negro protests	46	24	57
Negroes want to live off handouts	43	53	33
Negro education worse than white	40	27	58

Less privileged whites hold stereotyped beliefs about Negroes—that they smell different, have looser morals, and are lazy. There is far less willingness to have contact with blacks among poor whites. As Louis Harris notes: "If there are two races in this country poles apart on the race issue, then it is equally true there are two white societies just as far apart." [7]

THE DEVELOPMENT OF CIVIL RIGHTS POLICY

The initial goal in the struggle for equality in America was the elimination of Jim Crow. This required the development of a national civil rights policy to eliminate direct discrimination and segregaton in public and private life. First, discrimination and segregation practiced by governments had to be prohibited, particularly in voting and public education. Then, direct discrimination in all segments of American life—in transportation, theatres, parks, stores, restaurants, businesses, employment, and housing—came under legal attack.

At the outset it is important to realize that the elimination of Jim Crow, that is, the elimination of direct, lawful discrimination, does not in itself ensure equality. The civil rights policies of the national government do not affect the conditions of equality in America as directly as we might suppose. The recent civil rights gains of Negroes have not dramatically affected the living conditions of the masses of blacks in either the North or the South. The problem of racial inequality—inequality between blacks and whites in income, health, housing, employment, education, and so on—is more than a problem of direct legal discrimination even though the first important step toward equality was the elimination of Jim Crow. The movement to end direct discrimination laid the foundation for the politics of equality in the future.

The Fourteenth Amendment declares:

All persons born or naturalized in the United States, and subject to the Jurisdiction thereof, are citizens of the United States and of the State

[7] *Ibid.,* p. 137.

wherein they reside. No State shall make or enforce any law which shall abridge the privileges or immunities of citizens of the United States; nor shall any State deprive any person of life, liberty, or property, without due process of law; nor deny to any person within its jurisdiction the equal protection of the laws.

The language of the Fourteenth Amendment and its historical context leaves little doubt that its original purpose was to achieve the full measure of citizenship and equality for the American Negro. Some radical Republicans were prepared in 1867 to carry out in southern society the revolution this amendment implied. But by 1877, it was clear that Reconstruction had failed; the national government was not prepared to carry out the long, difficult, and disagreeable task of really reconstructing society in the eleven states of the former Confederacy. In what has been described as the compromise of 1877, the national government agreed to end military occupation of the South, give up its efforts to rearrange southern society, and lend tacit approval to white supremacy in that region. In return, the southern states pledged their support of the Union, accepted national supremacy, and, of course, agreed to permit the Republican candidate to assume the Presidency after the disputed election of 1876.

The Supreme Court adhered to the terms of the compromise. The result was a complete inversion of the meaning of the Fourteenth Amendment so that it became a bulwark of segregation. State laws segregating the races were upheld so long as persons in each of the separated races were protected equally. The constitutional argument on behalf of segregation under the Fourteenth Amendment was that the phrase "equal protection of the laws" did not prevent state-enforced separation of the races. Schools and other public facilities that were "separate but equal" won constitutional approval. This separate but equal doctrine became the Supreme Court's interpretation of the Equal Protection Clause of the Fourteenth Amendment in *Plessy* v. *Ferguson*:

> The object of the [14th] Amendment was undoubtedly to enforce the absolute equality of the two races before the law, but in the nature of things it could not have been intended to abolish distinctions based upon color, or to enforce social, as distinguished from political, equality, or a commingling of the two races upon terms unsatisfactory to either. Laws permitting, and even requiring, their separation in places where they are liable to be brought into contact do not necessarily imply the inferiority of either race to the other, and have been generally, if not universally, recognized as within the competency of the state legislatures in the exercise of their police power. The most common instance of this is connected with the establishment of separate schools for white and colored children, which has been held to be a valid exercise of the legislative power. . . .[8]

[8] *Plessy* v. *Ferguson*, 163, U.S. 537 (1896).

As a matter of fact, of course, segregated facilities, including public schools, were seldom if ever equal, even with respect to physical conditions. In practice, the doctrine of segregation was "separate and unequal." The Supreme Court began to take notice of this after World War II. While it declined to overrule the segregationist interpretation of the Fourteenth Amendment, it began to order the admission of individual Negroes to white public universities, where evidence indicated that separate Negro institutions were inferior or nonexistent.[9]

Leaders of the newly emerging civil rights movement in the 1940s and 1950s were not satisfied with court decisions that examined the circumstances in each case to determine if separate school facilities were really equal. Led by Roy Wilkins, Executive Director of the National Association for the Advancement of Colored People, and Thurgood Marshall, Chief Counsel for the NAACP, the civil rights movement pressed for a court decision that segregation itself meant inequality within the meaning of the Fourteenth Amendment, whether or not facilities were equal in all tangible respects. In short, they wanted a complete reversal of the "separate but equal" interpretation of the Fourteenth Amendment, and a holding that laws *separating* the races were unconstitutional.

The civil rights groups chose to bring suit for desegration in Topeka, Kansas, where segregated Negro and white schools were equal with respect to buildings, curricula, qualifications, and salaries of teachers, and other tangible factors. The object was to prevent the Court from ordering the admission of a Negro because *tangible* facilities were not equal, and to force the Court to review the doctrine of segregation itself.

On May 17, 1954, the Court rendered its decision in *Brown* v. *Board of Education of Topeka, Kansas*:

> Segregation of white and colored children in public schools has a detrimental effect upon the colored children. The impact is greater when it has the sanction of law, for the policy of separating the races is usually interpreted as denoting the inferiority of the Negro group. A form of inferiority affects the motivation of a child to learn. Segregation with the sanction of law, therefore, has a tendency to retard the educational and mental development of Negro children and to deprive them of some of the benefits they would receive in a racially integrated school system.
>
> Whatever may have been the extent of psychological knowledge of the time of *Plessy* v. *Ferguson*, this finding is amply supported by modern authority. Any language in *Plessy* vs. *Ferguson* contrary to this source is rejected.[10]

The symbolic importance of the original *Brown* v. *Topeka* decision cannot be overestimated. While it would be many years before any significant number of black children would attend formerly segre-

[9] *Sweatt* v. *Painter*, 339 U.S. 629 (1950).
[10] *Brown* v. *Board of Education of Topeka, Kansas*, 347 U.S. 483 (1954).

gated white schools, the decision by the nation's highest court un-
doubtedly stimulated black hopes and expectations. Sociologist Kenneth Clark writes:

> This [civil rights] movement would probably not have existed at all
> were it not for the 1954 Supreme Court school desegregation decision
> which provided a tremendous boost to the morale of Negroes by its
> *clear* affirmation that color is irrelevant to the rights of American citi-
> zens. Until this time the Southern Negro generally had accommodated to
> the separatism of the black from the white society.[11]

MASS RESISTANCE TO CIVIL RIGHTS POLICY

The Supreme Court had spoken forcefully in the Brown case in
1954 in declaring segregation unconstitutional. From a constitutional
viewpoint, any state-supported segregation of the races after 1954
was prohibited. Article VI of the Constitution declares that the words
of that document are "the supreme law of the land . . . anything in
the constitution or laws of any state to the contrary notwithstanding."

From a political viewpoint, however, the battle over segregation
was just beginning. Segregation would remain a part of American
life, regardless of its constitutionality, until effective elite power was
brought to bear to end it. The Supreme Court, by virtue of the
American system of federalism and separation of powers, has little
formal power at its disposal. Congress, the President, state governors
and legislatures, and the people have more power at their disposal
than the federal judiciary. The Supreme Court must rely largely on
the other branches of the federal government, on the states, and on
private individuals and orgnaizations to effectuate the law of the land.

Yet in 1954 the practice of segregation was widespread and deeply
ingrained in American life. Seventeen states required the segregation
of the races in public schools. These seventeen states were:

Alabama	North Carolina	Delaware
Arkansas	South Carolina	Kentucky
Florida	Tennessee	Maryland
Georgia	Texas	Missouri
Louisiana	Virginia	Oklahoma
Mississippi		West Virginia

The Congress of the United States required the segregation of the
races in the public schools of the District of Columbia. Four additional states—Arizona, Kansas, New Mexico, and Wyoming—authorized segregation upon the option of local school boards.

Thus, in deciding *Brown* v. *Topeka*, the Supreme Court struck
down the laws of twenty-one states and the District of Columbia in

---

[11] Kenneth B. Clark, *Dark Ghetto* (New York: Harper and Row, 1965), pp. 77-78.

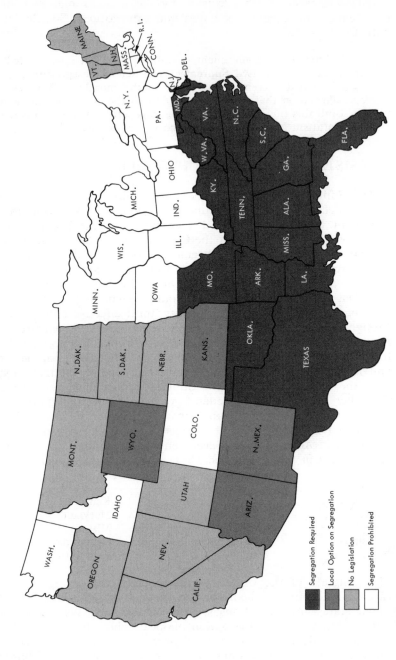

FIG. 3-1 SEGREGATION LAWS IN THE UNITED STATES IN 1954

Segregation Required

Local Option on Segregation

No Legislation

Segregation Prohibited

a single opinion. Such a far-reaching decision was bound to meet with difficulties in implementation. In an opinion delivered the following year regarding the question of relief for Brown and others similarly situated, the Supreme Court said:

> Full implementation of these constitutional principles may require solution of varied local school problems. School authorities have the primary responsibility for elucidating, assessing, and solving these problems; courts will have to consider whether the action of school authorities constitutes good faith implementation of the governing constitutional principles.

Thus, the Supreme Court did not order immediate nationwide desegregation, but instead turned over the responsibility for desegregation to state and local authorities under the supervision of federal district courts. The way was open for extensive litigation, obstruction, and delay by states that chose to resist desegregation.

The six border states with segregated school systems—Delaware, Kentucky, Maryland, Missouri, Oklahoma, West Virginia—together with the school districts in Kansas, Arizona, and New Mexico which had operated segregated schools, chose not to resist desegregation formally. The District of Columbia also desegregated its public schools the year following the Supreme Court's decision. Progress in desegregation in the border states proceeded fairly well; by 1964 over half of the Negro children in these states were attending integrated schools.

However, resistance to school integration was the policy choice of the eleven states of the Old Confederacy. Refusal of a school district to desegregate until it is faced with a federal court injunction was the most common form of delay. Segregationists also pressed for state laws which would create an endless chain of litigation in each of the nearly 3,000 school districts in the South, in the hope that these integration efforts would drown in a sea of protracted court controversy. Some other schemes included state payment of private school tuition in lieu of providing public schools, amending compulsory attendance laws to provide that no child shall be required to attend an integrated school, requiring schools faced with desegregation orders to cease operation, and the use of pupil placement laws to avoid or minimize the extent of integration. State officials attempted to prevent desegregation on the grounds that it would endanger public safety, and actually precipitated and encouraged violent resistance through attempts to "interpose" and "nullify" federal authority within their states.

Of all delaying tactics, the most successful was the pupil placement law. Under this law each child was guaranteed "freedom of choice" in the selection of his school. Prior to the fall term, all pupils, black and white, filled out a form indicating their choice of schools. School authorities then assigned pupils to the schools of their choice pro-

vided that space was available and that no other "problems" interfered. School authorities relied on the fact that most blacks and most
whites selected the schools they previously attended, that is, a
segregated school. Since pupil placement laws and freedom of choice
plans were at face value nondiscriminatory the Supreme Court held
them to be constitutional so long as there was no proof of discrimination in their administration. But by 1968 most federal district courts
had come to realize that little desegregation was occuring under freedom of choice plans. Increasingly, federal courts declined to accept
such plans from local school authorities as "good faith" implementation of desegregation. Gradually freedom of choice plans disappeared
in favor of unitary school districts with pupil assignment by school
officials.

On the whole, those states that chose to resist desegregation were
quite successful in doing so during the ten year period from 1954 to
1964. In late 1964 only about two percent of the Negro school children
in the eleven southern states were attending integrated schools! The
effectiveness of state and local governments in resisting the policy of
the Supreme Court for over a decade is an important commentary
on the power of states and communities in our federal system.

In the Civil Rights Act of 1964, Congress finally entered the civil
rights field in support of court efforts to achieve desegregation.
Among other things, the Civil Rights Act of 1964 provided that every
federal department and agency must take action to end segregation
in all programs or activities receiving federal financial assistance.
It was specified that this action was to include termination of financial
assistance if states and communities receiving federal funds refused
to comply with federal desegregation orders. Thus, in addition to
court orders requiring desegregation, states and communities faced
administrative orders or "guidelines" from federal executive agencies,
particularly the U.S. Office of Education, threatening loss of federal
funds for noncompliance. Acting under the authority of Title VI, the
U.S. Office of Education required all school districts in the seventeen
formerly segregated states to submit desegregation plans as a condition of federal assistance. "Guidelines" governing the acceptability of
these plans were frequently unclear, often contradictory, and always
changing, yet progress toward desegregation was speeded up.

In 1969 the last legal justification for delay in implementing school
desegregation collapsed when the Supreme Court rejected a request
by Mississippi school officials for a delay in implementing school desegregation in that state. School officials, with the support of the
Nixon Administration, contended that immediate desegregation in
several southern Mississippi counties would encounter "administrative and legislative difficulties." The Supreme Court stated that no
delay could be granted because "continued operation of segregated
school under a standard of allowing 'all deliberate speed' for de-

segregation is no longer constitutionally permissible." [12] The Court declared that every school district was obligated to end dual school systems "at once" and "now and hereafter" to operate only unitary schools. The effect of the decision—fifteen years after the original Brown case—was to eliminate any further legal justification for the continuation of segregation in public schools.

By 1970 southern school desegregation had proceeded to the point where more black pupils were attending integrated schools in the South than in the North. The Department of Health, Education, and Welfare reported that 58.3 percent of black pupils in the *South* were attending school with whites (up from 15.9 percent in 1967), whereas only 42.6 percent of black pupils in the *North* were attending integrated schools. Only 41.7 percent of black pupils were attending predominantly black schools in the South, but 57.4 percent of black pupils were attending predominantly black schools in the North. This is an important comparison between the diminishing impact of segregation by law in the South and the continuing impact of de facto segregation in the North. If the issue is posed as one of "racial isolation," then by 1970 the efforts of the federal courts and executive agencies toward eliminating the last vestiges of segregation by law had reduced racial isolation in the South to the point where it was less than racial isolation in the North.

The evidence is very strong that a large Negro population strengthens the position of segregationists. Southern states with large Negro populations have made less progress toward desegregation than states with smaller proportions of Negro residents. While large Negro populations appear to stimulate resistance to desegregation, wealth and urbanization appear to have the opposite effect. Donald R. Matthews and James Prothro systematically examined the envionmental and political factors associated with desegregation policy in 997 southern counties.[13] Their dependent variable was simply the presence or absence of some school desegregation in each county in 1960. The environmental variables that correlated most closely with this rough measure of desegregation were as follows:

1. Percent of population urban;
2. Nonwhite median income;
3. Nonwhite median school years completed;
4. White median income;
5. Percent of population Negro;
6. Percent of population increase in 1940-50;
7. Percent of church members Roman Catholic;

[12] *Alexander* v. *Holmes County Board of Education*, 396 U.S. 19 (1969).
[13] Donald R. Matthews and James W. Prothro, "Stateways versus Folkways: Critical Factors in Southern Reaction to Brown v. Board of Education," in *Essays on the American Constitution*, ed. Gottfried Dietze (Englewood Cliffs: Prentice-Hall, 1964), pp. 139-58.

8. Percent of church members Baptist;
9. Percent of nonwhite labor force in white collar jobs;
10. Percent of labor force in agriculture.

These variables are presented in the order of their strength of association with school desegregation. Matthews and Prothro concluded that
desegregation is most likely in an urban environment in which
Negroes and whites receive relatively high incomes and Negroes are
relatively well educated. In addition, a large Negro population was a
distinct barrier to desegregation.

Thus, the pattern of national enforcement and local resistance in
school desegregation suggested: (1) national policy could not be
implemented until Congress and the executive branch threatened
financial sanctions; (2) state and local resistance could be surprisingly
effective in frustrating national policy over a prolonged period of
time; (3) state and local resistance is *greater* where black populations
are greater; (4) well-educated, affluent, urban populations are less
likely to oppose black demands for equality than undereducated,
poor, rural populations.

LOCAL ELITES AND SOUTHERN SCHOOL DESEGREGATION

By the 1960s most southern school districts had come to realize
that desegregation was inevitable. This does not mean that they wel-
comed integration. On the contrary, there was a strong preference
for segregation. But most school board members, and most parents,
appeared to prefer some integration to a closing of the schools. And
the vast majority wanted to avoid violence. Robert L. Crain accurately portrays the typical southern school board's reaction to desegregation:

> Their first and least difficult problem was to find ways to put off
> desegregation as long as possible. The best solution was simply to find the
> most capable lawyer and let him use all the legal tricks he could borrow
> or invent. The second problem was to mobilize whatever resources were
> necessary to develop a favorable climate for desegregation and to mini-
> mize demonstrations, violence, and publicity. Third, the school board
> members had to decide whether they were willing to be labeled inte-
> grationists; if they were not, they had to decide how they could protect
> themselves by expressing public disapproval of integration and at the
> same time not give aid and comfort to the citizen's councils and the
> potential troublemakers. Finally the school board had to decide how to
> prevent the intervention of the state legislature or the governor.[14]

Crain examined school desegregation in seven southern cities. In
Crain's study, only New Orleans experienced conflict and violence

[14] Robert L. Crain, *The Politics of School Desegregation* (Chicago: Aldine,
1967), p. 232.

over desegregation. The reaction of segregationists in New Orleans in 1960 was so intense and went unchecked for such a long time that the city suffered serious dislocations. White children boycotted the two schools that were first selected for integration for an entire year, and unruly crowds cursed, stoned, and spat upon the few white children who continued to attend integrated schools. All of this occurred in full view of national television network cameras. School board members who had desegregated the school under the Federal Court order were ostracized by their friends, harrassed and threatened, and removed from office by the state legislature. Teachers and school personnel went unpaid for many months, while the legislature held up school funds and local banks refused to cash school checks. Despite the fact that New Orleans is one of America's most cosmopolitan cities—cultured, civilized, heterogeneous—it experienced one of the nation's most chaotic school desegregations.

In contrast, the desegregation in Atlanta was almost a model of civic action. Atlanta was the first city to desegregate in the deep south states of Mississippi, Alabama, Georgia and South Carolina. It desegregated despite a hostile state legislature and a governor, Ernest Vandiver, who had campaigned on the pledge that "No, not one" Negro would be admitted to a white school during his administration.

What explains the differences in desegregation politics in two cities as roughly comparable in size and socioeconomic character as Atlanta and New Orleans? Crain contends that the difference can be explained by the attitudes and sense of responsibility of each city's business and civic elite. School board members and elected officials are much too insecure in their positions and much too accessible to the opinions of white masses to be able to assume the leadership in desegregation. In contrast, the business and civic elite has sufficient power to influence the course of events and yet they are much more insulated from public opinion than are the elected officials. The power of the business and civic elite takes several forms: they have the money with which to influence political campaigns and to influence public opinion, and they enjoy positions of high prestige, especially in a southern city. They have personal influence over many leaders in the community. Moreover, they are not vulnerable to attack, whereas elected officials can be defeated at the polls, ministers can be fired, and employees can loose their jobs. Men with high positions in the business community are reasonably invulnerable to attacks from "rednecks" (lower class whites with the most hostile racial feelings). Crain concludes that "the ideology of the civic elite is the dominant factor in determining whether the city will acquiesce peacefully to the desegregation order, and . . . the composition of the school board is less important."

According to Crain, the elite of New Orleans had withdrawn from politics and had assumed no responsibility in the desegregation proceedings. This aloofness from politics and governmental affairs is part of a broader traditionalist ideology which seemed to characterize the old line elite of New Orleans. Atlanta's elite took a strong interest in economic development and in the national reputation of the city. However, in New Orleans the elite is not strongly committed to attracting new industry. In New Orleans the elite is truly "southern"; they disdain economic development efforts as brash money grubbing by the nouveaux riches. In Atlanta, money and achieved status account for elite membership, but in New Orleans being a native and coming from a "good family" are more important. According to Crain:

> New Orleans is an anachronism—a traditionalist society in mid-twentieth century America. We find attitudes in New Orleans which were prevalent in the traditionalist societies in the nineteenth century south, the most obvious of which is a resistance to new ideas and new values. Since new values are brought in by new wealth and by outsiders, the economic elite in New Orleans is predictably not as hospitable to new industry as the elites in other southern cities.[15]

It appears, then, that success in desegregation in southern cities may be a product of progressivism, cosmopolitanism, and responsibility of business and civic elites. These elites, insulated from public opinion, have the freedom, security, prestige, and power to achieve a political objective—desegregation—which is clearly at variance with the preferences of the masses.

"DE FACTO" SCHOOL SEGREGATION AND BUSSING

In *Brown* v. *Board of Education of Topeka*, the Supreme Court quoted approvingly the view that segregation had "a tendency to retard the educational and mental development of Negro children and to deprive them of some of the benefits they would receive in a racially integrated school system." In 1967 the U.S. Commission on Civil Rights reported that even when the segregation was *de facto*, that is, the product of segregated housing patterns and neighborhood schools rather than direct discrimination, the adverse effects on black students were still significant.[16] Black students attending predominantly black schools had lower achievement scores and lower levels of aspiration than blacks with comparable socioeconomic backgrounds who attended predominantly white schools. When a group of black students attending school with a majority of advantaged whites was compared to a group of blacks attending school with a majority of disadvantaged blacks, the average difference in levels of achievement

[15] *Ibid.*, p. 303.
[16] U.S. Commission on Civil Rights, *Racial Isolation in The Public Schools*, 2 vols. (Washington, D.C.: Government Printing Office, 1966).

amounted to more than two grade levels. On the other hand, the Commission found that the achievement levels of white students in classes roughly half white in composition were not substantially different from those of white students in all-white schools. This finding comprises perhaps the best single argument for ending de facto segregation in Northern urban systems.

Racial isolation of public school pupils is widespread throughout the nation. The U.S. Commission on Civil Rights reported that 75 percent of the black elementary school pupils in seventy-five large cities attended predominantly black schools (those with 90 percent or more black enrollment). However, ending de facto segregation would require drastic changes in the prevailing concept of "neighborhood schools." Schools would no longer be a part of the neighborhood or the local community but rather part of a larger city-wide or area-wide school system. Students would have to be bussed into and out of the ghettos on a massive scale. In several large cities where blacks comprise the overwhelming majority of public school students, desegregation would require city students to be bussed to the suburbs and suburban students to be bussed to the core city. Such a program would require the cooperation of independent suburban school districts, which seems very unlikely. Many suburbanites moved out of the central city in order to get their children out of city schools, and these persons are highly unlikely to favor any proposal to bus their children back into the ghettos. Finally, the ending of de facto segregation would require school districts to classify students on the basis of race and to use racial categories as a basis for school placement. Although this would supposedly be a benign form of racial classification, nevertheless it would represent a return to both government-sponsored racial classification and the differential application of laws to the separate races (in contrast to the notion that the law should be "color-blind").

To date the Supreme Court has *not* held that there is any affirmative duty to correct de facto racial imbalances in Northern schools. In other words, as yet there is no clear constitutional *duty* to eliminate de facto segregation in Northern cities, as long as school attendance lines are drawn with no real intention of segregating the races. De facto segregation in the North is not viewed as a product of state action, either present or past, and for this reason the state is not obligated under the Fourteenth Amendment to act affirmatively to end such segregation. Several U.S. circuit courts have held that the equal protection clause of the Fourteenth Amendment does not create an affirmative duty for school districts to correct imbalances resulting from neighborhood school plans not consciously devised to segregate the races. Of course Northern school districts may *choose* to end de facto segregation by bussing if they wish to do so. There is no constitutional barrier to racial classifications and bussing for the purpose of achieving integration (the Supreme Court has never adopted a "color-blind" policy), because such a scheme would be aimed at helping rather than harming the minority races.

In contrast to Northern schools, southern school districts have a special affirmative duty to elminate all vestiges of dual school systems, and this responsibility may include "bussing" and the breakup of neighborhood schools. Southern congressmen and governors have argued to no avail that Southern school districts should be given "equal" treatment with Northern school districts, and not be required to bus students out of their neighborhoods to achieve racial balancing. In 1970, President Richard Nixon announced his support of the neighborhood school concept. However, in an important case involving Charlotte and Mecklenburg County, North Carolina, in 1971, the Supreme Court held that school districts which had previously segregated students by law (Southern school districts) had a special constitutional mandate to end all vestiges of state-imposed segregation in their public schools.[17] The Court held that the racial composition of a school could be used as prima facie evidence of violation of constitutional rights under the Equal Protection Clause, and that bussing to achieve racial balance could be imposed upon Southern school districts as a means of ending all traces of dualism in the schools.

CONGRESS AND THE CIVIL RIGHTS ACT OF 1964

The initial objective of the civil rights movement in America was to prevent discrimination and segregation as practiced by or supported by *governments*, particularly states, municipalities, and school districts. But even while important victories for the civil rights movement were being recorded in the prevention of discrimination by governments, particularly in the Brown case, the movement began to broaden its objectives to include the elimination of discrimination in *all* segments of American life, private as well as public. Civil rights was redefined to mean not merely a legal but an actual possibility of developing human capacities and sharing in the goods a society has produced and the way of life it has built. This was a more positive concept of civil rights. It involved not merely restrictions on government, but a positive obligation of government to act forcefully to end discrimination in public accommodations, employment, housing, and all other sectors of private life. When the civil rights movement turned to combating private discrimination, it had to carry its fight into the legislative branch of government. The federal courts could help restrict discrimination by state and local governments and school authorities, but only Congress, state legislatures, and city councils could restrict discrimination practiced by private owners of restau-

[17] *Swann* v. *Charlotte-Mecklenburg Board of Education*, 39 L. W. 4437 (1971).

rants, hotels and motels, private employers, and other individuals who were not government officials.

Yet, prior to 1964, Congress was content to let the President and the courts struggle with the problem of civil rights. In 1957 and 1960, Congress passed weak civil rights bills which made it illegal for any person to interfere with the exercise of rights under a federal court order, or to use interstate commerce for the purpose of burning or bombing any building. So strong was the reluctance of Congress to enter the field of civil rights that even those bills were extensively debated and compromised before final passage. But by 1964 the demand for strong civil rights legislation was so great that Congress could no longer ignore the nation's most pressing domestic issue.

A new militancy, expressed in Martin Luther King's call for nonviolent direct action, appeared in the civil rights movement in the mid-1950s. Between 1941 and 1954, Negro protests were primarily in the form of legal cases brought by the NAACP to federal courts; negotiation and bargaining with white businessmen and government offiicals, often by the National Urban League; and local lobbying on behalf of Negro constituents by Negro political leaders in northern communities. But in 1955 the Negro community of Montgomery, Alabama, began a year-long boycott with frequent demonstrations against the Montgomery city buses over segregated seating practices. The dramatic appeal and the eventual success of the boycott in Montgomery brought nationwide attention to a local Negro minister, Martin Luther King, and led to the creation in 1956 of the Southern Christian Leadership Conference. In 1960, Negro students from the North Carolina Agricultural and Technical College began a "sit-in" demonstration at the segregated Woolworth lunch counter in Greensboro, North Carolina. Soon, "sit-ins" in restaurants, "read-ins" in libraries, "pray-ins" in white churches spread throughout the South, generally under the leadership of the Southern Christian Leadership Conference, which followed "nonviolent" techniques.

Perhaps the most dramatic confrontation between the civil rights movement and southern segregationists occurred in Birmingham, Alabama, in the spring of 1963. In support of a request for desegregation of downtown eating places and the formation of a biracial committee to work out the integration of public schools, Martin Luther King led several thousand Birmingham Negroes in a series of orderly street marches. The demonstrators were met with strong police action, including fire hoses, police dogs, and electric cattle prods. Newspaper pictures of Negroes being attacked by police and bitten by dogs were flashed all over the world. More than 25,000 demonstrators, including Dr. King, were jailed.

The year 1963 was probably the most important for nonviolent direct action. The Birmingham action set off demonstrations in many parts of the country; the theme remained one of nonviolence, and it was usually whites rather than Negroes who resorted to violence in these demonstrations. Responsible black elites remained in control of the movement and won widespread support from the white liberal community. The culmination of the nonviolent philosophy was a giant, yet orderly, march on Washington, held on August 28, 1963. More than 200,000 blacks and whites participated in the march, which was endorsed by many labor leaders, religious groups, and political figures. It was in response to this march that President Kennedy sent a strong civil rights bill to Congress, which was later passed, after his death— the famous Civil Rights Act of 1964.

The Civil Rights Act of 1964 passed both houses of Congress by better than a two-thirds favorable vote; it won the overwhelming support of both Republican and Democratic Congressmen. It was signed into law on July 4, 1964. It ranks with the Emancipation Proclamation, the Fourteenth Amendment, and *Brown* v. *Topeka* as one of the most important steps toward full equality for the Negro in America.

The Civil Rights Act of 1964 provides:

   I. That it is unlawful to apply unequal standards in voter registration procedures, or to deny registration for irrelevant errors or omissions on records or applications.
  II. That it is unlawful to discriminate or segregate persons on the grounds of race, color, religion, or national origin in any place or public accommodation, including hotels, motels, restaurants, movies, theatres, sports areas, entertainment houses, and other places which offer to serve the public. This prohibition extends to all establishments whose operations affect interstate commerce or whose discriminatory practices are supported by state action.
 III. That the Attorney General shall undertake civil action on behalf of any person denied equal access to a public accommodation to obtain a federal district court order to secure compliance with the act. If the owner or manager of a public accommodation should continue to discriminate, he would be in contempt of court and subject to peremptory fines and imprisonment without trial by jury. (This mode of enforcement gave establishments a chance to mend their ways without punishment, and it also avoided the possibility that southern juries would refuse to convict persons for violations of the act.)
  IV. That the Attorney General shall undertake civil actions on behalf of persons attempting orderly desegregation of public schools.
   V. That the Commission on Civil Rights, first established in the Civil Rights Act of 1957, shall be empowered to investigate deprivations of the right to vote, study and collect information regarding the discrimination in America, and make reports to the President and Congress.
  VI. That each federal department and agency shall take action to end discrimination in all programs or activities receiving federal financial assistance in any form. This action shall include termination of financial assistance.
 VII. That it shall be unlawful for any employer or labor union with 25 or more persons after 1965 to discriminate against any individual in any

fashion in employment, because of his race, color, religion, sex, or national origin, and that an Equal Employment Opportunity Commission shall be established to enforce this provision by investigation, conference, conciliation, persuasion, and, if need be, civil action in federal court.

The black revolution in the 1960s meant a turning away from the slowly moving machinery of the federal courts and the slow evolution of public law. The civil rights movement invented new political techniques for minorities in American politics. In 1963 a group of Alabama clergymen petitioned Martin Luther King, Jr., to call off mass demonstrations in Birmingham. King, who had been arrested in the demonstrations, replied in his famous "Letter from Birmingham Jail":

> You may well ask, "Why direct action? Why sit-ins, marches, etc.? Isn't negotiation a better path?" You are exactly right in your call for negotiation. Indeed, this is the purpose of direct action. Nonviolent direct action seeks to create such a crisis and establish such creative tension that a community that has constantly refused to negotiate is forced to confront the issue. It seeks to so dramatize the issue that it can no longer be ignored. . . .
>
> You express a great deal of anxiety over our willingness to break laws. . . . One may well ask, "How can you advocate breaking some laws and obeying others?" The answer is found in the fact that there are two types of laws: There are *just* laws and there are *unjust* laws. I would be the first to advocate obeying just laws. One has not only a legal but a moral responsibility to obey just laws. Conversely, one has a moral responsibility to disobey unjust laws. . . .
>
> All segregation statutes are unjust because segregation distorts the soul and damages the personality. It gives the segregator a false sense of superiority and the segregated a false sense of inferiority. . . .
>
> In no sense do I advocate evading or defying the law as the rabid segregationist would do. This would lead to anarchy. One who breaks an unjust law must do it *openly, lovingly* (not hatefully as the white mothers did in New Orleans when they were seen on television screaming "nigger, nigger, nigger") and with a willingness to accept the penalty. I submit that an individual who breaks a law that conscience tells him is unjust, and willingly accepts the penalty by staying in jail to arouse the conscience of the community over its injustice, is in reality expressing the very highest respect for law.[18]

It is important to note, however, that Martin Luther King's tactics relied primarily on an appeal to the conscience of white elites. The purpose of demonstrations was to call attention to injustice, and stimulate established elites to remedy the injustice by lawful means. The purpose of civil disobedience was to dramatize injustice; only *unjust* laws were to be broken "openly and lovingly," and punishment was

[18] A public letter by Martin Luther King, Jr., Birmingham, Alabama, April 16, 1963. Copyright © 1963 by Martin Luther King, Jr. Reprinted with permission of Joan Daves.

accepted to demonstrate sincerity. King did not urge black masses to remedy injustice themselves by any means necessary; and he did not urge the overthrow of established elites.

NATIONAL "FAIR HOUSING" POLICY

For many years "fair housing" had been considered the most sensitive area of civil rights legislation. Discrimination in the sale and rental of housing was the last major civil rights problem on which Congress took action. Discrimination in housing had not been mentioned in any previous legislation—not even in the comprehensive Civil Rights Act of 1964. It was not until 1966 that the President formally requested Congress to pass open housing legislation; but fair housing bills died in Congress in both the 1966 and 1967 sessions. Prohibiting discrimination in the sale or rental of housing affected the constituencies of northern members of Congress more than any of the earlier, southern-oriented legislation. The real estate industry in America was squarely opposed to the fair housing concept. The National Association of Real Estate Boards published a "Property Owners Bill of Rights" asserting the "right" of the individual American property owner

> . . . to determine the acceptability and desirability of any prospective buyer or tenant of his property. . . . To choose who, in his opinion, are congenial tenants in any property he owns—to maintain the stability and security of his income. . . . To enjoy the freedom to accept, reject, negotiate or not negotiate with, others.[19]

Moreover, there was reason to believe that a majority of white Americans agreed with the housing industry and opposed laws prohibiting discrimination in sale or rental housing. When the California legislature passed a fair housing law, the state's voters replied by overwhelmingly supporting a state constitutional amendment, known as Proposition 14, which prohibited the legislature from abridging the rights of citizens to sell, lease, or rent to the person of their choice. The effect of this constitutional amendment was to nullify the state's fair housing law, and it won a statewide referendum in California by a two to one margin of voters! Later the California Supreme Court held Proposition 14 to be a violation of the Fourteenth Amendment of the United States Constitution and in effect threw out the resuls of the referendum; but nonetheless the vote itself was clear evidence of widespread popular opposition to fair housing. Finally, the rioting in major cities in 1967 appeared to harden the attitudes of whites toward further civil rights legislation.

Thus, the prospects for a fair housing law were not very good at the beginning of 1968. However, when Martin Luther King, Jr. was

[19] National Association of Real Estate Boards, "Property Owners Bill of Rights," June 4, 1963.

assassinated on April 4 the mood of the nation and of Congress changed dramatically and many felt that Congress should pass a fair housing law as a tribute to the slain civil rights leader. The final version of the Civil Rights Bill of 1968 included amendments which made it a crime for persons to travel in interstate commerce with intent to incite or take part in a riot or to manufacture or transport firearms and explosives for use in a civil disorder. These "antiriot" amendments won crucial support for the bill.

The Civil Rights Act of 1968 prohibited the following forms of discrimination:

Refusal to sell or rent a dwelling to any person because of his race, color, religion, or national origin.
Discrimination against a person in the terms, conditions, or privileges of the sale or rental of a dwelling.
Advertising the sale or rental of a dwelling indicating a preference or discrimination based on race, color, religion, or national origin.
Inducing persons to sell or rent a dwelling by referring to the entry into the neighborhood of persons of a particular race, religion, or national origin (the "blockbusting" technique of real estate selling).

The Act applied to all apartments and houses, rented or sold, by either real estate developers or by private individuals who used the services of real estate agents. It exempted private individuals who sold their own home without the services of a real estate agent provided they did not indicate any preference or discrimination in advertising in the sale or rental of a house. It also exempted apartments with four or less units where the owner maintained his own residence. The enforcement provisions allowed a person who believed he had been discriminated against to file a complaint with the Secretary of Housing and Urban Development who would then investigate and attempt to conciliate the matter; if conciliation failed the individual could sue in a federal court for injunctive relief. But where state and local remedies were available, the individual was required to seek these local remedies first before federal court action. Thus, the enforcement procedure was quite cumbersome upon the individuals discriminated against.

EQUALITY AND BLACK-WHITE "LIFE CHANCES"

While the great gains of the civil rights movement were immensely important, it must be recognized that they are *symbolic* rather than *actual* changes in the conditions under which most blacks live in America. Racial politics today center about the actual inequalities between blacks and whites in incomes, jobs, housing, health, education, and other conditions of life.

The problem of inequality is usually posed as differences in the "life chances" of blacks and whites. Figures can reveal only the bare outline of the Negro's "life chances" in American society (see Table 3-3). In the 1960s the average income of a black family was only *half* the average white family's income. Nearly half of all black families were below the recognized poverty line of $3,000 annual income. Twice as many blacks lived in substandard housing as whites. The average black did not acquire as much education as the average white. Blacks are far less likely to hold prestigious white collar jobs in professional, managerial, clerical, or sales work. They did not hold many skilled craft jobs in industry, but were concentrated in operative, service, and laboring positions. Black women not only had more children, but they had them earlier. And too many children too early made it difficult for parents to finish school. Thus a cycle was at work in the ghettos; low education levels produced low income levels, which prevented parents from moving out of the ghettos, which deprived children of educational opportunities, and then the cycle repeated.

TABLE 3-3 ECONOMIC CHARACTERISTICS, NEGRO AND WHITE POPULATIONS
IN THE UNITED STATES, 1960 CENSUS

	Negro	*White*
Median family income	$2,520	$5,088
Percent families less than $3,000	39.6	18.6
Median school years completed by adults	8.2	10.9
Fertility rate	2,002	1,712
Percent female headed families	22.4	8.7
Male occupations in percent		
Professional	3.9	11.0
Managerial	2.3	11.5
Clerical	5.0	7.1
Sales	1.5	7.4
Farmers	4.4	5.6
Craftsmen	10.2	20.5
Operatives	23.5	19.5
Service	13.7	5.2
Farm labor	7.1	2.3
Labor	19.4	5.6
Not reported	8.4	4.2
Infant mortalities per 1,000 live births	43.2	22.9
Home ownership, percent	38.4	61.6
Size of family	4.3	3.6

Source: U.S. Bureau of the Census.

Daniel P. Moynihan has argued persuasively that one of the worst effects of slavery and segregation has been their impact on Negro family life.[20] The black male was most humiliated by segregationist practices. Segregation, with its implications of inferiority and submissiveness, damaged the male more than the female personality; the black female was a threat to no one. Not surprisingly, the female-headed black family emerges as one of the striking features of life in the ghetto. Over 25 percent of all black families are headed by women.

[20] Daniel P. Moynihan, *The Negro Family: The Case For National Action* (Washington, D.C.: Government Printing Office, 1965).

For the young black male brought up in a matriarchal setting in the ghetto, the future is often depressing, with defeat and frustration repeating themselves throughout his life. He may drop out of school in the ninth grade to protest his lack of success. If he fails his armed forces qualification tests (and a majority of young men from the ghetto do fail it), he may never again have an opportunity for further education or job training. Lacking parental supervision and with little to do, he may soon get into trouble with the police. A police record will further hurt his chances of getting a job. The ghetto male with limited job skills enters the job market seriously handicapped. His pay is usually not enough to support a family, and he has little hope of advancement. He may tie up much of his income in installment payments for a car, a television set, or the other conveniences that he sees in widespread use among middle class Americans. Because of his low credit rating, he will be forced to pay excessive interest rates, and sooner or later his creditors will garnish his salary. If he marries, he is likely to have five or more children, and he and his family will live in overcrowded substandard housing. As pressures and frustrations mount, he may decide to leave his family, either because he has found his inability to support his wife and children humiliating, or because only in this way will his wife and children be eligible for welfare payments. Welfare policy also strengthens the role of the female in the black family because she can get the family on welfare (particularly Aid to Families with Dependent Children) while the male cannot. In

TABLE 3-4 MEDIAN NONWHITE FAMILY INCOME AS A PERCENTAGE OF MEDIAN WHITE FAMILY INCOME FOR THE UNITED STATES, 1947 TO 1968

Year	Percent
1947	51
1948	53
1949	51
1950	54
1951	53
1952	57
1953	56
1954	56
1955	55
1956	53
1957	54
1958	51
1959	52
1960	55
1961	53
1962	53
1963	53
1964	56
1965	55
1966	60
1967	62
1968	63

Source: Bureau of the Census, *Consumer Income*, Dec. 23, 1969, p. 21.

fact, his remaining with his family is often an obstacle to its receiving welfare payments.

Despite these obstacles, blacks have made dramatic improvements in "life chances" over the last decade. Blacks have progressed in income, employment, education, home ownership, and other indicators of living standards—not only in absolute terms, but also relative to whites. Table 3–4 reveals that black family income has gradually moved closer to white family income over the last ten years. Thus, the gap between black and white life chances is narrowing; whether it is moving fast enough is another question. But the future is not as bleak as extreme rhetoric suggests. Blacks have made very impressive gains, both in absolute and relative terms, *within* the existing political and economic system.

PUBLIC POLICY AND BLACK-WHITE "LIFE CHANCES"

The civil rights movement opened up new opportunities for black Americans. But equality of *opportunity* is not the same as *absolute* equality. In a significant speech to the graduating class of Howard University in 1965, President Lyndon B. Johnson identified the fundamental problem of equality in America today:

> You do not take a person who for years has been hoveled by chains and liberate him, bring him up to the starting line of a race, and say, "You are free to compete with all the others," and still justly believe that you have been completely fair.
>
> Thus it is not enough to open the gates to opportunity. All our citizens must have the ability to walk through those gates.
>
> This is the next and most profound stage of the battle for civil rights . . . the task is to give twenty million Negroes the same choice as every other American to learn, to work, and share in society, to develop their abilities—physical, mental, and spiritual—and to pursue their individual happiness.[21]

But the complexity of this task is enormous. The problems are manifold—how to overcome the interlocking effects of deprivation in education, job training, health, housing, employment, crime and delinquency, and human motivation.

Can deprivation resulting from unequal treatment of Negroes in the past be eliminated without preferential treatment for present day victims? And if preferential programs are begun, how will we know when blacks have been brought to the starting line? What about blacks who do succeed in joining the affluent American middle class—will they suffer from feelings of guilt in leaving most of their black brothers behind in the ghetto? Will integration of middle-class Negroes result

---

[21] President Lyndon B. Johnson, address to graduating class, Howard University, June 4, 1965.

in a "skimming off of the cream" of potential leadership of Negro masses?

Another problem: "Integration" assumes that individual blacks will acquire the skills, education, jobs, and income requisite for a secure position in affluent middle-class America, and it assumes that the values and institutions of this America are looked upon as legitimate and desirable by most blacks. Negroes in the past have not had much of a share in shaping these institutions or determining these values; the most they can expect is a greater share in their joint determination in the future. Given these conditions, can we assume that blacks will voluntarily choose to join affluent white America? Once the right to choose has been established, will blacks choose to be "integrated," or will they choose separation?

It is not our intention here to review all of the proposed or existing public programs which may contribute to a reduction of inequality in American society. In Chapter 5 we will describe social insurance and welfare policies, and the difficulties involved in developing rational approaches to the care of the poor. In Chapter 6 we will examine the Economic Opportunity Act of 1964, the core of the widely heralded "war on poverty," which constituted the national government's most direct attempt to cope with the complex problems of poverty and inequality. The experience of the Economic Opportunity program is an instructive example of the complex political issues involved in public efforts aimed at equalizing "life chances." There is no guarantee that equality can be achieved *even if* the government embarks upon a multibillion dollar effort to do so.

The equalization of life chances of blacks and whites in America would most certainly involve a massive public effort in redistributing income, education, jobs, and other resources. Even at the present time there appears to be no real national commitment to this. In the wake of a series of urban riots the President's Commission on Civil Disorder recommended "A commitment to national action on an unprecedented scale" requiring "unprecedented levels of funding and performance." Among other things, the Commission called for two million new jobs, including one million government jobs; substantial federal aid to eliminate de facto segregation; a uniform national welfare program with assistance levels set above the poverty line; and six million federally financed units of low and moderate income housing. But the Commission's report was not favorably received in a great many political quarters, and no real effort has been made to implement the Commission's recommendations. No doubt the war in Vietnam had something to do with the failure of the national government to respond to the Commission's recommendations. But it may also be true that even without the Vietnam war there would be insufficient commitment by the American people to undertake a massive public effort to achieve absolute equality of blacks and whites in the near future.

SUMMARY

Let us try to set forth some propositions that are consistent with elite theory and assist in describing the development of civil rights policy:

1. Elites and masses in America differ in their attitudes towards blacks. Support for civil rights legislation has come from educated affluent whites in leadership positions. Working-class whites have formed the social basis of the Wallace movement.

2. Mass opinion toward civil rights has generally followed public policy, and not led it. Mass opinion did not oppose legally segregated schools until after elites had declared national policy in *Brown* v. *Topeka.*

3. The greatest impetus to the advancement of civil rights policy in this century was the U.S. Supreme Court's decision in *Brown* v. *Topeka.* Thus, a white elite group, nonelected and enjoying life terms in office, assumed the initiative in civil rights policy. Congress did not take significant action until ten years later.

4. Resistance to the implementation of *Brown* v. *Topeka* was centered in states and communities which had the *largest* black population percentages. Resistance to national policy was remarkably effective for over a decade, and blacks were not admitted to white schools in the South in large numbers until all segments of the national elite—Congress and the executive branch, as well as the judicial branch—acted in support of desegregation.

5. Within Southern communities success in desegregation depended upon a sense of responsibility on the part of the community's business and civic elite. Only community elites, insulated from mass opinion, had the freedom, security, prestige, and power to achieve a public policy—desegregation—which was clearly at variance with the preferences of the masses.

6. The elimination of legal discrimination and the guarantee of equality of opportunity in the Civil Rights Act of 1964 was achieved largely through the dramatic appeals of middle-class black leaders to consciences of white elites. Black leaders did not attempt to overthrow the established order, but to open opportunities for blacks to achieve success within the American system.

7. National elites legally guaranteed nondiscrimination in the sale or rental of housing in 1968, an action which was clearly at variance with the preferences of white masses. Enforcement is likely to be difficult until mass opinion is brought into conformity with public policy.

8. Elite support for *equality of opportunity* does not satisfy the demands of black masses for *absolute* equality. White elites are not yet prepared to undertake a massive public effort to redistribute income, education, jobs, housing, and other resources in order to achieve the equalization of "life chances" among blacks and whites.

BIBLIOGRAPHY

BERMAN, DANIEL M., *It Is So Ordered*. New York: W. W. Norton, 1966.

CARMICHAEL, STOKELY and CHARLES V. HAMILTON, *Black Power*. New York: Random House, 1968.

CLARK, KENNETH B., *Dark Ghetto*. New York: Harper & Row, 1965.

CRAIN, ROBERT, *The Politics of School Desegregation*. Chicago: Aldine, 1968.

DYE, THOMAS R., *The Politics of Equality*. New York: Bobbs-Merrill, 1971.

PARSONS, TALCOTT and KENNETH B. CLARK (eds.), *The Negro American*. Boston: Beacon Press, 1965.

VIOLENCE AND REPRESSION:
elite response to mass disorder

The civil rights movement of the 1960s functioned within the established "rules of the game" of the American political system. The purpose of mass demonstrations, sit-ins, marches, and other nonviolent direct action tactics was to move the existing system to eliminate the injustices of discrimination and segregation. These activities were not designed to replace the existing system but to make it *work* on behalf of blacks as well as whites. Demonstrations were designed "to bear witness" to the existence of injustice—"to dramatize the issue so that it could no longer be ignored," in order to stir the conscience of white elites and to shame them into taking action to remedy injustice by lawful means. National elites responded to these appeals with the passage of the Civil Rights Act of 1964, the Voting Right Act of 1965, and the Fair Housing of 1968.

But the civil rights legislation of the 1960s had relatively little impact on the black masses in urban ghettos. The breakthroughs that the civil rights movement made in open public accommodations, fair employment, fair housing, and voting rights may have opened new opportunities for the educated black middle class, but the undereducated black poor living in the ghetto environment could not really take advantage of these new opportunities. The victories of the civil rights movement were primarily *symbolic* victories; the *actual* conditions of ghetto blacks in income, education, health, employment, housing, and other conditions of life were left unchanged. It was inevitable that the resentment, bitterness, and frustration of the ghetto masses would find expression in some fashion. And it was inevitable that this expression would not always stay with the established "rules of the game."

THE GHETTO RIOTS

Civil disorder and violence are not new on the American scene. On the night of December 16, 1773, a group of "agitators" in Boston, Massachusetts, illegally destroyed 342 chests of tea. The nation itself was founded in armed revolution. And violence as a form of political protest has continued intermittently in America to the present day. Yet even though domestic violence has played a prominent role in America's history, the ghetto riots of the 1960s shocked the nation with massive and widespread civil disorders. All of these riots involved Negro attacks on established authority—policemen, firemen, National Guardsmen, whites in general, and property owned by whites. Three of these riots—Watts, California, in 1965 and Newark and Detroit in 1967—amounted to major civil disorders.

The Watts riot in August 1965 was described in the McCone Commission's report:

In the ugliest interval . . . perhaps as many as 10,000 Negroes took to the streets in neurotic bands. They looted stores, set fires, beat up white passers-by whom they had hauled from stopped cars, many of which were turned upside-down and burned, exchanged shots with law enforcement officers, and stoned and shot at firemen. The rioters seemed to have been caught up in an insensate rage of destruction. By Friday, disorder spread to adjoining areas, and ultimately, an area covering 46.5 square miles had to be controlled with the aid of military authority before public order was restored. . . .

Of the 34 killed, one was a fireman, one was a deputy sheriff, and one a Long Beach policeman. . . . [the remainder were Negroes.]

More than 600 buildings were damaged by burning and looting. Out of this number, more than 200 were completely destroyed by fire. The rioters concentrated primarily on food markets, liquor stores, furniture stores, clothing stores, department stores, and pawn shops.

. . . We note with interest that no residences were deliberately burned, that damage to schools, libraries, churches and public buildings was minimal, and that certain types of business establishments, notably service stations and automobile dealers, were for the most part unharmed.[1]

For four consecutive days and nights, in the summer of 1967, snipers

[1] Governor's Commission on the Los Angeles Riots, John A. McCone, Chairman, *Violence in the City—An End or a Beginning* (Sacramento, Calif.: Office of the Governor of California, 1965), pp. 3-5.

Michigan National Guardsmen in Detroit's Riot-Torn West Side, July 1967. UPI Photo

fired at police and firemen, looters made off with the inventories of scores of stores, and arsonists set fire to large portions of commercial property in the black section of Newark. New Jersey's governor proclaimed Newark a city "in open rebellion," declared a state of emergency, and called out the National Guard. More than four thousand city policemen, state troopers, and National Guardsmen were required to restore order. Before the riot was over, twenty-three persons had been killed, and property damage was widespread. Of the dead, only two were white—a policeman and a fireman. Of the Negro dead, two were children and six were women.

But it was Detroit which became the scene of the bloodiest racial violence of the twentieth century. A week of rioting in Detroit, July 23-28, 1967, left 43 dead, and more than 1,000 injured. Whole sections of the city were reduced to charred, smoky ruins. Firemen who tried to fight fires were stoned and occasionally shot by ghetto residents. Over 1,300 buildings were totally demolished and 2,700 businesses sacked.

Detroit's upheaval began when police raided an after-hours club and arrested the bartender and several customers for selling and consuming alcoholic beverages after authorized closing hours. A force of 15,000 city and state police, National Guardsmen, and finally federal troops fought to quell the violence. Most of the looted retail businesses were liquor stores, groceries, and furniture stores. Many Negro merchants scrawled "Soul Brother" on their windows in an attempt to escape the wrath of the black mobs.

In the end, homes and shops covering a total area of fourteen square miles were gutted by fire. Of the 43 persons killed during the riot, 33 were Negro and 10 were white. Among the dead were one National Guardsman, one fireman, one policeman, and one Negro private guard. Both the violence and the pathos of the ghetto riots were reflected in the following report from Detroit:

> . . . a spirit of carefree nihilism was taking hold. To riot and destroy

appeared more and more to become ends in themselves. Late Sunday afternoon it appeared to one observer that the young people were "dancing amidst the flames."

A Negro plain clothes officer was standing in an intersection when a man threw a Molotov cocktail into a business establishment on the corner. In the heat of the afternoon, fanned by the 20–25 mile per hour winds of both Sunday and Monday, the fire reached the home next door within minutes. As its residents uselessly sprayed the flames with garden hoses, the fire jumped from roof to roof of adjacent two and three-story buildings. Within the hour the entire block was in flames. The ninth house in the burning row belonged to the arsonist who had thrown the Molotov cocktail. . . .

. . . Employed as a private guard, fifty-five year old Julius L. Dorsey, a Negro, was standing in front of a market, when accosted by two Negro men and a woman. They demanded he permit them to loot the market. He ignored their demands. They began to berate him. He asked a neighbor to call the police. As the argument grew more heated, Dorsey fired three shots from his pistol in the air.

The police radio reported: "Looters, they have rifles." A patrol car driven by a police officer and carrying three National Guardsmen arrived. As the looters fled, the law enforcement personnel opened fire. When the firing ceased, one person lay dead. He was Julius L. Dorsey. . . .[2]

The National Advisory Commission on Civil Disorders concluded:

1. No civil disorder was "typical" in all respects . . .
2. While civil disorders of 1967 were racial in character, they were not *inter*-racial. The 1967 disorders, as well as earlier disorders of the recent period, involved action within Negro neighborhoods against symbols of white American society—authority and property—rather than against white persons.
3. Despite extremist rhetoric there was no attempt to subvert the social order of the United States. Instead, most of those who attacked white authority and property seemed to be demanding fuller participation in the social order and the material benefits enjoyed by the vast majority of American citizens.
4. Disorder did not typically erupt without pre-existing causes, as a result of a single "triggering" or "precipitating" incident. Instead, it developed out of an increasingly social atmosphere, in which typically a series of tension-heightening incidents over a period of weeks or months became linked in the minds of many in the Negro community with a shared network of underlying grievances.
5. There was, typically, a complex relationship between the series of incidents, and the underlying grievances. For example, grievances about allegedly abusive police practices . . . were often aggravated in the minds of many Negroes by incidents involving the police, or the inaction of municipal authorities on Negro complaints about police action.
6. Many grievances in the Negro community resulted from discrimination, prejudice, and powerlessness which Negroes often experience. . . .
7. Characteristically the typical rioter was not a hoodlum, habitual criminal, or riff-raff. . . . Instead, he was a teenager or young adult, a life-long

resident of the city in which he rioted, high school drop-out—but somewhat better than his Negro neighbor—and almost invariably underemployed or employed in a menial job. He was proud of his race, extremely hostile to both whites and middle class negroes and, though informed about politics, highly distrustful of the political system and of political leaders.

8. Numerous Negro counter-rioters walked the street, urging the rioters to "cool it." . . .

9. Negotiation between Negro and white officials occurred during virtually all of this disorder. . . .

10. . . . Some rioters may have shared neither the conditions nor the grievance of their Negro neighbors; some may have coolly and deliberately exploited the chaos created by others; some may have been drawn into the melee merely because they identified with, or wished to emulate, others.

11. The background of disorder in the riot cities was typically characterized by severely disadvantaged conditions for Negroes, especially as compared with those of whites. . . .

12. In the immediate aftermath of disorder, the status quo of daily life before the disorder generally was quickly restored. Yet despite some notable public and private efforts, little basic change took place in the conditions underlying the disorder. In some cases, the result was increased dislike between blacks and whites, diminished inter-racial communication, and the growth of Negro and white extremist groups.[3]

ASSESSING THE CAUSES OF RIOTS

One explanation of urban violence is that it is a product of the "relative deprivation" of ghetto residents.[4] "Relative deprivation" is the discrepancy between people's expectations about the goods and conditions of life to which they are justifiably entitled and what they perceive to be their *chances* for getting and keeping what they feel they deserve. Relative deprivation is not just a complicated way of saying that people are deprived and therefore angry, because they have less than what they want; it is more complex than that. Relative deprivation focuses on (1) what people think they *deserve*, not just what they want in an ideal sense, and (2) what they think they have a *chance of getting*, not just what they have.

Relative deprivation differs considerably from the "absolute deprivation" hypothesis. The absolute deprivation idea suggests that the individuals who are most deprived are most likely to rise up. Of course, it is true that conditions in America's ghettos provide the

[2] National Advisory Commission on Civil Disorders, *Report* (Washington, D.C.: Government Printing Office, 1968), p. 4.

[3] *Ibid.*, pp. 110-12.

[4] For a full discussion of the "relative deprivation" explanation as well as alternative explanations, see Dan R. Bowen and Louis H. Masotti, "Civil Violence: A Theoretical Overview," in *Riots and Rebellion* (Beverly Hills, Calif.: Sage Publications, 1968), Masotti and Bowen, eds.; see also James C. Davies, "Toward a Theory of Revolution," *American Sociological Review*, Vol. 27 (February 1962), 6; and Ted Gurr, *Why Men Rebel* (Princeton: Princeton University Press, 1970).

necessary environment for violence. Racial imbalance, de facto segregation, slum housing, discrimination, unemployment, poor schools, and poverty, all provide excellent kindling for the flames of violence. But these underlying conditions for violence existed for decades in America, and the nation never experienced simultaneous violent uprisings in nearly all its major cities before the 1960s. This suggests the deprivation itself is not a sufficient condition for violence. Some new ingredients were added to the incendiary conditions in American cities which touched off the violence of the 1960s.

Relative deprivation focuses on the distance between one's current status and his expectation level. According to this hypothesis, it is neither the wholly downtrodden—who have no aspirations—nor the very well off—who can satisfy theirs—who represent a threat to civil order. The threat is posed by those whose expectations about what they deserve outdistance the capacity of the political system to satisfy them. Often rapid increases in expectations are a product of minor or symbolic improvements in conditions. This leads to the apparent paradox of violence and disorder occurring at the very time that improvements in the conditions of blacks are being made. It is hope, not despair, which generates civil violence and disorder. Masotti and Bowen remark: "The reason why black Americans riot is because there has been just enough improvement in their condition to generate hopes, expectations, or aspirations beyond the capacities of the system to meet them." [5]

The civil rights movement made many blacks acutely aware of discrimination in American society and reduced their tolerance for injustice. The civil rights movement increased the aspiration level of Negro masses, and inspired impatience and hostility toward the "white establishment." The civil rights movement had to awaken blacks to their plight in American society before progress could be made in eliminating discrimination; but the price of this awakening was a major increase in aspiration levels and the risk of frustration and bitterness when aspirations were unfulfilled. The breakthroughs made by the established civil rights movement in public accommodations, employment, voting, and office holding in the 1960s may have opened new opportunities for the educated middle class. But the undereducated Negro poor, living in the ghetto environment, could not really take advantage of many of these opportunities. The movement increased their expectation level, but it failed to alter significantly their condition in life. Thus, it is no coincidence that the urban disorders followed on the heels of some of the most significant legislative gains in the civil rights struggle.

Once racial violence has broken out anywhere in the nation, the mass media play an important role in disseminating images of violence as well as the symbols and rationalizations of the rioters. Television offers the rioter a mass audience. It was not unknown for rioters to leave the scene temporarily to hurry to their TV sets to see them-

---

[5] Masotti and Bowen, *Riots and Rebellion*, pp. 24-25.

selves. Moreover, television images may reinforce predispositions to participate and even to legitimate participation. Television enables blacks in one ghetto to see what blacks in another ghetto are doing, and explains simultaneously rioting in ghettoes across the nation.

THE NATIONAL ADVISORY COMMISSION ON CIVIL DISORDERS

In July 1967, in the midst of widespread urban disorder, President Lyndon B. Johnson appointed a National Advisory Commission on Civil Disorders to study the riots and to make necessary recommendations. In its official report the Commission enumerated "three of the most bitter fruits of white racial attitudes":

> *Pervasive discrimination and segregation.* The first is surely the continuing exclusion of great numbers of Negroes from the benefits of economic progress through discrimination in employment and education, and their enforced confinement in segregated housing and schools. The corrosive and degrading effects of this condition and the attitudes that underlie it are the source of the deepest bitterness and at the center of the problem of racial disorder.

> *Black migration and white exodus.* The second is the massive and growing concentration of impoverished Negroes in our major cities resulting from Negro migration from the rural South, rapid population growth and the continuing movement of the white middle-class to the suburbs. The consequence is a greatly increased burden on the already depleted resources of cities, creating a growing crisis of deteriorating facilities and services and unmet human needs.

> *Black ghettos.* Third, in the teeming racial ghettos, segregation and poverty have intersected to destroy opportunity and hope and to enforce failure. The ghettos too often mean men and women without jobs, families without men, and schools where children are processed instead of educated, until they return to the street—to crime, to narcotics, to dependency on welfare, and to bitterness and resentment against society in general and white society in particular.[6]

However, the Commission admitted that "these facts alone—fundamental as they are—cannot be said to have caused the disorders." The Commission identified three "powerful ingredients" that had "begun to catalyze the mixture":

> *Frustrated hopes.* The expectations aroused by the great judicial and legislative victories of the civil rights movement have led to frustration, hostility and cynicism in the fact of the persistent gap between promise and fulfillment. The dramatic struggle for equal rights in the South has sensitized Northern Negroes to the economic inequalities reflected in the deprivations of ghetto life.

> *Legitimation of violence.* A climate that tends toward the approval and encouragement of violence as a form of protest has been created by white terrorism directed against nonviolent protest, including instances of abuse and even murder of some civil rights workers in the South;

[6] National Advisory Commission in Civil Disorders, *Report*, pp. 203-4.

by the open defiance of law and federal authority by state and local officials resisting desegregation; and by some protest groups engaging in civil disobedience who turn their backs on nonviolence, go beyond the Constitutionally protected rights of petition and free assembly, and resort to violence to attempt to compel alteration of laws and policies with which they disagree. This condition has been reinforced by a general erosion of respect for authority in American society and reduced effectiveness of social standards and community restraints on violence and crime. This in turn has largely resulted from rapid urbanization and the dramatic reduction in the average age of the total population.

Powerlessness. Finally, many Negroes have come to believe that they are being exploited politically and economically by the white "power structure." Negroes, like people in poverty everywhere, in fact, lack the channels of communication, influence and appeal that traditionally have been available to ethnic minorities within the city and which enabled them—unburdened by color—to scale the walls of the white ghettos in an earlier era. The frustrations of powerlessness have led some to the conviction that there is no effective alternative to violence as a means of expression and redress, as a way of "moving the system." More generally, the result is alienation and hostility toward the institutions of law and government and the white society which controls them. This is reflected in the reach toward racial consciousness and solidarity reflected in the slogan "Black Power." [7]

The Commission warned that "our nation is moving toward two societies, one black, one white—separate and unequal." The principle "blame" for the riots was placed upon whites rather than blacks: "What white Americans have never fully understood—but what the Negro can never forget—is that white society is deeply implicated in the ghetto. White institutions created it, white institutions maintain it, and white society condones it." [8] The Commission recommended massive federal aid programs in employment, education, welfare, and housing, but it suggested no new departures from traditional programs in these areas. The Commission called for the creation of two million new jobs in the ghettos, the elimination of de facto segregation, the construction of six million new units of public housing, and more liberal welfare benefits. In the Commission's words: "These programs will require unprecedented levels of funding and performance, but they neither probe deeper nor demand more than the problems which called them forth. There can be no higher priority for national action and no higher claim on the nation's conscience."

POLICE IN THE GHETTO

Nearly all riots are accompanied by charges of "police brutality." Incidents involving police action have often been the trigger for riots. Police-black tensions are always high in ghetto areas since to many

[7] *Ibid.*, pp. 204-5.
[8] *Ibid.*, p. 2.

ghetto dwellers the police are a symbol of white oppression. "Police brutality" has become a theme with enormous emotional impact among blacks.

While the actual events at any particular riot can probably never be untangled to the full satisfaction of both sides, perceptually the policeman stands as a symbol of oppression for blacks and a symbol of law and order for whites. Police themselves are not immune to social prejudice. The policeman's attitude toward ghetto residents is often affected by the high crime rates in ghetto areas. The policeman is suspicious of ghetto residents because crime rates tell him that his suspicions are often justified. Sociologists interviewing policemen in the cities that experienced riots in 1967 reported that 79 percent of the policemen did not think that Negroes were treated unequally.[9] However, police accurately perceived the hostility directed at them in the ghettos. They believed that only a small minority of blacks, as compared to substantial majority of whites, regard them as friends. Moreover, the police viewed themselves much as blacks view them—as unwelcome aliens in the ghetto: they reported feeling isolated in a hostile atmosphere, but could not understand why blacks resent them. Finally, antiblack attitudes among the policemen interviewed were fairly strong; for example, 49 percent did not approve of socializing between whites and blacks, and 56 percent were disturbed by the movement of blacks into white neighborhoods.

Policemen tend to view ghetto riots as acts of criminal irresponsibility rather than social or political protest. A large majority of the policemen interviewed in 1967 believed that the riots "are caused by nationalists and militants" (77 percent) and that "criminal elements are involved in riots" (69 percent); fewer than one-third of the policemen (31 percent) believed that "unheard Negro complaints are involved in riots."[10] Policemen are not particularly sensitive to the underlying social and economic problems of the ghetto. They tend to regard a riot as primarily a problem in mob control and the suppression of criminal activity. Policemen frequently view judges as too lenient in law enforcement. They often look upon civil rights groups as contributors to violence and upon social agencies as misguided social reform institutions that do not understand the legitimacy of force. Policemen are recruited from those social classes most likely to have anti-Negro prejudices, the lower-middle and working classes. Very few have had college training. It would be unrealistic to expect policemen to possess more tolerant social attitudes than the middle- and lower-class high school educated white populations from which most of them are recruited. High crime rates in the ghettos and the element of danger in the policeman's job make him naturally suspicious of ghetto residents, particularly young people. Policemen are engaged

[9] *Supplemental Studies for the National Advisory Commission on Civil Disorders* (Washington, D.C.: Government Printing Office, 1968), p. 44.
[10] *Ibid.*, p. 96.

in rule enforcement as members of a semimilitary organization. They are concerned with authority themselves, and they expect ghetto residents to respect authority. It is often difficult for even the most well-meaning police officer to develop respect or sympathy for ghetto residents. One policeman described this problem as follows:

> The police have to associate with lower class people, slobs, drunks, criminals, riff-raff of the worst sort. Most of these . . . are Negroes. The police officers see these people through middle class or lower middle class eye-balls. But even if he saw them through highly sophisticated eye-balls he can't go in the street and take this night after night. When some Negro criminal says to you a few times, "you white mother-fucker, take that badge off and I'll shove it up your ass," well it's bound to affect you after a while. Pretty soon you decide they're all just niggers and they'll never be anything but niggers. It would take not just an average man to resist this feeling, it would take an extraordinary man to resist it, and there are very few ways by which the police department can attract extraordinary men to join them.[11]

One commentator described the dilemma of police-ghetto relations as follows:

> First, the police department recruits from a population (the working class) whose numbers are more likely than the average population to hold anti-Negro attitudes; second, the recruits are given a basic classroom training program that is unlikely to change the anti-Negro sentiments; third, the recruit goes out on the street as a patrolman and is more likely than not to have his anti-Negro attitudes reinforced and hardened by the older officer; fourth, in the best departments, the most able officers are soon transferred to specialized administrative duties in training, recruitment, juvenile work, etc., or are promoted after three to five years to supervisory positions; fifth, after five years the patrolman on street duty significantly increases in levels of cynicism, authoritarianism, and generalized hostility to the non-police world. Finally, it is highly likely that the worst of the patrolmen will wind up patroling the ghetto because that tends to be the least wanted assignment.

> If this is an accurate description of the urban police system (and my personal observations over the past five years tell me this is so), then the reason is clear why every poll of black citizens shows the same high level of distrust and hostility against policemen.[12]

The National Advisory Commission on Civil Disorders found that even most routine and legitimate police action can lead to disorder in the ghetto. On sweltering summer nights the front steps and the streets become a refuge from the stifling, non-air-conditioned unventilated rooms of tenement houses in the ghettos. A large number

[11] James Q. Wilson, *Varieties of Police Behavior* (Chambridge: Harvard University Press, 1968), p. 43.
[12] Burton Levy, "Cops in the Ghetto," in *Riots and Rebellion*, Masotti and Bowen, eds., p. 353; See also Arthur Niederhoffer, *Behind the Shield: The Police in Urban Society* (New York: Doubleday, 1967); and J. H. Skolnick, *Justice Without Trial* (New York: John Wiley, 1967).

of people are on the streets on such nights, including a high proportion of young people. Attracting a crowd is easy in this setting. Though stopping a car for speeding might be a routine police action that would pass unnoticed anywhere else, in the ghetto that action can attract a crowd immediately. Ghetto residents watching a white policeman arrest a black man in their neighborhood are "quick to misunderstand, quick to characterize the police action as unfair, quick to abandon curiosity for anger." The Commission made a series of recommendations regarding city police and law enforcement, including the following:

> The police department should have a clear and enforced policy that the standard of law enforcement in ghetto areas is the same as in other communities. . . .
>
> A specialized agency with adequate funds and staff should be created separate from other municipal agencies, to handle, investigate and to make recommendations on city complaints [against policemen].
>
> Police departments should intensify their efforts to recruit more Negroes. . . .
>
> Police officers should be so assigned as to insure that the police department is fully and visibly integrated. Some cities have adopted a policy of assigning one white and one Negro officer to patrol cars, especially in ghetto areas. . . .
>
> The basic rule, when applying force, is to use only the minimum force necessary to effectively control the situation. Unwarranted application of force will incite the mob to further violence, as well as kindle seeds of resentment for police that, in turn, could cause a riot to recur. Ill-advised or excessive application of force will not only result in charges of police brutality, but also may prolong the disturbance.[13]

URBAN WARFARE—COPS AND PANTHERS

The ghetto riots were unplanned, property-oriented, mass disorders. But a new form of ghetto violence is now haunting the nation's cities. It is planned, deliberate, person-oriented violence involving small numbers of well-armed blacks in conflict with the police. Loosely organized Black Panther groups have sprung up in the nation's largest cities, and tension between these militant armed blacks and the city police has resulted in several bloody "shoot-outs."

The Black Panther leaders speak the rhetoric of violence. Panther newspapers contain "recipes" for molotov cocktails and "peoples' hand grenades"—aerosal cans filled with explosives. They declare "All self-defense groups must strike blows against the slavemaster until we have secured our survival as a people, and if this takes shooting every pig and blowing up every pigsty, then let's get on with it." And there has been enough association of Panthers with violence (Eldridge Cleaver, Huey Newton, Bobby Seale, and others) to suggest that many Panthers are prepared to go beyond the mere rhetoric of

[13] National Advisory Commission on Civil Disorders, p. 325.

violence. Large quantities of weapons have been seized at various Panther headquarters.

Since police are generally the objects of Panther wrath, they are understandably touchy in approaching Panther "turf." In several violent confrontations between police and Panthers, most notably in Chicago in December 1969, police have not hesitated to use heavy fire power against Panthers. The result has been the development of some sympathy for the Panthers among blacks. Louis Harris reported in 1970 that a majority of blacks agree that "Panthers give me a sense of pride." [14]

Violence erupted in Cleveland in 1968 that was similar in nature to several later violent confrontations between Black Panthers and policemen.[15] On the night of July 24, 1968, a small well-equipped army of black nationalists led by Fred "Ahmed" Evans engaged in a two-hour gun battle with Cleveland policemen. Blacks with automatic weapons and bandoliers of ammunition strapped around their chests killed three policemen and wounded twelve others; a civilian who attempted to help a wounded policeman was also killed; at least three black nationalists were killed. Ahmed Evans was later convicted of conspiring with other black nationalists to purchase weapons and to plan their attack on the police. The anger and extremism of the small band of black nationalists in Cleveland was apparently unaffected by the fact that the city's mayor, Carl Stokes, was a black. Since earlier violence both in Cleveland and elsewhere had been spontaneous and unplanned, the deliberate and premediated nature of the violence of the black nationalists in Cleveland signaled an ominous development in race relations.

ELITE AND MASS REACTION TO RACIAL VIOLENCE

Blacks and whites disagree over the causes and cures of urban violence. Whites are far more likely to believe that the main cause of civil disorder has been "radicals," looters and other undesirables, and "communists." Very few blacks take this view. Blacks tended to cite discrimination and unfair treatment, unemployment, inferior jobs, and housing. Only about half as many whites cited these underlying, socioeconomic conditions as "the main cause" of riots. A clear majority of blacks believed that the civil disturbances were "mainly a protest against unfair conditions" and very few blacks believed that the riots were "mainly a way of looting and things like that." While many whites recognized the protest nature of the riots, whites were far more likely to believe that disturbances were mainly a way of looting.

Blacks and whites differed even more sharply on how to prevent riots. Whites tended to call for more repressive measures, "more police control," while blacks called for improvements in socioeconomic con-

[14] *Time*, May 11, 1970, p. 30.
[15] See Louis H. Masotti and Jerome R. Corsi, *Shoot-Out in Cleveland: Report to the National Commission on the Causes and Prevention of Violence* (Washington, D.C.: Government Printing Office, 1968).

ditions, "better employment," and "discrimination." Whites and blacks also differed substantially in their assessment of the impact of the riots. More blacks believed the disturbances helped rather than hurt the cause of Negro rights. In contrast, the overwhelming majority of whites believed the riots hurt the Negro cause (see Table 4–1).

While more blacks believed the riots helped rather than hurt their cause, it is important to point out that the great majority of blacks in cities do not believe that violence is "the best way for Negroes to gain their rights." On the contrary, most blacks are prepared to put their faith in "laws and persuasion" and "nonviolent protest." When asked "if a disturbance like the one in Detroit or Newark last

TABLE 4-1 BLACK AND WHITE PERCEPTIONS OF CIVIL DISORDER IN LARGE CITIES

Some people say these disturbances are mainly a protest by Negroes against unfair conditions. Others say they are mainly a way of looting and things like that. Which seems more correct to you?	*Negro*		*White*	
	Men	*Women*	*Men*	*Women*
Mainly protest	56	59	38	48
Mainly looting	9	10	33	24
50/50 mixture	30	25	25	24
Don't know	5	6	4	4
On the whole, do you think the disturbances have helped or hurt the cause of Negro rights, or would you say they haven't made much difference?				
Helped	37	30	13	14
Hurt	22	24	69	59
Helped and hurt equally	12	11	7	7
Made no difference	21	28	9	17
Don't know	8	7	2	3
What do you think was the main cause of these disturbances?				
Discrimination, unfair treatment	49	48	22	27
Unemployment	23	22	13	13
Inferior jobs	13	10	5	5
Bad housing	23	20	15	15
Poor education	10	9	7	7
Poverty	10	8	11	9
Police brutality	10	4	2	1
Black power, "radicals," Communists	4	5	33	26
Looters and other undesirables	11	11	34	34
What do you think is the most important thing the city government could do to keep a disturbance like the one in Detroit from breaking out here?				
Better employment	26	24	11	9
End discrimination	14	15	2	3
Better housing	8	8	4	4
Other social and economic improvements	7	5	4	3
Better police treatment	6	1	0	1
Improve communication between Negroes and whites	12	13	10	13
More police control	9	8	51	42
Can't do anything	3	5	8	8
Don't know	15	21	10	17

Source: *Supplemental Studies for the National Commission on Civil Disorders* (Washington, D.C.: Government Printing Office, 1968).

summer broke out here, do you think you would join, or would try to stop it, or would you stay away from it," three out of every four urban blacks said they would "stay away." Only a tiny fraction said they would join in, and a nearly equal fraction said they would try to stop it. Yet even though the overwhelming majority of Negroes renounced violence, they expressed sympathy for those who do join in riots. In summary most urban blacks look upon the riots as protest activity (see Table 4–2). A majority feel sympathetic toward the rioters, but only a small minority are willing to join the riots themselves. Most blacks reject violence as a means of securing their rights, but more believe that the riots helped rather than hurt their cause.

The reaction of elites to rioting was mixed. It was not until July, 1967, that President Johnson publicly acknowledged the extent of civil disorder and condemned rioting. His statement was typical of those of many public officials who were actively engaged in the suppression of a riot:

> Let there be no mistake about it—the looting, arson, plunder, and pillage which have occurred are not part of the civil rights protest. There is no American right to loot stores, burn buildings, to fire rifles from rooftops. This is a crime. . . .
>
> Criminals who have committed these acts of violence against the people deserve to be punished—they must be punished.[16]

TABLE 4-2   Black Attitudes Toward Violence in Large Cities

As you see it, what is the best way for Negroes to try to gain their rights—use laws and persuasion, use nonviolent protest, or be ready to use violence?	Negro Total (percent)
Laws and persuasion	39
Nonviolent protest	38
Be ready to use violence	15
Don't know	8
If a disturbance like the one in Detroit or Newark last summer broke out here, do you think you would join in, or would try to stop it, or would you stay away from it?	
Join in	8
Try to stop it	9
Stay away	76
Don't know	6
Other	1
Even if you didn't join in, would you feel in sympathy with Negroes who did choose to join in, or would you feel unsympathetic toward them?	
Sympathetic	54
Unsympathetic	24
Inappropriate; willing to join in	8
Other; Don't know	14

Source: Supplemental Studies for the National Commission on Civil Disorders (Washington, D.C.: Government Printing Office, 1968).

[16] President Lyndon B. Johnson in a speech broadcast over national television networks, July 27, 1967.

Later the President cited the riots as an additional reason for Congress to pass Administration-backed urban programs to alleviate the ills of cities. But many Congressmen were concerned that large-scale increases in federal expenditures in the ghettos might appear to reward rioting. Congress reacted by passing overwhelmingly a bipartisan antiriot bill, making it a federal crime to cross state lines to incite a riot. The Administration had opposed the bill as repressive and unlikely to contribute a solution to the underlying causes of riots. No new federal programs were devised by the President or passed by the Congress in response to the riots. Nor were already existing federal programs greatly expanded, despite suggestions by the Commission on Civil Disorders. Perhaps the financial pressure of the Vietnam war made such a course of action appear to be unfeasible at the time. Or perhaps neither the President nor the Congress had any really new ideas about how to solve the complex problems of the ghettos.

Most important social movements in American history have been accompanied by violence. The American political system is frequently moved by *crises* when it is unmoved by anything else. The civil rights protest movement sought to create *nonviolent* crises which would move the elites to end direct discrimination. But the argument of the black militant is that white elites will not respond to black demands for real equality unless their own physical well-being is directly threatened. In commenting on the role of violence in the struggle for equality, Masotti and others note:

> Perhaps the black power advocates understand better than most whites that Americans have traditionally paid only lip service to their notion of consensus when critical issues arose; that, in fact, when critical issues arise, they can no longer be solved through the normal political channels based on common understandings; that, indeed, the only common interest a challenging minority and an unresponsive majority have is violence, with the minority offering peace only when the majority makes the requisite concessions.[17]

Yet there is little likelihood that violence will produce the attitude change among white elites necessary for progress in the struggle for equality. Violence has resulted in a negative reaction among whites. It has served to reinforce prejudice and to justify antagonisms against blacks rather than to affect any attitude changes. Violence in the urban ghettos in the 1960s failed to shock white Americans into action on behalf of equality or even to scare them into such action. Instead, the urban violence led to a strong "law and order" movement which was reflected in local, state, and national politics. The violence provided white masses with an opportunity to express hostile stereotypes about Negroes, e.g., that the riots were "mainly a way of looting

[17] Louis H. Masotti, Jeffrey K. Hadden, Kenneth F. Semmatore, Jerome R. Corsi, *A Time To Burn?* (Chicago: Rand McNally, 1969), p. 162.

and things like that." The riots also gave white elites a new political theme—"law and order."

The reaction of most government officials was negative also. Both the President and Congress pointedly ignored the recommendations of the Advisory Commission on Civil Disorders for more jobs, housing, and educational programs in the ghettos. There was substantial fear that new public programs might appear to "reward violence." No more money was poured into the ghettos. Both Congress and the President became disenchanted with the Poverty Program. The rhetoric of government officials emphasized "law and order," rather than massive programs aimed at equalizing black and white living standards.

SUMMARY

Urban violence is a form of political activity on the part of black masses in the ghetto. The violence expresses the hostility which many blacks feel toward white people in general and toward established authority. White elites who had supported the elimination of legal discrimination reacted negatively when black masses violated the established "rules of the game." White elites, both "liberal" and "conservative," have taken steps to insure "law and order," but they have been unwilling to undertake massive governmental programs to achieve absolute equality in society. All of this is consistent with elite theory.

1. The civil rights movement, although well within the established elite consensus in goals and tactics, awakened black masses to their condition in American society. The result was a major increase in their aspiration levels and subsequent frustration and bitterness because these new aspirations were unfulfilled. The traditional apathy of the black masses was replaced with an activism that was unstable and violence prone.

2. The change from apathy to activism occurred as a result of rising expectations of black masses. The civil rights movement had to awaken blacks to their plight in American society to begin to make progress in the elimination of discrimination. But the price of this awakening was a major increase of aspiration levels of the masses and a subsequent frustration and bitterness when these aspirations were not fulfilled.

3. Black violence was directed against the symbols of white authority in the ghetto. Mass violence was irrational and self-defeating in that the great majority of the casualties—the dead, the injured, and the arrested—were black ghetto residents. But mass activism is frequently unpredictable and irrational.

4. Police in the ghetto are recruited from white masses rather than white elites, and thus reflect white mass attitudes toward blacks.

Police are frequently unsympathetic toward black aspirations, and their experiences in the ghetto reinforce unsympathetic attitudes. Police tend to see black activism as a problem in law enforcement, rather than as political or social protest. Blacks tend to see white police as agents of repression.

5. Some blacks espouse an ideology of violence as the only means of dealing with white society. Their use of the rhetoric and symbols of violence has intensified police opposition, and several violent confrontations have taken place.

6. White masses reacted with hostility toward mass riots by blacks, even though white masses were not the direct objects of rioters. The violence gave white masses an opportunity to express hostile stereotypes about blacks. White masses called for more repressive measures and provided mass support for a strong "law and order" movement.

7. Elite reaction was mixed. Some white elites cited rioting and violence as evidence of the social maladies of cities and called for massive public programs to improve housing, health, education, employment, and so on. But no new massive public programs were undertaken.

8. Generally established elites, who had supported the elimination of legal discrimination and efforts to achieve equality of opportunity, reacted negatively when black masses violated the accepted consensus about "rules of the game." They condemned rioters as "criminals," passed a law making it a federal crime to cross a state line to incite the masses to riot, and called for improved police tactics and training in quelling mass disturbances. A strong "law and order" movement developed in local, state, and national politics.

BIBLIOGRAPHY

GURR, TED, *Why Men Rebel?* Princeton: Princeton University Press, 1970.
MASOTTI, LOUIS H. and DON R. BOWEN, eds., *Riots and Rebellion.* Beverly Hills: Sage Publications, 1960.
National Advisory Commission on Civil Disorders, *Report.* Washington, D.C.: Government Printing Office, 1968.
Supplemental Studies for the National Advisory Commission on Civil Disorders. Washington, D.C.: Government Printing Office, 1968.
WILSON, JAMES Q., *Varieties of Police Behavior.* Cambridge, Mass.: Harvard University Press, 1968.

WELFARE:
the limits of rationalism

CHAPTER 5

SOCIAL DEPENDENCY IN AMERICA

Social dependency in America is rising at a truly alarming rate. Approximately 7 percent of the nation's population—14 million people—is on welfare rolls. This is nearly twice the number of people on welfare rolls five years ago. The welfare population of New York City exceeds the total population of a city the size of Baltimore. In Boston, one person out of every five receives some form of public assistance; in Newark the figure is one person out of every four. In New York and San Francisco, one out of every seven persons receives welfare. And these figures may represent only *half* of the persons eligible for welfare assistance in this nation! Maximum monthly payments for a family of four on welfare in New York or New Jersey exceed $350 per month—more than the cash income of many working families. The costs of welfare have brought some cities to the brink of bankruptcy; and many states have been forced to cut back on planned educational spending in order to fund growing welfare programs.

The costs of welfare and the growth of social dependency outrage many working, tax-paying Americans, but their outrage is matched by that of the recipients themselves who claim that the payments are

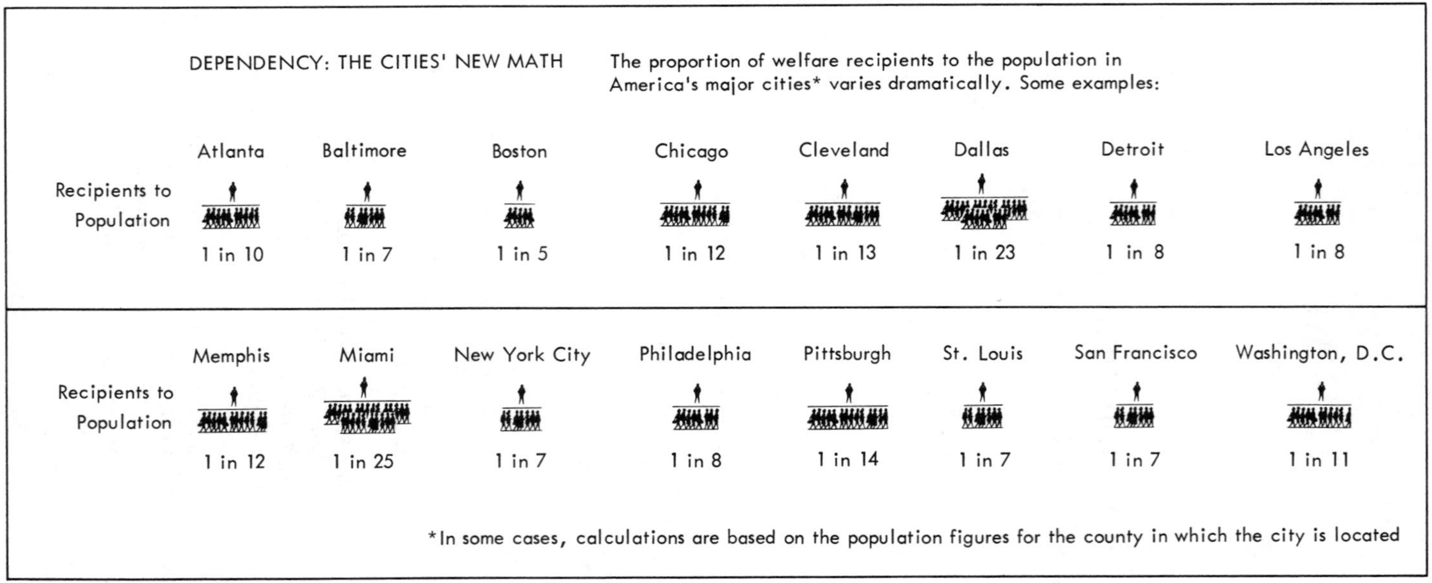

DEPENDENCY: THE CITIES' NEW MATH

The proportion of welfare recipients to the population in America's major cities* varies dramatically. Some examples:

	Atlanta	Baltimore	Boston	Chicago	Cleveland	Dallas	Detroit	Los Angeles
Recipients to Population	1 in 10	1 in 7	1 in 5	1 in 12	1 in 13	1 in 23	1 in 8	1 in 8

	Memphis	Miami	New York City	Philadelphia	Pittsburgh	St. Louis	San Francisco	Washington, D.C.
Recipients to Population	1 in 12	1 in 25	1 in 7	1 in 8	1 in 14	1 in 7	1 in 7	1 in 11

*In some cases, calculations are based on the population figures for the county in which the city is located

FIG. 5-1

Source: Newsweek, February 8, 1971, p. 23.

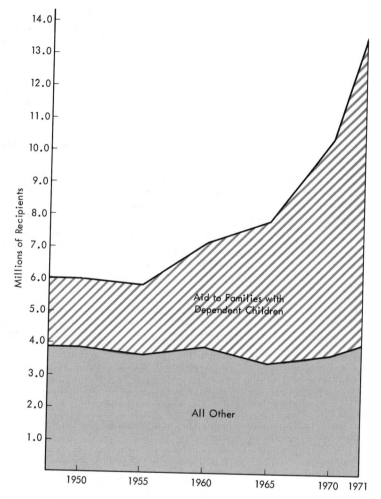

FIG. 5-2 THE WELFARE EXPLOSION

inadequate to maintain a decent standard of living. Nationwide, welfare payments are well below poverty levels established by the government (for example, the Social Security Administration's poverty line of $3500 in 1970 for a family of four). In Alabama and Mississippi the maximum monthly cash payment for a family of four is less than $100. The welfare bureaucracy is a nightmare—long lines, endless forms, insensitive officials, and pointless regulations. No one is more bitter about the welfare system in America than the recipients themselves. Even the welfare officials who operate the system are offended by it. Turnover among caseworkers is high. Caseworkers are assigned so many cases that they can rarely be of direct assistance to families.

All they can do is process forms and send checks. Finally, the greatest inequity in the welfare system is its total exclusion of the *working* poor —those millions of American families who live in poverty but cannot receive government assistance because one member of the family is working.

Racial antagonisms are another part of the welfare dilemma. About 25 percent of the nation's black population receives public assistance of one kind or another; only about 4 percent of the white population is on welfare. In the nation's large cities the welfare rolls are overwhelmingly black. Hence, conflict over welfare is closely related to racial problems.

Incredibly enough, today's welfare dilemma is the product of more than thirty years of rational planning. Social security, public assistance, medicaid and medicare, manpower training, the "war on poverty," and a variety of other programs and policies, were initially presented to the nation as rational approaches to the problems of the poor. Yet none of these programs have succeeded in eliminating poverty or even reducing public demands that "something be done" about "the welfare mess." All of these programs have produced serious, unanticipated consequences. Welfare rolls continue to rise, both in absolute numbers and in percentage of the population. This is true despite an expanding economy and the absence of any national economic depression. The rapidly rising costs of many current welfare programs are resented by working taxpayers. Many current welfare policies are denounced by the officials and caseworkers who must administer them. Welfare assistance does not get to many Americans who deserve it. It is frequently accepted with bitterness by those who were intended to benefit from it.

It is not really possible in this chapter to describe all of the problems of the poor in America or to describe all of the difficulties in developing rational health and welfare policies. But it is possible to describe the general design of alternative strategies to deal with poverty in America, to observe how these strategies were implemented in public policy, and to outline some of the obstacles to a rational approach to the problems of the poor.

THE PUNITIVE STRATEGY—EARLY WELFARE POLICY

Public welfare has been a recognized responsibility of governments in English-speaking nations for almost four hundred years. Prior to the 1930s, care of the poor in the United States resembled the early patterns of poor relief established as far back as the Poor Relief Act of 1601 by the English Parliament. Early "Elizabethan" welfare policy was a combination of punitive as well as alleviative strategies which discouraged all but the most desperately poor from seeking aid, and provided only minimal assistance to those persons clearly unable to care for themselves. Primary reliance was placed upon institutional care—county work houses, poor houses, or alms houses. The "able-bodied poor," those we call the unemployed, were sent to county work houses; while the "worthy poor," widows, aged, orphans, and handicapped, were sent to poor houses. Indigent persons who were mentally or physically ill were often kept in the same institutions. Destitute children were kept in county orphanages or sent to foster homes. Thus, public welfare was limited almost exclusively to institutional care; the distribution of food or clothing or other aid to homes of the poor was left to private charities. Whatever relief was provided by the public could never exceed the value of the income of the lowest paid person in the community who was not on relief. Poor rolls were made public, and relief was forthcoming only if there were no living relatives who could be legally required to support a destitute member of their family.

Under Elizabethan law, the care of the poor was the responsibility of the local governments rather than the state and local governments. The parish in England, and the township and county in the United States, had to care for their poor out of their general tax funds. Since local governments wished to make certain that they were not caring for the poor of other communities, residence requirements were established for welfare care, and communities generally limited their support to those who had been born in the area or who had lived there for some time.

The rationale behind Elizabethan policy—a rationale which has not altogether disappeared from the welfare scene today—was that poverty was a product of moral or character deficiencies in the individual. Only a punitive strategy would dissuade people from indolence and keep poverty to a minimum. The great English economist of the nineteenth century, T. R. Malthus, wrote that the poor

> . . . are themselves the causes of their own poverty; that the means of redress are in their own hands, and in the hands of no other person whatever; that the society in which they live and the government which presides over it, are without any direct power in this respect.[1]

In America, the popular sociologist Herbert Spencer opposed any public assistance because it interfered with the natural laws of selection. Natural evolution would wipe out poverty over time, he believed, by simply wiping out the poor, who were "good-for-nothings, who . . . live on the good-for-somethings—vagrants and sots, criminals and those who are on their way to crime. . . ."[2] However, Spencer's simple solution never really prevailed in public policy. Soft-hearted public

---

[1] T. R. Malthus, *An Essay on the Principle of Population* (London, 1826); quoted by Sidney Fine, *Laissez Faire and the General Welfare State* (Ann Arbor: University of Michigan Press, 1956), p. 7.
[2] Herbert Spencer, *The Man Versus the State* (London, 1892); quoted by Fine, *Laissez Faire*, p. 38.

officials and charitable organizations contrived to keep the poor alive with a trickle of public and private aid.

During the period of rapid industrialization and heavy immigration, roughly 1870 to 1920, the big city political "machines" and "bosses" also interfered with natural selection by assisting the impoverished (according to the bosses' own sense of political rationality). The political machine operated as a large, although inefficient, brokerage organization. It traded off baskets of food, bushels of coal, minor patronage, and petty favors, in exchange for the votes of the poor. To get funds to pay for this primitive welfare assistance, it traded off city contracts, protection, and privileges to business interests, who paid off in cash. The machine was not very efficient as a welfare organization, since a great many middle men came between the cash paid for a business franchise to the Christmas turkey sent to Widow O'Leary. But it worked. Recipients of such assistance were spared much of the red tape and delays experienced by recipients of public assistance today. More importantly, the aid was provided in a very personal fashion without making the recipient feel inferior or dependent. They were trading something valuable—their vote—for the assistance they received.

Prior to the 1930s most people believed the federal government had no legitimate role to play in the welfare field. The federal government provided only for needy veterans, Indians, and merchant seamen.

The Depression brought about significant changes in attitudes toward public welfare and in the policies and administration of welfare programs. Millions who had previously considered welfare recipients to be unworthy of public concern now joined in the breadlines themselves. One out of four Americans was unemployed and one out of six was receiving some sort of welfare care. No longer were many people willing to believe that poverty was a product of the individual's moral or character faults. This widespread experience with poverty changed public attitudes toward welfare and led to a change away from Elizabethan policy.

THE PREVENTATIVE STRATEGY—SOCIAL SECURITY

The administration of President Franklin D. Roosevelt lent legitimacy to the concept of national planning. In the broadest sense national planning meant attempts by the federal government to develop rational programs to achieve societal goals. Roosevelt himself was a master at articulating broad national purposes which could enlist the support of a large cross-section of the national public. However, Roosevelt was something less than a master in devising specific rational policy alternatives to achieve these purposes. Despite a great deal of New Deal rhetoric implying rationality and consistency in solving national problems, the actual record of the Roosevelt administration indicated pragmatism, experimentalism, and improvisation. According to Roosevelt, the times required

> Full, persistent experimentation. If it fails, admit it frankly and try something else. But above all, try something. The millions who are in want will not stand by silently forever until the things to satisfy their needs are within easy reach.[3]

Yet there was an underlying logic to the most important piece of legislation of the New Deal—the Social Security Act of 1935. In this Act, the federal government undertook to establish the basic framework for welfare policies at the federal, state, and local level, and, more importantly, to set forth a new approach to the problem of poverty. The Depression convinced the national leadership, and a great many citizens, that indigency could result from forces over which the individual had no control—loss of his job, old age, death of the family breadwinner, or physical disability. The solution was to require individuals to purchase insurance against their own indigency resulting from any of these misfortunes.

The *social insurance* concept, devised by the New Deal planners, was designed to prevent poverty resulting from unemployment, old age, death of a family breadwinner, or physical disability. Social insurance was based on the same notion as private insurance—the sharing of risks and the setting aside of money for a rainy day. Social insurance was not to be charity or public assistance. Social insurance was to be preventative. It relied upon the individual's (compulsory) contribution to his own protection. In contrast, public assistance is only alleviative, and relies upon general tax revenues from all taxpayers. Indeed, when the Roosevelt administration presented the social insurance plan to Congress in the Social Security Act of 1935, they contended it would eventually abolish the need for any public assistance program, since individuals would be compelled to protect themselves against poverty!

The distinction between a *social insurance* program and a *public assistance* program is an important one, which has on occasion been a major political issue. If the beneficiaries of a government program are required to have made contributions to it before claiming any of its benefits, and if they are entitled to the benefits regardless of their personal wealth, then the program is said to be financed on the *social insurance* principle. On the other hand, if a program is financed out of general tax revenues, and if the recipients are required to show they are poor before claiming its benefits, then the program is said to be financed on the *public assistance* principle. One of the key features of the Social Security Act is the Old Age Survivors' Disability Insurance (OASDI) program; this is a compulsory social insurance program financed by regular deductions from earnings, which gives

[3] Richard Hofstadter, *American Political Tradition* (New York: Alfred A. Knopf, 1948), p. 316.

individuals a legal right to benefits in the event of certain occurrences that cause a reduction of their income: old age, death of the head of household, or permanent disability. OASDI is based on the same principle as private insurance—sharing the risk of the loss of income—except that it is a government program that is compulsory for all workers. OASDI is not public *charity*, but a way of compelling people to provide *insurance* against a loss of income. OASDI now covers about nine out of every ten workers in the United States. Both employees and employers must pay equal amounts toward the employees' OASDI insurance. Upon retirement, an insured worker is entitled to monthly benefit payments based upon his age at retirement and the amount he has earned during his working years. However, average monthly payments are really quite modest: the average monthly amount for a retired worker, aged sixty-five, with a wife, is less than $200. So OASDI has not eliminated poverty from the ranks of the retired in America.

OASDI also insures benefit payments to survivors of an insured worker, including his widow if she has dependent children. But if she has no dependent children, her benefits will not begin until she herself reaches retirement age. Finally, OASDI insures benefit payments to persons who suffer permanent and total disabilities that prevent them from working more than one year. However, on the whole, payments to survivors and disabled workers are just as modest as those provided retired workers.

OASDI is a completely federal program, administered by the Social Security Administration in the Department of Health, Education, and Welfare. But OASDI has an important indirect effect on state and local welfare programs: by compelling people to insure themselves against the possibility of their own poverty, social security has doubtlessly reduced the welfare problems which state and local governments would otherwise face.

The second feature of the Social Security Act of 1935 was that it induced states to enact unemployment compensation programs through the imposition of the payroll tax on all employers. A federal unemployment tax is levied on the payroll of employers of four or more workers, but employers paying into state insurance programs that meet federal standards may use these state payments to offset most of their federal unemployment tax. In other words, the federal government threatens to undertake an unemployment compensation program and tax, if the states do not do so themselves. This federal program succeeded in inducing all fifty states to establish unemployment compensation programs. However, the federal standards are flexible and the states have considerable freedom in shaping their own unemployment programs. In all cases, unemployed workers must report in person and show that they are willing and able to work in order to receive unemployment compensation benefits, and states cannot deny workers benefits for refusing to work as strike breakers or refusing to work for rates lower than prevailing rates. But basic decisions concerning the amount of benefits, eligibility, and the length of time that benefits can be drawn are largely left to the states.

Even before the Social Security Act of 1935, persons concerned with the state of the nation's health, and particularly the medical care problems of the poor and the aged, had urged the federal government to undertake a broad national health care program. Proponents of the national health program generally shunned the English system of government-owned and operated hospitals and government-employed doctors, in favor of a compulsory medical *insurance* program closely linked to the Social Security Act. They envisoned a program in which all Americans would be required to insure themselves against the possibility of their medical indigency; the program would resemble private medical and hospital insurance, except that it would be compulsory. Individuals would continue to choose their own doctors, but their bills would be paid in whole or in part through their government medical insurance policy. Opponents of a national health program, led by the prestigious American Medical Association representing the nation's physicians, strongly opposed a national health program linked to social security. They deemed it "socialized medicine" and argued that it would interfere with the "sacred doctor-patient relationship." They argued that a large proportion of the population was already covered by voluntary private medical insurance plans, and that charity hospitals and charitable services of doctors were readily available to the poor. Basically the physicians worried that if the Social Security Administration paid insured persons' doctor bills, the Social Security Administration would begin to set maximum prices for physicians' services; the AMA feared that this would lead to the subservience of physicians to a government agency.

In 1965, after more than thirty years of unsuccessful efforts, Congress finally enacted an historic comprehensive medical care act for persons over sixty-five, which became known as "Medicare." Passed over the opposition of the American Medical Association, Medicare provided for prepaid hospital insurance for the aged under social security, and low cost voluntary medical insurance for the aged under federal administration. Medicare includes: (1) a compulsory basic health insurance plan covering hospital costs for the aged, financed through payroll taxes collected under the social security system; and (2) a voluntary but supplemental medical program that will pay doctors' bills and additional medical expenses, financed in part by contributions from the aged and in part by the general tax revenues. It is not yet clear what the impact of this act will be at the local level, in terms of reducing state and local burdens of providing for charitable hospital and medical care. Social security never eliminated the need for welfare rolls, and it is doubtful that Medicare will ever eliminate the need for tax-supported hospitals and health care. So far only aged persons are covered by Medicare provisions.

INTENDED AND UNINTENDED CONSEQUENCES
OF SOCIAL SECURITY

The framers of the Social Security Act of 1935 created an OASDI trust fund with the expectation that a reserve would be built up from social insurance premiums from working persons. The reserve would earn interest, and the interest and principal would be used in later years to pay benefits. Benefits for an individual would be in proportion to his contributions. General tax revenues would not be used at all. It was intended that the system would resemble the financing of private insurance. But it turned out not to work that way at all.

The social insurance system is now financed on a pay-as-you-go, rather than a reserve, system. Political pressure to raise benefit levels while keeping payments low, reduced the reserve to a very minor role in social security finance. Today the income from social security premiums—over $35 billion—matches the outgo in social security benefits. Today, this generation of workingmen is paying for the benefits of the last generation, and it is expected that this generation's benefits will be financed by the next generation of workers. Social security trust fund revenues are now lumped together with general tax revenues in the federal budget.

Congress has gradually increased the social security payroll tax from three percent combined employee and employer contributions on the first $3,000 of wages, to an expected twelve per cent combined contribution on the first $9,000 by the 1980s. To keep up with the generous benefits which Congress finds politically expedient to vote year after year, the social security tax is now the *third largest source of federal revenue.* More important, it is also *the fastest growing source of federal revenue.* Social insurance payments are now the *second largest expenditure of the federal government* after national defense.

The decline of the insurance concept began in the very first years of the program when FDR's planners quickly realized that building a reserve was taking money from the economy and adding to the Depression. The plan to build a large self-financing reserve fund was abandoned in 1939. The generosity of Congress has raised benefit levels an average of four hundred per cent since 1940. Now Congress regularly alters the levels of benefits and the formula for their computation, a practice very much at variance with sound insurance practices. More and more groups of workers have been given coverage under social security. Benefits are no longer really proportionate to contributions; they are figured more generously for those whose wages were low than those whose wages were high. The proportion of benefits actually purchased by the contributions of those retiring in the system to date have averaged less than ten per cent! The only remaining aspect of an insurance program is that individuals must have paid into the system to receive its benefits, and beneficiaries are not required to prove they are needy. Most Americans view their benefits as a right.

The social security tax is highly regressive. It takes a much larger share of the income of the poor than the rich. This was not a serious factor when the payments amounted to very little, but today the size of social security revenues—fully one-quarter of the federal government's income—have an important impact on the total revenue structure. The tax is only on wages, not total *income*. And wages *above* certain levels ($7,800 in 1970) are completely untaxed.

Despite rises in benefit levels, the average monthly payment for a retired couple remains below $200. This is well below the recognized poverty level of the 1960s of $3,500 per year. Without additional retirement or investment income, all social security recipients would live in poverty, and a significant proportion of them have no such additional income. While there is no question that social security has reduced the amount of poverty which would exist in the absence of the program, it has failed to eliminate poverty.

THE ALLEVIATIVE STRATEGY—PUBLIC ASSISTANCE

The social security, unemployment compensation, and medicare programs were based upon the insurance strategy for preventing indigency, but the federal government also undertook in the Social Security Act of 1935 to help the states in providing public assistance payments to certain needy persons to alleviate the conditions of poverty. The strategy was clearly alleviative; there was no effort to attack the causes of poverty. The notion was to provide a minimum level of subsistence to certain categories of needy adults—the aged, blind, and disabled—and to provide for the care of dependent children. This was to be done by providing small amounts of cash in monthly payments through state-administered welfare programs. The grant-in-aid device was employed because welfare functions traditionally had been the responsibility of state and local governments, and the constitutional arrangements under American federalism made direct federal administration improbable. The entire federal effort in public assistance was supposed to be temporary in duration, declining in importance as social insurance took over the burden of assuring security.

The federal share of public assistance is determined by a formula that attempts to equalize welfare efforts among the states by having the federal government pay a larger share to states with higher needs and less wealth. The federal aid formula authorizes the federal government to pay a large share of minimum benefits and a lesser share of benefits above the minimum, up to a maximum amount, above which the federal government pays no share. The federal government also pays half of the cost of administering the programs.

All of the states divide welfare assistance among the four categories of recipients aided by the government—the aged, the blind, the disabled, and dependent children. Within broad outlines of the federal policy, states retain considerable discretion in their welfare programs, in terms of the amounts of money appropriated, benefits to be paid to recipients, rules of eligibility, and rules of the programs. Each state may choose to grant assistance beyond the amounts supported by the national government, or it may choose to have no welfare programs at all. Each state establishes its own standards to determine "need." Later we shall examine variations in average benefit payments in these categorical assistance programs.

It is important to note that the federal government aids only four categories of welfare recipients. Only persons who are aged, blind, or disabled, or dependent children fall within the categories of recipients eligible for federal support. Aid to persons who do *not* fall in any of these categories but who, for one reason or another, are "needy" is referred to as *general assistance*. General assistance programs are entirely state financed and state administered. Without federal participation, these programs differ radically from state to state in terms of the persons aided, the criteria for eligibility, the amount and nature of benefits, and administration of financing. Many of these programs continue to resemble Elizabethan welfare policy. The average general assistance payment is lower than comparable payments in federally supported programs.

States also continue to maintain institutions to care for those individuals who are so destitute, alone, or ill that money payments cannot meet their needs. These institutions include state orphanages, homes for the aged, and homes for the ill. They are, for the most part, state financed as well as state administered. Persons living in these tax supported institutions normally are not eligible for federal assistance, although they may receive old age payments for medical care received in a nursing home. This feature of federal welfare policy has provided incentive for the states to turn their indigent institutions into nursing homes. The quality of these homes and of the people employed to care for their residents varies enormously from state to state.

Federal standards for state public assistance programs, which are established as a prerequisite to receiving federal aid, allow considerable flexibility in state programs. Federal law requires the states to make financial contributions to their public assistance programs and to supervise these programs either directly or through local agencies. Whatever standards a state adopts must be applicable throughout the state, and there must be no discrimination in these welfare programs. The Social Security Administration demands periodic reporting from the states, insists that states administer federally supported programs under a merit personnel system, and prevents the states from imposing unreasonable residence requirements on recipients. But in important questions of administration, standards of eligibility, residence, types of assistance, and amounts of payments, the states are free to determine their own welfare programs.

In 1965, Congress also passed a Medical Assistance Program (Medicaid) which provided federal funds to enable states to guarantee medical services to all public assistance recipients. Each state operates its own Medicaid program. Unlike Medicare, Medicaid is a welfare program designed for needy persons; no prior contributions are required, but recipients of Medicaid services must be eligible for welfare assistance. States can assist *other* medically needy persons if they choose to do so. The cost of this program has far exceeded all original estimates, suggesting that the poor in America require much more medical attention than they have received in the past.

TABLE 5-1 SOCIAL SECURITY, 1940-1972

	1940	1950	1960	1965	1970	1972
Numbers of beneficiaries (in thousands)	222	3,477	14,845	20,867	25,312	30,556
Average monthly benefit, retired worker	$23	$44	$74	$84	$100	$117
Percent of payrolls covered	74.7	77.2	86.5	86.0	88.5	89.0
Social insurance receipts of federal government (in millions)	n.a.	$5,500	$11,248	$17,359	$38,914	$50,225
Social insurance receipts as percent of all federal receipts				15.9	19.1	22.5	24.0
Medicare expenditures (in millions)	0	0	0	0	$ 6,800	$ 8,600

Source: The Budget of the United States Government, 1972 (Washington, D.C.: Government Printing Office, 1971); and past issues of U.S. Bureau of the Census, *Statistical Abstract of the United States.*

THE WELFARE MESS: CONSEQUENCES UNINTENDED

Public assistance turned out to be politically one of the most unpopular programs ever adopted by Congress. It is disliked by national, state, and local legislators who must vote the skyrocketing appropriations for it; it is resented by the taxpayers who must bear the ever increasing burdens of it; it is denounced by the officials and caseworkers who must administer it; and it is accepted with bitterness by those who were intended to benefit from it.

Photo by Fred W. McDarrah, © 1971

First of all, dependence upon public assistance in America is increasing at a very rapid rate. Whether or not the public assistance program itself encourages dependency, one thing is certain: more Americans depend upon public assistance today then ever before, despite a healthy national economy. Certainly our public assistance programs have not succeeded in reducing dependency. In the last decade the number of welfare recipients have more than doubled, and public assistance costs have quadrupled. Interestingly, it has not been programs for the aged, blind, or disabled, or even the general assistance programs which have incurred the greatest burdens. It is the Aid to Families with Dependent Children (AFDC) program which

TABLE 5-2 GROWTH OF PUBLIC ASSISTANCE PROGRAMS

	Total	AFDC	Aged	Disabled	Blind	General Assistance
			(Millions of Recipients)			
1950	6.0	2.2	2.8	.1	.1	.9
1955	5.8	2.2	2.5	.2	.1	.7
1960	7.0	3.1	2.3	.4	.1	1.2
1965	7.8	4.4	2.1	.6	.1	.7
1970	10.4	6.7	2.0	.87	.1	.8
1971	13.5	9.5	2.0	1.0	.1	.9
1972	15.0	10.8	2.1	1.0	.1	1.0

Source: Special Analysis of the Budget of the United States, 1972 (Washington, D.C.: Government Printing Office, 1971); and past issues of U.S. Bureau of the Census, *Statistical Abstract of the United States.*

is the largest, most expensive, and most rapidly growing of all welfare programs, and the most controversial. Today approximately five percent of all children under eighteen years of age are under AFDC coverage. If the present trends continue, one out of every ten children will be under AFDC by 1975.

This growth in welfare rolls has occurred during a period of high employment; it cannot be attributed to economic depression. The acceleration has occurred because more people are applying for public assistance. They have been aided by the activities of civil rights and welfare rights organizations, Office of Economic Opportunity-supported community action groups, and comparable groups, which have informed eligible persons of the law and encouraged them to apply for assistance. Increases in assistance levels, relaxation of eligibility requirements, and a more sympathetic attitude on the part of welfare administrators, have also contributed to the increase in welfare rolls. So also has the movement of persons from southern and rural areas, where welfare administration is tighter, to northern urban areas, where access to welfare rolls is less restricted.

Despite increased dependency upon welfare, and the growing burden of welfare costs, a majority of the nation's poor do *not* receive public

assistance Depending on one's definition of poverty there were between twenty-five and forty million poor people in America in 1970,
yet only fourteen million persons on welfare rolls. Most of the nation's
poor are *working poor*, who are ineligible for welfare assistance
because they hold jobs, even though these jobs pay very little. A low-
income family, headed by the father, is not eligible to receive AFDC
payments if the father is working, regardless of how poor the family
may be.

Not only does welfare fail to assist most of the nation's poor, it
does not provide enough in the way of assistance to recipients to raise
them out of poverty. While welfare benefits differ from state to state,
in every state the level of benefits falls well below the recognized
poverty line.

State administration of welfare has resulted in wide disparities
among the states in eligibility requirements and benefits levels. For
example, in 1970 average AFDC monthly payments ranged from a
high of $66.40 per child in New Jersey to a low of $10.20 per child
in Mississippi. Monthly old age assistance payments ranged from a
high of $116 in New Hampshire to a low of $39 in Mississippi. A state's
income is the single most important variable determining the level
of welfare benefits. In terms of welfare payments, it is far better
to be poor in a wealthy state than in a poor one.

Poorer states have large proportions of their populations on public
assistance rolls, and poorer states have lower welfare benefit payments. This means they pay smaller amounts of money to larger
numbers of people. It is not surprising that economic development
levels are closely related to benefits paid to recipients of *general
assistance*, since relief in this area is paid for exclusively from state
and local fiscal sources. But it is surprising that economic development
in the states has such a great impact on benefit programs in which
the federal government bears part of the cost (see Figure 5–3). We
would expect federal participation to reduce inequalities among the
states. Actually the federal government does make larger health and
welfare grants to the poorer states, and therefore helps offset disparities among the states based upon levels of wealth. However, the
reason federal participation does not equalize welfare payments among
the states is to be found in the formula that allocates federal money
to the states for public assistance. The federal government, under its
public assistance formula, pays a larger share of minimum benefits
and a lesser share of additional benefits up to a certain maximum
benefit level, after which the federal government pays nothing. The
object of this formula is to help poorer states provide a minimum
level of welfare service. However, since the formula results in a
higher proportion of federal support to states with lower welfare
benefits, the federal government actually rewards states for low
payments per recipient. Poorer states can get the most federal aid
by paying smaller amounts of money to large numbers of people.

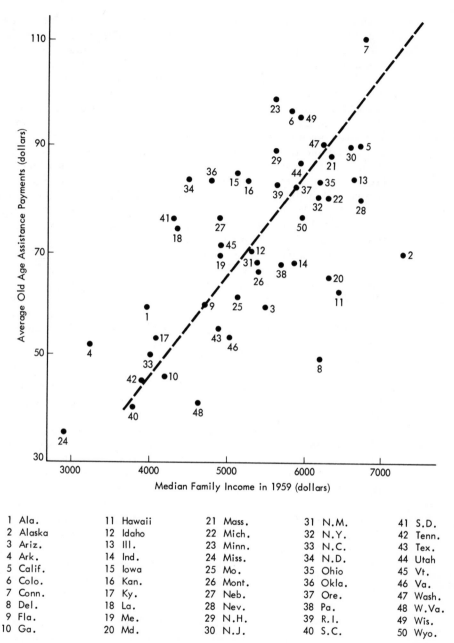

FIG. 5-3 THE FIFTY STATES ARRANGED ACCORDING TO MEDIAN FAMILY INCOME AND
AVERAGE OLD AGE ASSISTANCE PAYMENTS

Source: Thomas R. Dye, *Politics, Economics, and the Public* (Chicago: Rand
McNally & Co., © 1966), p. 126. Reproduced by permission.

Operating policies and administration of welfare have produced a whole series of problems, including disincentives to family life and work. Until recently, most states denied AFDC benefits if a man was living with his family, even though he had no work. This denial was based on the assumption that an employable man in the household meant that children were no longer "dependent" upon the state. Thus, if a man lived with his family, he could watch them go hungry; if he abandoned them, public assistance would enable them to eat. Moreover, an unmarried mother could get on welfare rolls easier than a married mother (who had to prove she was not receiving support from her husband). Occasionally enforcement of the "man in the house" rule led to sensational reports of welfare caseworkers making surprise nighttime calls to discover whether a woman had a partner in her bed. These rules have been relaxed in recent years, but it is still more difficult for whole families to get on public assistance than for fatherless families.

In most states, if a recipient of assistance takes a full time job, assistance checks are reduced or stopped. If the recipient is then laid off, it may take some time to get back on the welfare roll. In other words, employment is uncertain, while assistance is not. More importantly, the jobs available to most recipients are very low-paying jobs which do not produce much more income than assistance, particularly when transportation, child care, and other costs of working are considered. All of these facts discourage work.

The merits of cash versus goods and services as a form of public assistance have long been debated. It is frequently argued that cash payments are ineffective in alleviating poverty because recipients are often unable to manage household money. They fall prey to advertising and business which encourage them to spend money for non-essential items, and to overlook the food and clothing needs of themselves and their children. Assistance in the form of goods (for example, food stamps which could only be used to purchase basic food items) and services (for example, health care, day care for children, home management counseling) might represent a more effective approach. However, recipients themselves resent the goods and services approach, charging that it is paternalistic, that it curtails flexibility in family spending, and that it implies irresponsibility on the part of the recipient. Today most caseworkers argue for joint provision of cash and goods and services; they contend that cash is more effective when accompanied by services, and services are more effective when accompanied by cash.

Welfare administration is made difficult by the heavy load assigned to caseworkers, many of whom are recent college graduates. They spend much of their time determining eligibility, computing payments, and filling out an avalanche of proper forms. With case loads averaging up to 100 or 200 families, their contacts with recipients must be hurried, infrequent, and impersonal. Caseworkers are unable to develop any close bonds of friendship or rapport with persons in need of help. Recipients often come to view caseworkers with distrust or worse. The strain on caseworkers is very great; big city welfare departments report 50 percent turnover among caseworkers each year.

While these problems are serious, it is important to note that some of the charges leveled against public assistance are unfounded. For example, there are very few individuals for whom welfare has become "a permanent way of life." The median length of time on AFDC is less than three years; only one-tenth of the persons aided have been receiving assistance for more than ten years. The number of "welfare chislers"—able-bodied employable adults who prefer public assisted idleness to work—is probably quite small. The bulk of recipients are either aged, blind, disabled, women, or children; few employable men are on welfare rolls. The work alternative for the large numbers of AFDC mothers is fraught with problems—child care, lack of skills, no work experience, etc. It might be more costly to society to prepare these women for work than to support them.

PROSPECTS FOR WELFARE REFORM

President Richard M. Nixon summarized the nation's welfare policies as "a colossal failure":

> Whether measured by the anguish of the poor themselves or by the drastically mounting burden on the taxpayer, the present welfare system has to be judged a colossal failure.
>
> Our states and cities find themselves sinking in a welfare quagmire as caseloads increase, as costs escalate and as the welfare system stagnates enterprise and perpetuates dependency. What began on a small scale in the depression '30's has become a monster in the prosperous '60's. The tragedy is not only that it is bringing states and cities to the brink of financial disaster, but also that it is failing to meet the elementary human, social and financial needs of the poor.
>
> It breaks up homes. It often penalizes work. It robs recipients of dignity. And it grows.
>
> Benefit levels are grossly unequal. . . .
>
> The present system creates an incentive for desertion. . . .
>
> The present system often makes it possible to receive more money on welfare than on a low-paying job. This creates an incentive not to work; it also is unfair to the working poor. . . .[4]

The president proposed a new "family assistance plan" which paralleled so-called "guaranteed annual income" proposals which had been discussed for years in liberal circles.

[4] President Richard M. Nixon, speech on national television networks, August 12, 1969.

I propose that we abolish the present welfare system and adopt in its place a new family assistance system. Initially, this new system would cost more than welfare. But unlike welfare, it is designed to correct the condition it deals with and thus to lessen the long-range burden.

Under this plan, the so-called "adult categories" of aid—aid to the aged, the blind and disabled—would be continued and a national minimum standard for benefits would be set, with the Federal Government contributing to its cost and also sharing the cost of additional state payments above that amount.

But the program now called "Aid to Families with Dependent Children"—the program we normally think of when we think of "welfare"—would be done away with completely. . . .

Its benefits would go to the working poor as well as the non-working; to families with dependent children headed by a father as well as to those headed by a mother, and a basic federal minimum would be provided, the same in every state.

I propose that the Federal Government build a foundation under the income of every American family with dependent children that cannot care for itself—wherever in America that family may live.

For a family of four now on welfare, with no outside income the basic federal payment would be $1,600 a year. States could add to that amount, and most would do so. In no case would anyone's present level of benefits be lowered. At the same time, this foundation would be one on which the family itself could build. Outside earnings would be encouraged, not discouraged. The new worker could keep the first $60 a month of outside earnings with no reduction in his benefits, and beyond that his benefits would be reduced by only 50 cents for each dollar earned.

By the same token, a family head already employed at low wages could get a family assistance supplement, those who work would no longer be discriminated against. A family of five in which the father earns $2,000 a year—which is the hard fact of life for many families—would get family assistance payments of $1,260 for a total income of $3,260. A family of seven earning $3,000 a year would have its income raised to $4,360.

Thus, for the first time, the government would recognize that it has no less of an obligation to the working poor than to the nonworking poor, and for the first time, benefits would be scaled in such a way that it would always pay to work.

With such incentive, most recipients who can work will want to work. This is part of the American character.

But what of the others—those who can work but choose not to?

The answer is very simple.

Under this proposal, everyone who accepts benefits must also accept work or training provided suitable jobs are available, either locally or at some distance if transportation is provided. The only exceptions would be those unable to work and mothers of preschool children. Even mothers of preschool children, however, would have the opportunity to work—because I am also proposing along with this a major expansion of day-care centers to make it possible for mothers to take jobs by which they can support themselves and their children.[5]

---

[5] *Ibid.*

The proposed Family Assistance Program is clearly designed to remedy many of the dysfunctional consequences of previous welfare policy—disincentives to work, discouragement of family life, inequalities among the states, and discrimination against the working poor. But the long run impact of such a policy reform is difficult to predict.

The first problem with the Nixon proposal is the increase in welfare costs which would be involved.[6] The Nixon Administration itself estimated that an *additional* $4 billion per year would be required in federal funds to pay the minimum national guarantee of only $1,600 for needy families. But this estimate may be very low; the actual costs might turn out to be more than twice as great. Moreover, it is likely that Congress will increase this guarantee to $2,400 or more. There is no really reliable information on the number of working poor who would apply or what this would cost. Presumably the costs of AFDC would be eliminated; but the costs of old age, blind, and disabled assistance would continue, not to mention the spiraling cost of "Medicaid" for the poor.

Despite the heavy costs involved in a federally guaranteed $1,600 or $2,400 income for a family of four, there is no doubt that this is an inadequate income by anyone's standards. It is well below the Social Security Administration's recognized "poverty" line of $3,500. It is likely that Congress would be under great pressure to increase this guarantee over the years, adding further to the costs of the program.

Moreover, it is not certain whether this expansion of welfare assistance to many working families would increase or reduce economic dependency in America. It is conceivable that such an expansion in welfare assistance would encourage dependency by making the acceptance of such assistance a common family practice, extending well up into the middle class. Certainly the percentage of the population receiving some form of public assistance would be greatly increased; it is conceivable that 20 percent of the population would eventually gain access to welfare rolls under a family assistance program.

The work incentives of the Nixon proposal have been attacked as useless, and perhaps demeaning. Previous work incentive amendments to public assistance programs have not succeeded in reducing dependency. If welfare recipients could find good jobs they would have done so long ago; the real problem is that they are unskilled, uneducated, and unprepared to function effectively in the work force. Perhaps the work incentives would encourage some recipients to accept more poorly-paid, economically marginal jobs—maid service, gardening, window washing, etc. But the social value of these jobs is limited, and this aspect of the reform proposal has been attacked as demeaning to the poor.

[6] For an excellent example of a rational analysis of welfare reform, see Theodore Marmor, "On Comparing Income Maintenance Alternatives," *American Political Science Review*, Vol. 65 (March 1971), 83-96.

SUMMARY

A variety of seemingly "rational" strategies for dealing with the poor have been attempted over the years. Yet each strategy produced many unintended consequences, and none succeeded in eliminating poverty or even reducing the political controversy surrounding welfare efforts. Let us summarize the major directions of welfare policy in America and some of the difficulties encountered in coping effectively with the problems of the poor:

1. The strategy of early welfare policy was to discourage poverty by providing only minimal assistance, generally in institutions, to the most destitute in society. Heavy reliance was placed on local governments and upon private charity. Poverty was viewed as a product of moral deficiency in the individual, and it was reasoned that only a punitive strategy would dissuade people from indolence.

2. The widespread experience with poverty in the Depression led many people to reason that poverty was a product of personal misfortunes or economic conditions over which the individual had little control. Thus, the Depression discredited the punitive strategy.

3. The social insurance concept was designed as a preventive strategy to insure persons against indigency arising from old age, death of a family breadwinner or physical disability. It was hoped that social security would eventually abolish the need for public welfare, since individuals would be insured against poverty.

4. Despite the fact that social insurance is now the second largest expenditure item of the federal government, welfare rolls are rising rapidly rather than declining. Average monthly payments under social security fall below recognized poverty levels. The trust fund concept has been abandoned. And the tax itself is highly regressive.

5. The federal government also undertook an alleviative strategy in helping the states provide public assistance payments to certain categories of needy persons—aged, blind, disabled, and dependent children. Federal grants-in-aid to the states assisted them in providing monthly cash payments to the needy.

6. Dependence upon public assistance in America is growing at a very rapid rate, despite a reasonably healthy economy. Aid to families with dependent children is the largest, most expensive, and most rapidly growing of all welfare programs. Yet a majority of the nation's poor do not receive welfare payments,

notably the working poor. Welfare benefits fall well below poverty levels and they are uneven among the states. Program policies include disincentives to both family life and work. Cash payments are frequently misspent. Caseworkers are too overloaded for effective counseling. Administration is heavy with red tape.

7. A national strategy for health care was finally adopted in 1965. It included "Medicare" for the aged under the social security program, and "Medicaid" for welfare recipients under federal-state public assistance programs. The costs of both programs greatly exceed expectations.

8. Welfare reform—in terms of a family assistance plan or guaranteed annual income—is another attempt at rationalizing welfare policy. It is designed to assist the working as well as the non-working poor, to provide a federally guaranteed floor on minimum incomes, and to reduce dependency by work incentives. However, the outcomes are difficult to predict; the number of participants and future costs are difficult to estimate; the impact on social dependency is difficult to foresee; and the work incentives may turn out to be inappropriate or ineffective.

BIBLIOGRAPHY

Advisory Council on Public Welfare, *Having the Power, We Have the Duty*, Report to the Secretary of Health, Education and Welfare. Washington: Government Printing Office, 1966.

FISHMAN, LEO, ed., *Poverty Amid Affluence.* New Haven: Yale University Press, 1966.

HARRINGTON, MICHAEL, *The Other America: Poverty in the United States.* New York: Macmillan, 1962.

President's Commission on Income Maintenance Programs, *Poverty Amid Plenty.* Washington, D.C.: Government Printing Office, 1969.

POVERTY:
the search for a rational strategy

CHAPTER 6

POVERTY IN AMERICA

Measuring the extent of poverty in America is itself a political activity. Proponents of programs for the poor frequently make high estimates of the number of poor. They view the problem of poverty as a persistent one, even in an affluent society; they contend that many millions of poor people suffer from hunger, exposure, and remedial illness, and that some of them even starve to death. Their definition of the problem practically mandates immediate and massive public programs.

On the other hand others minimize the number of poor in America. They see poverty diminishing over time without major public programs; they view the poor in America as considerably better off than the middle-class of fifty years ago and even wealthy by the standards of most other societies in the world; and they deny that anyone needs to suffer from hunger, exposure, remedial illness, or starvation if they make use of the services and facilities available to them. This definition of the problem minimizes demands for public programs to fight poverty. Hence the first obstacle to a rational approach to poverty lies in the conflict over the definition of the problem.

According to the U.S. Social Security Administration there are about 25 million poor people in the United States. This is approximately 13 percent of the population. This is the number of Americans falling *below* the poverty line which is set at: [1]

	Annual Cash Income, 1968	
Family Size	*Urban*	*Rural–Farms*
1	$1,748	$1,487
2	2,262	1,904
3	2,774	2,352
4	3,553	3,034
5	4,188	3,577
6	4,706	4,021
7	5,789	4,916

This definition of the poverty line was derived by careful calculation of costs of food, housing, clothing, and other items for rural and urban families of different sizes. The dollar amounts on these lines are flexible to take into account the effect of inflation; these amounts can be expected to rise each year with the rate of inflation.

There are several problems in this definition of poverty. First of all, it does not account for regional differences in the costs of living, or climate, or accepted style of living. Second, it does not account for family assets—for example, a family which owns its own home does not usually devote as much income to housing as a family which rents. Third, there are many families and individuals whose particular circumstances may place them officially among the poor but who do not think of themselves as "poor people"—students, for example. Doubtless there are others whose income is above the poverty line but who have special problems—such as serious or chronic sickness—which leave them impoverished. Finally, the official definition of poverty does not recognize the problems of those who spend their incomes unwisely. If money goes for liquor, or dope, or expensive used cars, or if money is siphoned off by loan sharks, impoverished relatives and friends, or high prices charged by ghetto storeowners, then even a reasonably high income family can live in poverty. Yet despite these problems, the Social Security Administration definition has provided the best available estimate of poverty in America.

How poor is "poor"? There is reason to believe that the 25 million Americans living in official poverty do not all suffer hardship and privation.[2] About 45 percent own cars, 42 percent own their own homes, and more than half have some savings. Nearly 80 percent of the poor have television sets and 75 percent have refrigerators or freezers. Over three-quarters have hot water, access to a telephone for receiving calls, kitchen with cooking equipment, a flush toilet,

[1] U.S. Bureau of the Census, *Current Population Reports*, Series P-60 "Poverty in the United States: 1959-1968" (1969), p. 11. See also *Economic Report of the President, January, 1965* (Washington, D.C.: Government Printing Office, 1965).
[2] Herman P. Miller, "The Dimensions of Poverty," in Ben B. Seligman, ed., *Poverty as a Public Issue* (New York: Free Press, 1965).

and a bath. Yet the diets of the poor are nutritionally bad, whether from ignorance or poverty. The poor do not seek medical attention except in emergencies. The result is a great deal of preventable illness and malnutrition.

TABLE 6-1   POPULATION, BY CATEGORIES, WITH INCOME BELOW POVERTY LEVEL
(Based on Total Population)

	Number (in millions)	Percent of Total in Category
Total	25.4	12.8
White population	17.4	10.0
Black population	8.0	34.7
Those living in central cities	7.8	13.4
Those living in suburbs	5.1	7.3
Those living in rural	12.5	18.0
Under age 25	13.1	14.3
Ages 25-65	7.6	8.7
Over age 65	4.6	25.0
Families with male head	15.0	8.8
Families with female head	10.4	38.9

Source: U.S. Bureau of the Census, *Statistical Abstract of the United States: 1970* (Washington, D.C.: Government Printing Office, 1970), p. 328.

Who are the poor? Poverty occurs in many different kinds of families and in all environmental settings. However, the incidence of poverty varies sharply among groups living under different circumstances, and several groups experience poverty in greater proportions than the national average.[3] First of all, the likelihood of *blacks* experiencing poverty is three times greater than whites; the percentage of the black population of the United States falling under the poverty line is 34.7, compared to 10.0 percent for the white population. Second, *female-headed families* experience poverty far more frequently than male-headed families; 38.9 percent of all female-headed families live below the poverty line. Third, the *aged* experience more poverty than persons of working age; 25.0 percent of the population over 65 lives below the poverty line. While we think of poverty as a characteristic of persons living in large, central city ghettos, actually *rural* families experience more poverty more frequently than central city families. On the other hand, central cities have more poverty than their surrounding suburbs..

Are the poor disappearing? In Franklin D. Roosevelt's second inaugural address in 1937 he said, "I see one-third of a nation ill-housed, ill-clad, ill-nourished." Since that time the American political and economic system has succeeded in reducing the proportion of poor to less than 13 percent. If current rates in the reduction of poverty in America continue in the future, there will be virtually no poverty remaining in 25 to 50 years.

[3] U.S. Bureau of the Census, "Poverty in the United States."

POVERTY IN THE UNITED STATES

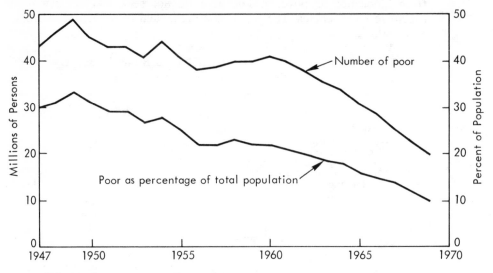

FIG. 6-1 POVERTY IN THE UNITED STATES

Source: Redrawn after G. Bach, *Economics*, 7th Ed. (Englewood Cliffs, N.J.: Prentice-Hall, Inc., © 1971), Fig. 37-1, p. 535. Data from Council of Economic Advisers and Social Security Administration.

Table 6-2 provides a closer look at the change in the number and percentage of poor over the last decade.[4] All of these figures account for the effect of inflation, so there is no question that the number and percentage of the population living in poverty is declining, despite increases in the population. Both white and black poverty is declining, although the rate of decline among blacks has not been as great as the rate of decline among whites.

TABLE 6-2 CHANGES IN THE NUMBER OF POOR
1959-1967

Pop. Living Below Poverty Level	1959 Millions	1963 Millions	1963 Change from '59	1967 Millions	1967 Change from '63
Total	39.5	36.4	—2.0	27.8	—6.5
White	28.5	25.2	—3.0	19.0	—6.8
Nonwhite	11.0	11.2	0.4	8.8	—5.9

Source: U.S. Bureau of the Census, *Current Population Reports,* Series P-60, No. 68, "Poverty in the United States" (Washington, D.C.: Government Printing Office, 1969), p. 21.

4 *Ibid.*

POVERTY AS RELATIVE DEPRIVATION

It is possible to define poverty as "a state of mind"—some people think they have less income or material possessions than most Americans, and they believe they are entitled to more. Their sense of deprivation is not tied to any *absolute* level of income. Instead, their sense of deprivation is *relative* to what most Americans have, and what they, therefore, feel they are entitled to. Even fairly substantial incomes may result in a sense of relative deprivation in a very affluent society when commercial advertising and the mass media portray the "average American" as having a high level of consumption and material well-being.

Today the poor are not any more deprived, relative to the nonpoor, than in the past. However, they *feel* more deprived—they perceive the gap to be wider, and they no longer accept the gap as legitimate. Blacks are unequally overrepresented among the poor; the civil rights movement made blacks acutely aware of their position in American society relative to whites. Thus, the black revolution contributed to a new awareness of the problem of poverty in terms of relative differences in income and conditions of life.

Defining poverty as relative deprivation really defines it as *inequality* in society. As Victor Fuchs explains:

> By the standards that have prevailed over most of history, and still prevail over large areas of the world, there are very few poor in the United States today. Nevertheless, there are millions of American families who, both in their own eyes and in those of others, are poor. As our nation prospers, our judgment as to what constitutes poverty will inevitably change. When we talk about poverty in America, we are talking about families and individuals who have much less income than most of us. When we talk about reducing or eliminating poverty, we are really talking about changing the distribution of income.[5]

Thus, eliminating poverty if it is defined as relative deprivation would mean achieving absolute equality of incomes and material possessions in America.

Let us try systematically to examine poverty as relative deprivation. Economists have already provided us with a way of measuring income distributions within political systems.[6] Income distributions may be observed by means of a Lorenz curve, which shows the cumulative proportions of aggregate income (on the verical or y axis) accruing to cumulative proportions of the population ranging in order

[5] Victor R. Fuchs, "Redefining Poverty and Redistributing Income," *The Public Interest* (Summer 1967), p. 91.
[6] See James Morgan, "The Anatomy of Income Distributions," *The Review of Economics and Statistics*, Vol. 44 (August 1962), 270-80.

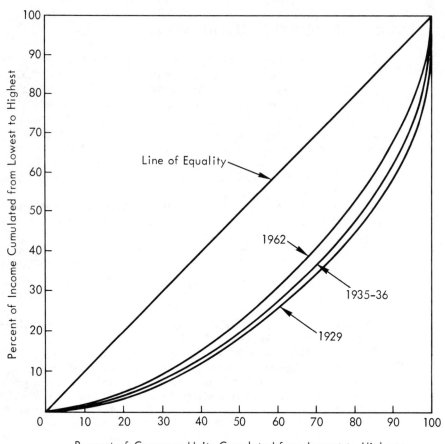

FIG. 6-2 Lorenz Curves for the Distribution of Family Personal Income

from the lowest to highest income earners (on the horizontal or *x* axis). The total area on a diagram that falls between the Lorenz curve, representing the actual income distribution, and the straight diagonal line, representing perfect income equality, expresses the extent of income inequality within a political system. This area is measured by Gini coefficient or a Gini index, which ranges from a plus 1.00 (theoretically perfect inequality) to 0.00 (theoretically perfect equality) as illustrated in Figure 6-2. Inequality in America is decreasing over time. However, the rate of decrease is not very rapid. Certainly poverty as relative deprivation is not disappearing at the same rate as absolute poverty. Figure 6.2 shows that the Lorenz curve is moving closer to the line of perfect equality over time, but that changes in the curve are not very great.

A closer view of changes in income inequality over time is presented in Table 6-3. This table divides all American families into five groups—from the lowest one-fifth, in personal income, to the highest one-fifth—and shows the percentage of total family personal income received by each of these groups over the years. (If perfect income equality existed, each fifth of American families would receive 20 percent of all family personal income, and it would not even be possible to rank fifths from highest to lowest.) The poorest one-fifth received 3.5 percent of all family personal income in 1929; in 1962, however, this group had increased its percentage of all family personal income to 4.6. (Most of this increase occurred during World War II.) The highest one-fifth of American families in personal income received 54.4 percent of all family personal income in 1929; in 1962, however, this percentage had declined to 45.5. This was the only income group to lose in relation to other income groups. The middle classes improved their relative income position even more than the poor. Another measure of income equalization over time is

TABLE 6-3   PERCENT DISTRIBUTION OF FAMILY PERSONAL INCOME [1] BY QUINTILES AND TOP 5 PERCENT OF CONSUMER UNITS,[2] SELECTED YEARS, 1929–1962

Quintiles	1929	1935-1936	1941	1944	1947	1950	1951	1954	1956	1959	1962	1968
Lowest	3.5	4.1	4.1	4.9	5.0	4.8	5.0	.48	.48	4.6	4.6	5.7
Second	9.0	9.2	9.5	10.9	11.0	10.9	11.3	11.1	11.3	10.9	10.9	12.4
Third	13.8	14.1	15.3	16.2	16.0	16.1	16.5	16.4	16.3	16.3	16.3	17.7
Fourth	19.3	20.9	22.3	22.2	22.0	22.1	22.3	22.5	22.3	22.6	22.7	23.7
Highest	54.4	51.7	48.8	45.8	46.0	46.1	44.9	45.2	45.3	45.6	45.5	40.6
Total	100.0	100.0	100.0	100.0	100.0	100.0	100.0	100.0	100.0	100.0	100.0	100.0
Top 5 percent ratio	30.0	26.5	24.0	20.7	20.9	21.4	20.7	20.3	20.2	20.2	19.6	14.0
Gini concentration	.49	.47	.44	.39	.40	.40		.39	.39		.40	.37

[1] Family personal income includes wage and salary receipts (net of social insurance contributions), other labor income, proprietors' and rental income, dividends, personal interest income, and transfer payments. In addition to monetary income flows, it includes certain nonmonetary or imputed income such as wages in kind, the value of food and fuel produced and consumed on farms, net imputed rental value of owner-occupied homes, and imputed interest. Personal income differs from national income in that it excludes corporate profits taxes, corporate saving (inclusive of inventory valuation adjustment), and social security contributions of employers and employees, and includes transfer payments (mostly governmental) and interest on consumer and government debt.

[2] Consumer units include farm operator and nonfarm families and unattached individuals. A family is defined as a group of two or more persons related by blood, marriage, or adoption, and residing together.

Source: Edward C. Budd, *Inequality and Poverty* (New York: W. W. Norton & Co., © 1967), p. xiii., reprinted by permission of W. W. Norton & Co., Inc.; and U.S. Bureau of the Census, *Consumer Income*, December 23, 1969 (Series P-60), p. 22.

the decline in the percentage of income received by the top 5 percent in America. The top 5 percent received 30.0 percent of all family personal incomes in 1929, but only 19.6 percent in 1962. The Gini coefficient of income inequality declined from .49 to .40 in that same time period. There is no doubt that income differences in America are decreasing over time.

However, it is unlikely that income differences will ever disappear completely—at least not in a society that rewards skill, talent, risk taking, and ingenuity. If the problem of poverty is defined as relative deprivation—that is, *inequality*—then the problem is not really capable of solution. Regardless of how well off the poor may be in absolute terms, there will always be a lowest one-fifth of the population receiving something less than 20 percent of all income. Income differences may decline over time, but *some* differences will remain, and even minor differences can acquire great importance and hence pose a "problem."

In describing federal antipoverty programs, we will be dealing with policies that were designed primarily to raise the poor above the poverty line. Policies dealing with income redistribution are discussed in Chapter 10.

THE CURATIVE STRATEGY—THE WAR ON POVERTY

The war on poverty is an attempt to apply a "curative strategy" to the problems of the poor. In contrast to the alleviative strategy of public assistance, or the preventative strategy of social security, the curative strategy stresses efforts to help the poor and unemployed become self-supporting and capable of earning adequate incomes by bringing about changes in the individuals themselves or in their environment. The curative strategy was the prevailing approach to poverty in the administrations of Presidents John F. Kennedy and Lyndon B. Johnson. It is represented in the Economic Development Act of 1965, Appalachian Regional Development Act of 1965, the Manpower Training and Development Act of 1962, and the Economic Opportunity Act of 1964, all of which are discussed below.

The rationale of the curative strategy was described in a very influential book, *The Affluent Society*, by economist and presidential advisor John Kenneth Galbraith.[7] Writing in 1957, Galbraith first called the attention of the intellectual community to the existence of widespread poverty in the midst of an affluent society. Although only a small minority of Americans are poor, the poverty they experience is a very bitter kind of poverty because the majority of Americans are so rich.

[7] John K. Galbraith, *The Affluent Society* (Boston: Houghton Mifflin, 1958).

In attempting to identify the causes of poverty in America, Galbraith distinguishes between "case poverty" and "area poverty." Case poverty is largely a product of the personal characteristics of affected persons. Some persons have been unable to participate in the nation's prosperity because of old age, illiteracy, inadequate education, lack of job skills, poor health, inadequate motivation, or racial discrimination. Area poverty is a product of economic deficiency relating to a particular sector of the nation, such as West Virginia or much of the rest of Appalachia, and large parts of rural America. Urbanization, industrialization, and technological development appear to have passed up many of these areas, creating high rates of unemployment and large numbers of low income families. The decline in employment in the coal industry, the exhaustion of iron ore mines, the squeezing out of the small farmer from the agricultural market, and other such economic factors create "pockets of poverty" or "depressed areas" throughout the nation. People in these areas suffer many of the problems of case poverty because the two types of poverty are not mutually exclusive. But both case poverty and area poverty differ from the "mass poverty" of the 1930s or the mass poverty predicted for capitalist societies by Marxian doctrine. Today's poverty afflicts only a minority of Americans, and it does not disappear even when the economy expands and the nation is prosperous.

The federal government launched its campaign against area poverty with the Area Redevelopment Act of 1961.[8] This was a four-year program of assistance for depressed areas, in which the Area Redevelopment Administration in the Department of Commerce provided long term loans at low interest to attract businesses to these areas, loans and grants to local governments for public facilities needed to attract businesses, and support for other community economic development and worker-retraining programs. The Act was essentially a "trickle-down" approach to poverty, with most of the direct benefits going to businesses rather than the poor. Republicans charged that the program was a pork barrel to help elect Democrats, and many specific ARA projects were criticized for failing to alleviate poverty. In 1965, President Johnson requested Congress to replace ARA with an expanded and broadened program for depressed areas under the Economic Development Act of 1965. It authorized grants and loans for public works, development facilities, technical assistance, and other activities to help economically depressed areas and to stimulate planning for economic development. In this Act, the responsibility is

[8] For an excellent summary of public policies in the war on poverty, see James E. Anderson, "Poverty, Unemployment, and Economic Development: The Search for a National Anti-Poverty Policy," *Journal of Politics*, Vol. 29 (February 1967), 70-93.

placed upon local and state governments to apply for economic development assistance from the Economic Development Administration and to create multicounty and multistate development areas and districts for the purposes of planning economic development. The Economic Development Administration can make direct grants to communities for such projects as water systems, waste disposal plants, industrial development parks, airports, or other facilities that will improve employment opportunities in a depressed area; but it insists on regional planning and requires any community proposal to "substantially further the objectives of the war on poverty."

The Appalachian Regional Redevelopment Act in 1965 was another federal approach to the problem of area poverty. The name "Appalachia" denoted an eleven-state region centering around the Appalachian mountains from southern New York to mid-Alabama. It was generally conceded to be the largest economically depressed area in the nation, although it did contain "pockets of prosperity." The focus of the Appalachia Act is on highway construction, which was be-

Shacks, Appalachia. Photo by Michael Mauney

lieved necessary to open up the region to economic development although it may make it even easier for the residents to leave. Programs under the Appalachia Act will be carried out by existing national and state agencies, such as the U.S. Bureau of Public Roads and state highway departments. However, the entire program is coordinated by the Appalachian Regional Commission, comprised of the governor of each state in the region or his representative, and a federal representative chosen by the President. This arrangement was designed to secure state participation and better adaptation of programs to local conditions. Needless to say, the Appalachian program stirred the interest of congressmen from *other* regional areas.

As an approach to case poverty, the federal government passed the Manpower Training and Development Act of 1962, which authorizes federal grants to state employment agencies and private enterprise for on-the-job training programs to help workers in depressed areas, or elsewhere, acquire new job skills. Originally the act called for matching funds on a 50–50 basis by state governments after the first two years of the program; but when it appeared certain that states would drop the program altogether rather than share its costs, the federal government amended the act to authorize 100 percent federal financing. It seems safe to conclude that state and local governments will not undertake manpower training programs for unskilled workers without full federal financial support.

The most important legislation in the "war on poverty" is the Economic Opportunity Act of 1964.[9] The Office of Economic Opportunity (OEO) was established directly under the President with authority to support varied and highly experimental techniques for combating poverty at the community level. The focus was upon case poverty and the objective was to help the poor and unemployed become self-supporting and capable of earning adequate incomes by bringing about changes in the individuals themselves or in their environment. The strategy was one of "rehabilitation, not relief." OEO was given no authority to make direct grants to the poor as relief or public assistance. All of its programs were aimed, whether accurately or inaccurately, at curing the causes of poverty rather than alleviating its symptoms.

THE JOB CORPS, NEIGHBORHOOD YOUTH CORPS, WORK-STUDY, AND VISTA

The Economic Opportunity Act established several programs oriented toward youth. The strategy appeared to be aimed at breaking the cycle of poverty at an early age. The Job Corps is designed to

---

[9] For a description of the programs under the Economic Opportunity Act, see Joseph A. Kershaw, *Government Against Poverty* (Chicago: Markham, 1970).

provide education, vocational training, and work experience in rural conservation camps for unemployable youth between the ages of sixteen and twenty-one. It is not a simple manpower training effort; Job Corps enrollees are considered to lack the attitudes and basic education required to gain and hold a job. Reading and basic arithmetic are taught, as well as auto mechanics, clerical work, and the use of tools. Health care and personal guidance and counseling are also provided. Removing the enrollees from their home environment is considered helpful in breaking habits and associations that are obstacles to useful employment. It is very difficult to measure the effectiveness of the program; the program's dropout rate is very high; the cost of the program per enrollee is very high (in 1966 Congress mandated that operating costs be kept at $7,500 per man), and there is no solid evidence that Job Corps' alumni do better in the labor market than they would have done without Job Corps' experience. At its peak, Job Corps had 40,000 enrollees, but by 1970 it was down to less than 20,000.

Another program for teenage youth is the Neighborhood Youth Corps. It is designed to provide some work, counseling, and on-the-job training for youth who are living at home. Participating youths may be in school or out of school. The Neighborhood Youth Corps was intended for youths who were somewhat more employable than those who were expected to enter Job Corps. But the programs were never really coordinated, and youths with different problems and backgrounds found their way into both programs. Evaluations of the Neighborhood Youth Corps are no more positive than evaluations of the Job Corps. At its peak there were 500,000 youths enrolled in Neighborhood Youth Corps projects throughout the nation.

A Work-Study Program helps students from low-income families remain in school by giving them federally paid part-time employment with cooperating public or private agencies. Many universities and colleges are participants in this program; they benefit from the federally paid labor and students benefit from the part-time jobs created.

The Volunteers in Service to America (VISTA) was modeled after the popular Peace Corps idea, but volunteers were to work in domestic, poverty-impacted areas rather than in foreign countries. Volunteers normally give one year of service—frequently in migrant labor camps, Indian reservations, neighborhood service centers, and so on. Of course, a fundamental problem in the program is determining what services the idealistic, young, middle-class volunteers can provide. Unless VISTA workers have some special skills, they are not very useful to poor people.

COMMUNITY ACTION PROGRAMS

The core of the Economic Opportunity Act was a grassroots "Community Action Program" to be carried on at the local level with federal financial assistance, by public or private nonprofit agencies. Communities were urged to form a "Community Action Agency," composed of representatives of government, private organizations, and most importantly, the poor themselves. It was originally intended that OEO would *support antipoverty programs* devised by the local community action agency. Projects might include (but were not limited to) literacy training, health services, homemaker services, legal aid for the poor, neighborhood service centers, manpower vocational training, and childhood development activties. The Act also envisioned that a community action agency would help *organize the poor* so that they could become participating members of the community and avail themselves of the many public programs designed to serve the poor. Finally, the Act attempted to *coordinate federal and state programs for the poor* in each community.

Community action was to be "developed, conducted, and administered with the maximum feasible participation of the residents of the areas and members of the groups served." This was one of the more controversial phases in the Act itself. Militants within the OEO administration frequently cited this phase as authority to "mobilize" the poor "to have immediate and irreversable impact on the communities." This language implied that the poor were to be organized as a political force, by federal antipoverty warriors using federal funds. Needless to say neither Congress nor the Democratic Administration of President Lyndon Johnson intended to create in these communities rival political organizations that would compete for power with local governments. But some OEO administrators thought that the language of the Act gave them this authority.

The typical Community Action Agency was governed by a board consisting of public officials (perhaps the mayor, a county commissioner, a school board member, public health officer, etc.), prominent public citizens (from business, labor, civil rights, religious, and civil affairs organizations), and representatives of the poor (in some cases elected in agency-sponsored elections but more often hand picked by ministers, social workers, civil rights leaders, etc.) A staff was to be hired, including a full-time director, and paid from an OEO grant for administrative expenses. A target area would be defined—generally it was the low income area of the county or the ghetto of a city. Neighborhood centers were established in the target area, perhaps with general counselors, employment assistance, a recreation hall, a child care center, and some sort of health clinic. These centers assisted the poor in contacting the school system, the welfare department, employment agencies, the public housing authority, and so on. Frequently, the centers and the antipoverty workers who manned them acted as intermediaries between the poor and public agencies. The jargon describing this activity was "outreach."

Community Action Agencies also devised specific antipoverty projects for submission to Washington offices of OEO for funding. The most popular of these projects was "Operation Head Start"—usually a cooperative program between the community action agency and the local school district. Preschool children from poor families were given six to eight weeks of special summer preparation before entering kindergarten or first grade. The idea was to give these disadvantaged children a "head start" on formal schooling. Congress (as well as the general public) was favorably disposed toward this program and emphasized it in later budget appropriations to OEO. However, studies of the academic progress of disadvantaged children who participated in Head Start revealed that these children did no better in the long run than disadvantaged children who had not participated in the program.

Another type of antipoverty project was the "legal services program." Many community action agencies established free legal services to the poor to assist them in rent disputes, contracts, welfare rules, minor police actions, housing regulations, and so on. The idea was that the poor seldom have access to legal counsel and they are frequently taken advantage of because they do not understand their rights. Congress amended the Act in 1967 to insure that no OEO funds would be used to defend any person in a criminal case. But antipoverty lawyers using federal funds have been active in bringing suit against city welfare departments, housing authorities, public health agencies, and other government bodies.

Other kinds of antipoverty projects funded by OEO include family planning programs—the provision of advice and devices to facilitate family planning by the poor; homemaker services—advice to poor families on how to stretch low family budgets; manpower training—special outreach efforts to bring hard core unemployed into more established manpower programs; "Follow Through"—to remedy the recognized failures of Head Start and continue special educational experiences for poor children after they enter school; "Upward Bound"—educational counseling for poor children; etc.

WHY WE LOST THE WAR ON POVERTY

In 1969 the Office of Economic Opportunity was "reorganized" by the Nixon Administration, transferring its educational and manpower training programs—the Head Start Program, the Job Corps, and

Manpower Training—to other federal agencies and relegating OEO to the status of a "laboratory agency." Funds for the war on poverty —never more than $2 billion per year—faced gradual reallocation. President Nixon declared:

> In the past, OEO suffered from a confusion of roles and from a massive attempt to do everything at once, with the same people performing many conflicting functions: coordinating old programs, doing new research, setting up demonstration projects, evaluating results and serving as advocates for the poor. As a result, inefficiency, waste and resentment too often clouded the record of even its best accomplishments.[10]

The demise of the economic opportunity programs cannot be attributed to political partisanship. The war on poverty had become the unpopular stepchild of the Johnson Administration long before LBJ left office. The reasons for the failure of this effort to implement a curative strategy are complex.[11]

The Office of Economic Opportunity was always the scene of great confusion. New and untried programs were organized at breakneck speed. There was a high turnover in personnel. There was delay and confusion in releasing funds to local community action agencies. There was an excess of scandal and corruption particularly at the local level. Community action agencies with young and inexperienced personnel frequently offended experienced governmental administrators as well as local political figures. Congressional action was uncertain, the Agency's life was extended for a year at a time, and appropriations were often delayed. But most damaging of all, even though programs were put in operation, there was little concrete evidence that these programs were successful in their objectives, that is, in eliminating the causes of poverty.

The community action effort in Syracuse, New York, was illustrative of the difficulties which all too frequently plagued the war on poverty. In a city of 222,000, with only 16,000 Negroes, the Syracuse Crusade for Opportunity, the local community action agency, was established with a white majority on its governing board. Simultaneously, however, the OEO gave Syracuse University a grant to establish a Community Action Training Center to experiment with new approaches for enabling the poor to participate in the management of antipoverty programs such as the Crusade for Opportunity. The Training Center worked primarily with blacks, and soon agitation was begun among the Negro poor that Negroes "take over"

---

[10] President Richard M. Nixon, Message to Congress, October 2, 1969.
[11] The most important and controversial analysis of the difficulties in the war on poverty is Daniel P. Moynihan, *Maximum Feasible Misunderstanding: Community Action in the War on Poverty* (New York: Free Press, 1969), on which the following analysis relies.

Crusade for Opportunity. Early in 1966 the white Jewish executive director resigned the $19,000 job (a very substantial salary from the perspective of the poor clientele) and was replaced by a militant black. Soon blacks acquired a majority on the Board. In the eyes of the public the war on poverty was now a "black program." At this point the public demands and the rhetoric emanating from Crusade for Opportunity became more and more abrasive to the white community. For example, remedial reading manuals in literacy classes informed readers: "no ends are accomplished without the use of force. . . . Squeamishness about force is the mark not of idealistic but moonstruck morals." The local NAACP charged that such materials were "geared to rioting," but militant poverty workers responded that the NAACP head was a "house nigger."

While the struggle for power went on over Crusade for Opportunity, the actual antipoverty projects floundered. A job training program was rated "a dismal failure" by its head. Politically the organization failed to assist the poor in bringing about a more responsive government. A Republican Mayor was reelected, not only in spite of, but probably because of, the intense opposition, even harassment, by antipoverty workers. The finances of the organization soon became a scandal; substantial sums went unaccounted for. Then it was revealed that $7 million of the $8 million expended by Crusade for Opportunity up to mid-1967 went for salaries of antipoverty workers. It was difficult to see what the organization had done for the poor of Syracuse.

Daniel P. Moynihan summarized the community action experiences as follows:

> Over and again the attempts by official and quasi-official agencies (such as the Ford Foundation) to organize poor communities led first to the radicalization of the middle-class persons who began the effort; next to a certain amount of stirring among the poor, but accompanied by heightened radical antagonism *on the part of the poor* if they happened to be black; next to retaliation from the larger white community; whereupon it would emerge that the community action agency, which had talked so much, been so much in the headlines, promised so much in the way of change in the fundamentals of things, was powerless. A creature of a Washington bureaucracy, subject to discontinuation without notice. Finally, much bitterness all around.[12]

Community experiences such as that in Syracuse were bound to reverbrate in Washington. The Democratic administration under President Johnson had never intended to finance a conflict between poor blacks and Democratic big-city mayors and party organization.

[12] *Ibid.*, p. 134-35.

The Democratic administration did not wish to stir up antagonism in cities between blacks and low-income white labor and ethnic groups which made up the winning Democratic party coalition since the days of FDR. Local power structures are not without influence in Washington; they could strike at the financial roots of the program in Washington without risking direct confrontation at the local level. Even before Johnson left office, the war on poverty had been substantially downgraded in policy priorities. The Nixon administration began a gradual dismantling of OEO. The final verdict on the war on poverty is not yet in. But the interim report is very negative.

In an obvious reference to public policies affecting the poor and the black in America, Aaron Wildavsky wrote:

> A recipe for violence: Promise a lot; deliver a little. Lead people to believe they will be much better off, but let there be no dramatic improvement. Try a variety of small programs, each interesting but marginal in impact and severely underfinanced. Avoid any attempted solution remotely comparable in size to the dimensions of the problem you are trying to solve. Have middle-class civil servants hire upper-class student radicals to use lower-class Negroes as a battering ram against the existing local political systems; then complain that people are going around disrupting things and chastise local politicians for not cooperating with those out to do them in. Get some poor people involved in local decision-making, only to discover that there is not enough at stake to be worth bothering about. Feel guilty about what has happened to black people; tell them you are surprised they have not revolted before; express shock and dismay when they follow your advice. Go in for a little force, just enough to anger, not enough to discourage. Feel guilty again; say you are surprised that worse has not happened. Alternate with a little suppression. Mix well, apply a match, and run. . . .[13]

It would be difficult to find a better summary of the unintended consequences of public programs for the poor and the black.

SUMMARY

The difficulties in national policy making are evidenced in policies and programs dealing with the poor.

1. Contrasting definitions of the problem of poverty constitute an obstacle to national policy making. Official government sources define poverty in terms of minimum dollar amounts required

---

[13] Aaron Wildavsky, "The Empty-Headed Blues: Black Rebellion and White Reaction," *The Public Interest* (Spring 1968), p. 3.

for food, housing, clothing, and other necessary items. Poverty, by this definition, is declining over time.

2. If poverty is defined in relative terms, then the problem of poverty is nearly insoluble. Income inequality is slowly decreasing over time. However, unless all incomes in America are equalized among all persons, there will always be some individuals who fall below average income levels. Even if incomes are substantially narrowed, small differences may come to have great symbolic value and the problem of "poverty" will remain.

3. The "War on Poverty" was designed as a curative strategy to help poverty-stricken individuals and areas become self-supporting. The Economic Development Act and the Appalachian Regional Devolpment Act were designed to cure area poverty, while the Manpower Training and Development Act and the Economic Opportunity Act were designed to assist individuals in fighting poverty.

4. Several antipoverty programs dealt with young people—Job Corps, Work Study, Head Start, etc. The strategy appeared to be aimed at breaking the cycle of poverty at an early age. However, the impact of these programs is difficult to discern.

5. Community action programs had multiple objectives—mobilize the poor to become participating members of the community and to pressure community agencies to better serve their needs; coordinate federal and state progams for the poor in each community; and support a variety of local antipoverty projects. Frequently these objectives conflicted, particularly when community action agencies threatened to mobilze the poor as a political force in competition with existing community political structures.

6. The War on Poverty promised the poor, especially the poor blacks, a great deal—but it failed to bring about any significant change in their condition. Frustration and bitterness was a frequent product of antipoverty efforts. Community action programs were characterized by confusion, turnover, inexperience, scandal, and racial and political controversy.

BIBLIOGRAPHY

Budd, Edward C., *Inequality and Poverty*. New York: Norton, 1967.
Galbraith, John K., *The Affluent Society*. Boston: Houghton Mifflin, 1958.
Kershaw, Joseph A., *Government Against Poverty*. Chicago: Markham, 1970.

LEVINE, ROBERT A., *The Poor Ye Need Not Have With You.* Cambridge, Mass.: M.I.T. Press, 1970.

MOYNIHAN, DANIEL P., *Maximum Feasible Misunderstanding: Community Action and the War on Poverty.* New York: Fress Press, 1969.

WILCOX, CLAIR, *Toward Social Welfare.* Homewood, Ill.: Richard D. Irwin, 1969.

EDUCATION:
the group struggle

Perhaps the most widely recommended "solution" to the problems that confront American society is more and better schooling. If there ever was a time when schools were only expected to combat ignorance and illiteracy that time is far behind us. Today schools are expected to do many things: resolve racial conflict and build an integrated society; inspire patriotism and good citizenship; provide values, aspirations, and a sense of identity to disadvantaged children; offer various forms of recreation and mass entertainment (football games, bands, choruses, majorettes, and the like); reduce conflict in society by teaching children to get along well with others and to adjust to group living; reduce the highway accident toll by teaching students to be good drivers; fight disease and ill health through physical education, health training, and even medical treatment; eliminate unemployment and poverty by teaching job skills; end malnutrition and hunger through school lunch and milk programs; produce scientists and other technicians to continue America's progress in science and technology; fight drug abuse and educate children about sex; and act as custodians for teenagers who have no interest in education but whom we do not permit either to work or to roam the streets unsupervised. In other words, nearly all of the nation's problems are reflected in demands placed on the nation's schools. And, of course, these demands are frequently conflicting.

Thus, educational policy affects a wide variety of interests, and stimulates a great deal of interest-group activity. We will describe the major interests involved in federal educational policy and examine the group struggle over federal aid to education. We will examine the constitutional provisions and Court policies dealing with religion in the public schools. We shall observe how both racial and religious group interests are mobilized in educational policy making, and we will see the importance of resolving group conflict in the development of educational policy. We shall also describe the structure of educational decision making and the resulting multiple points of group access in a fragmented federal-state-local educational system. We shall attempt to describe the broad categories of group interests —teachers, taxpayers, school board members, school administrators —involved in educational policy at the local level. Finally, we will attempt to unravel the complex issues and interests involved in providing equality of educational opportunity for children in the nation's black ghettos.

THE FEDERAL ROLE IN EDUCATION

The total cost of education in America is less than 4 percent of the nation's total personal income. The primary responsibility for administration and finance of public schools rests with the fifty *state* governments and their subdivisions. In the 1970s Americans will spend over $40 billion per year on their elementary and secondary public schools. Currently the federal government pays only about 10 percent of that cost; 90 percent of the cost of public schools is born by state and local governments (see Figure 7-1).

The federal government's role in education is a long-standing one. In the famous Northwest Ordinance of 1787, Congress offered land grants for public schools in the new territories and gave succeeding generations words to be forever etched on grammar school cornerstones: "Religion, morality, and knoweldge, being necessary to good government and the happiness of mankind, schools and the means for education should ever be encouraged." The earliest democrats believed that the safest repository of the ultimate powers of society was the people themselves. If the people made mistakes, the remedy was not to remove power from their hands but to help them in forming their judgment through education. If the common man was to be granted the right to vote, he must be educated to his task. This meant that public education had to be universal, free, and compulsory. Compulsory education began in Massachusetts in 1852 and was eventually adopted by Mississippi in 1918.

In 1862 the Morrill Land Grant Act provided grants of federal land

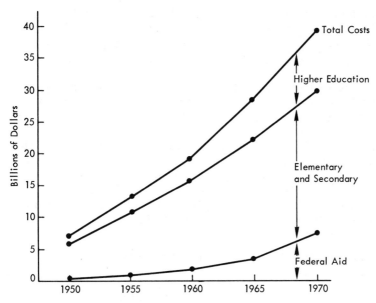

FIG. 7-1   THE GROWING COSTS OF EDUCATION

to each state for the establishment of colleges specializing in agricultural and mechanical arts. These became known as "Land Grant Colleges." In 1867 Congress established a U.S. Office of Education which is now a part of the Department of Health, Education, and Welfare. The Smith-Hughes Act of 1917 set up the first program of federal grants-in-aid to promote vocational education, enabling schools to provide training in agriculture, home economics, trades, and industries. In the National School Lunch and Milk Programs, begun in 1946, federal grants and commodity donations are made for non-profit lunches and milk served in public and private schools. In the Federal Impacted Areas Aid Program begun in 1950, federal aid is authorized for "federally impacted" areas of the nation. These are areas where federal activities create a substantial increase in school enrollments or a reduction in taxable resources because of a federally owned property. Federal funds can be used for construction, operation, and maintenance of schools in these public school districts. This program is an outgrowth of the defense-impacted area aid legislation in World War II.

In response to the Soviet Union's success in launching the first satellite into space, Congress became concerned that the American educational system might not be keeping abreast of advances being made in other nations, particularly in science and technology. The Russian space shot created an intensive debate over education in America, and prompted Congress to reexamine the responsibilites of the national government in public education. "Sputnik" made everyone realize that education was closely related to national defense. In the National Defense Education Act of 1958 Congress provided financial aid to states and public school districts to improve instruction in science, mathematics, and foreign languages; to strengthen guidance counseling and testing; and to improve statistical services. And also to establish a system of loans to undergraduates, fellowships to graduate students, and funds to colleges—all in an effort to improve the training of teachers in America.

The costs of higher education have grown even faster than the costs of elementary and secondary education. Not only has the number of young people of college age dramatically increased in the past decade, but so also has the *proportion* of college-age persons who enter college. In the 1970s 55 percent of all college-age persons are expected to enroll in college (see Table 7-1).

TABLE 7-1 GROWTH OF HIGHER EDUCATION ENROLLMENT

	College Age Population (millions)	Higher Education Enrollment (millions)	Percentage Enrolled
1955	8.3	2.7	32
1960	9.7	3.6	37
1965	12.3	5.5	45
1970	14.5	7.3	50
1975	16.3	9.0	55

Source: U.S. Department of Health, Education, and Welfare, Office of Education, *Projections of Educational Statistics to 1975-76* (Washington, D.C.: Government Printing Office, 1966).

Federal aid to colleges and universites comes in a variety of forms. Historically, the Morrill Act of 1862 provided the groundwork for federal assistance to higher education. In 1890 Congress activated several federal grants to support the operations of the land grant colleges, and this aid, although very modest, continues to the present. The GI Bills following World War II and the Korean War (enacted in 1944 and 1952 respectively) were not, strictly speaking, aid-to-education bills, but rather a form of assistance to veterans to help them adjust to civilian life. Nevertheless, these bills had a great impact on higher education in terms of the millions of veterans who were able to enroll in college. In 1966 Congress finally acted to make veterans education benefits a permanent program for "all those who risk their lives in our armed forces." The National Defense Education Act of 1958 also affected higher education by assisting superior students through loans and grants to continue undergraduate and graduate education, and directly assisting institutions in which they enroll. Preference was given to undergraduate students intending to teach in elementary or secondary schools, particularly in science, mathematics, and modern foreign languages, and to graduate students preparing to teach in colleges.

Federal support for scientific research has also had an important impact on higher education. In 1950 Congress established the National Science Foundation to promote scientific research and education. NSF has provided fellowships for graduate education in the sciences, supported the development of science institutes and centers at universities, funded training institutes for science teachers at all levels, supported many specific scientific research projects, and supported other miscellaneous scientific enterprises. In addition to NSF, many other federal agencies—the Department of Defense, Atomic Energy Commission, Office of Education, Public Health Service, etc.—have granted research contracts to universities for specific projects. So many and varied are the relationships between universities and government agencies that it is difficult to determine the full impact of research contracts and grants. However, the total of these contracts and grants in 1970 probably exceeded $5 billion dollars; this amount was spent by institutions of higher education over and above the $10 billion spent for general education. Thus, research has become a very big item in university life.

The federal government directly assists institutions of higher education through the Higher Education Facilities Act of 1963 and Higher Education Act of 1965. The first of these general support measures authorizes federal grants and loans for construction and improvement of both public and private higher education facilities; generally matching grants are required from the institution. The 1965 Act was much broader in scope providing for federally insured student loans and scholarships, a National Teacher Corps, funds for library materials and specialized equipment, grants to expand university extension programs, and grants to strengthen colleges which "are struggling for survival and are isolated from the main currents of academic life."

Despite these many individual federal programs in education, prior to 1965 the overall contribution of the federal government to education was very small. No general federal aid to education bill was able to win Congressional approval, for reasons which we will explore later. Federal programs were only peripheral in character and limited in impact—some aid to federally impacted areas; assistance in school lunch and milk programs, some support for vocational-technical education; some grants for science, mathematics, and foreign language projects, etc.—but no real general assistance to public and private schools in building classrooms or paying teacher salaries. Building costs and teachers' salaries are the really burdensome costs in education.

The Elementary and Secondary Education Act of 1965 marked the first real breakthrough in large scale federal-aid-to-education. ESEA doubled federal education funds in a single year and is now the largest federal-aid-to-education program. Yet, even ESEA cannot be termed a *general* aid-to-education program—one which would assist all public and private schools with costs of school construction and teachers' salaries. The main thrust of ESEA is in "poverty-impacted" schools, instructional materials, and educational research and training.

The Elementary and Secondary Education Act provided for the following:

Title   I: Financial assistance to "local educational agencies serving areas with concentrations of children from low-income families" for programs "which contribute particularly to meeting the special needs of educationally deprived children." Grants would be made on application to the Office of Education on the basis of the number of children from poverty stricken families.

Title   II: Grants to "public and private elementary and secondary schools" for the acquisition of school library resources, textbooks, and other instructional materials.

Title III: Grants for public and private schools for "supplementary educational centers and services" including remedial programs, counseling, adult education, specialized instruction and equipment, etc.

Title IV: Grants to universities, colleges, or other nonprofit organizations for research or demonstration projects in education.

Title V: Grants to stimulate and strengthen state educational agencies.

Note that the Act does include private, church-related schools in some of its benefits, so long as the federal aid money is used for non-religious purposes within such schools. However, the greatest amounts of money distributed under ESEA have been to public schools in poverty-impacted areas.

FEDERAL AID TO EDUCATION AND THE GROUP STRUGGLE

The long struggle for federal-aid-to-education is an excellent example of the power of interest groups in blocking legislation which has widespread public support, and the necessity of accommodating specific interest groups and finding workable compromises before a bill can be passed. Every year from 1945 to 1965—a period spanning two decades and the administrations of both Democratic and Republican Presidents and both Democratic and Republican Congressional majorities—federal-aid-to-education bills were introduced and debated at great length. Yet no general aid-to-education bill passed the Congress in this period. These bills were lost *despite* overwhelming public support for federal aid to education revealed in all national opinion polls during this period, and *despite* announced Presidential support for such aid. The failure of federal aid to education under these conditions can be attributed to the conflict between major *racial* and *religious* group interests in America over the character of such aid. Federal aid to education became lost in the major racial and religious controversies in the nation. Not until these issues were resolved, and bargains struck with the influential interest groups involved, was it possible to secure the passage of the Elementary and Secondary Education Act of 1965.[1]

Leading the fight for federal aid to education was the National Education Association. The NEA represents school administrators, state departments of education, university schools of education, and often the interests of the dues-paying teachers as well. Whatever differences existed within these various categories of members, the NEA was united in its support of federal aid to education. The national office of NEA, located in a modern well-equipped office building in Washington, works closely with the Office of Education, located only a few blocks away. The NEA also has affiliates in every one of the fifty states and most local school districts in the nation. While NEA was a strong advocate of federal aid, it actively opposed public funds for private church-related schools. Other groups supporting federal aid were the AFL–CIO (particularly its constituent union, the American Federation of Teachers, which frequently competes with NEA for the loyalties of classroom teachers), Americans for Democratic Action, National Congress of Parents and Teachers, and other library and professional groups.

The arguments by NEA and others in support of federal aid were:

1. Education is a national responsibility rather than a matter of mere local concern:

> Nations with the highest general level of education are those with the highest economic development. Schools more than natural resources are the basis of prosperity. . . .
>
> Where ignorance generates poverty, poverty perpetuates ignorance, and the whole nation is weaker. . . .
>
> A similar relationship appears in draft rejections. . . . The ability of American society to conduct its essential affairs—political, economic, and military—depends directly upon education.[2]

2. States and local school districts are already strained to the limits of their financial capacities. Only the national government has the tax resources—individual and corporate income taxes—to raise funds for education.

3. Only the national government can equalize educational opportunities throughout the country:

---

[1] A detailed account of the long struggle leading to the passage of the Elementary and Secondary Education Act of 1965 is found in Eugene Eidenberg and Roy D. Morey, *An Act of Congress* (New York: Norton & Co., 1969).

[2] Educational Policies Commission, National Education Association, *National Policy and the Financing of Public Schools* (Washington, D.C.: National Education Assiciation, 1962), p. 7.

The operation of the national industrial economy appears to insure that average per capita income will be unequal among the states. The poorest states, if left to their own resources have no reasonable prospect of raising the funds to provide adequate education. Some form of equalization is needed, because it is vital to the nation that the children in the poorest states also be well-educated. Therefore, federal participation in the financing of their schools is essential.[3]

Opposition to the general idea of federal aid to education was limited to conservative groups, including the U.S. Chamber of Commerce, National Association of Manufacturers, American Farm Bureau Federation, American Legion, and the Daughters of the American Revolution. Generally this opposition argued:

1. The progress of states and school districts in meeting educational needs is impressive. The "educational crisis" is overrated.
2. Federal aid would inevitably lead to federal control, the creation of a powerful national education bureaucracy, and the dangerous erosion of state and local powers and responsibilities.

But this opposition was never really very strong in itself. Responsible conservatives, for many years under the leadership of Senator Robert A. Taft of Ohio, supported the idea of federal aid. The only hope for the opposition was to divide the proponents of federal aid.

The first divisive issue was that of *race*. The question of whether or not the federal government would assist racially segregated Southern schools was raised very early in the debates on federal aid. Southern Congressmen stood to gain from any federal aid program designed to equalize educational expenditures among the states, since Southern states are among the poorest in the nation. But the prospect of federal aid money being used as a leverage to achieve integration was an anathema to this group. On the other hand, the National Association for the Advancement of Colored People (NAACP), and many liberal groups and Congressmen, opposed any federal aid to schools operated on a racially segregated basis. The 1954 decision, in *Brown* v. *Board of Education of Topeka, Kansas*, that racial segregation in public schools was unconstitutional strengthened the resolve of the liberals to deny federal aid to segregated schools. In 1956 Representative Adam Clayton Powell of Harlem introduced an amendment to the federal aid-to-education bill barring such aid for segregated schools. The NEA, the AFL–CIO, and President Dwight Eisenhower opposed the Powell Amendment, believing correctly that such an amendment would involve federal school aid in the sensitive segregation issue and thereby lead to its defeat. But the Powell Amendment was accepted in the House by a 225–192 vote, with Democrats voting against the amendment 77 to 146 and Republicans for it 148–46. Then on the question of *final passage* with the Powell Amendment included,

---

[3] *Ibid.*, p. 11.

the House defeated the bill 194–224 (Democrats 119–105, Republicans 75–119). Southern Democrats who had voted against the Powell Amendment felt obliged to vote against final passage with that amendment tacked on. It turned out that 96 Republicans who voted *for* the Powell Amendment voted *against* final passage! This was the hard core opposition to federal aid. The Powell Amendment had been supported as a tactic to divide Southern and Northern supporters of the bill. Once the Powell Amendment was part of the bill, the coalition of conservative Republicans and Southern Democrats defeated it. Similar cross pressures affected federal aid bills in other years.

The Civil Rights Act of 1964 greatly assisted the movement for federal aid to education, even though it made no direct mention of such aid. Title VI of that Act specified that:

> No person in the United States shall, on the grounds of race, color, or national origin, be excluded from participation in, be denied the benefits of, or be subjected to discrimination under any program or activity receiving federal financial assistance.

In effect, this was a "Powell Amendment" covering *every* federal aid program. The Act also specified that every federal department and agency must take action to end segregation by issuing rules, regulations, and orders (later known as "guidelines"), and withholding federal aid from any programs which have failed to comply with terms. The Act was supported by large majorities of both Democrats and Republicans in the House and the Senate. The effect of the Act was to resolve the issue raised by Representative Powell and others, and clear the track of at least one obstacle to federal aid to education.

The second divisive issue in federal aid to education was *religion*, i. e., whether or not federal aid should go to private, church-related schools. The Catholic Church operates a very large elementary and secondary school system in the United States. Catholic groups, particularly the National Catholic Welfare Conference, generally refused to support any federal aid bill which did not include aid to parochial schools. The leading Catholic spokesman in two decades of struggle over federal aid to education was Francis Cardinal Spellman of New York. Early in the struggle (1949), Mrs. Eleanor Roosevelt wrote:

> Those who believe in the right of any human being to belong to whatever church he sees fit . . . cannot be accused of prejudice when we do not want to see public education connected with religious control of the schools.

Cardinal Spellman responded that "Mrs. Roosevelt's record of anti-Catholicism stands for all to see." [4] When President John F. Kennedy excluded church schools from his 1961 aid to education bill, Spellman responded:

[4] Eidenberg and Morey, *An Act of Congress*, p. 20.

I believe that I state that these recommendations are unfair to most parents of the nation's 6,800,000 parochial and private school children. Such legislation would discriminate against a multitude of America's children because their parents choose to exercise their constitutional right to educate them in accordance with their religious beliefs.

The requirements of the national defense as well as the general welfare of our country demand that, in educational opportunities, no child be treated as a second-class citizen. Hence, it is unthinkable that any American child be denied the Federal funds allotted to other children which are necessary for his mental development because his parents choose for him a God-centered education. . . .

I cannot believe that Congress would enact a program of financial assistance and secondary education unless all children were granted equal educational privileges, regardless of the school they attend.

By denying this measure of equality to church-related school children and their parents, the task force proposals are blatantly discriminating against them, depriving them of freedom of mind and freedom of religion.[5]

Yet, many Protestant groups were equally convinced that federal aid to church-related schools would destroy the historic concept of separation of church and state. Many Protestant denominations, as well as the National Council of Churches, went on record against federal aid for parochial schools. A spokesman for the influential group of Protestants and Other Americans United for Separation of Church and State, stated:

Cardinal Spellman has not changed his mind. His aim is still to compel Protestants, Jews, and others to support a wholly controlled function of the Roman Catholic Church. The compulsion lies in the use of the taxing powers of the Federal Government to raise funds for Catholic schools. He has given us fair warning, so he should have our answer. American Protestants will never pay taxes to support Catholic schools. We will oppose enactment of laws which require such payments. If Congress is pressured into enacting such laws, we will contest them in the courts. If the courts reverse themselves and declare such laws constitutional, we will still refuse to pay these taxes, paying whatever price is necessary to preserve religious liberty in a pluralistic society.[6]

The failure of President Kennedy's aid-to-education bill in 1961 is generally attributed to the religious conflict which it engendered. In honoring a 1960 campaign pledge to Protestants, the nation's first Catholic President introduced a federal aid to education bill which *excluded* parochial schools.[7] To the school aid bill's usual enemies

[5] Quoted in Hugh D. Price, "Race, Religion and the Rules Committee," in Alan F. Westin, ed., *The Uses of Power* (New York: Harcourt Brace Jovanovich, 1962), p. 23.
[6] *Ibid.*, p. 36-37.
[7] In a speech before the Greater Houston Ministerial Association in 1960 Kennedy stated: "I believe in an America where separation of Church and State is absolute . . . where no church or church school is granted any public funds or political preference."

—conservative Republicans wary of federal bureaucracy and Southern Democrats wary of integration efforts—President Kennedy added a substantial bloc of Catholic Congressmen, many of whom had supported aid to education in the past. To reduce Southern fears, the Administration pledged *not* to withhold funds from segregated schools, and Representative Powell obliged a Presidential request not to introduce the desegregation issue in the interest of passing a bill. But on crucial votes in the all-important Rules Committee of the House, Catholic Democratic committee members, who previously supported the Administration, joined the Republicans and some still skeptical Southern Democrats to defeat the bill.

By 1965, twenty years of group struggle over federal aid to education convinced proponents of the policy that compromise between major interest groups was essential to its adoption.

ESEA AND GROUP COMPROMISE

There is no doubt that President Lyndon B. Johnson's overwhelming victory in the Presidential election of 1964 against Republican Barry Goldwater improved the chances for federal aid to education. A great many House and Senate Democrats rode into Congress in the Democratic sweep of the 1964 elections, giving the President's party an extraordinary 295 to 140 margin in the House and 68 to 32 margin in the Senate. Yet despite this popular mandate, it is unlikely that the Johnson federal aid-to-education bill would have become law had the President not taken great pains to arrange a compromise among the major interest groups involved.

Since the Civil Rights Act of 1964 was the law of the land, it was unnecessary for the President to fight the civil rights issue directly. While Southern Democrats would remain cool to voting for federal money that they knew would be used later as desegregation leverage, they were not placed in a position of voting directly on a bill to advance desegregation. Over 40 percent of Southern Democrats in the Congress would end up supporting the President's bill. In 1965 it was the *religious* issue which required the greatest skill in group negotiation and compromise.

Congress, particularly members of the House and Senate committees most directly concerned with education legislation, expected the Administration to work out the appropriate group compromise before Congress would consider a federal aid bill. In effect, Congress stood ready to legitimatize whatever compromise could be arranged among the major interests. Political scientists Eidenberg and Morey explained it as follows:

> The Congress and particularly the members of the committee who had experienced education fights before, feared they would have to resolve the church-state issue on Capitol Hill. The political consequences of tak-

ing sides on the "religious issue" was the greatest concern of most members. One Democratic member of the committee put it this way: "We were all sensitive to the start of another holy war. Politically, not many of us can afford a religious war—at least those of us from two-religion districts."

In effect, the Democrats on the committee wanted and expected the Administration to work out the necessary agreements (whatever they might be) so that the principal factions were satisfied. Their failure on so many prior occasions to find agreement predisposed the leading congressional figures to leave these delicate negotiations in the hands of the Administration. Then the committee and the House would act to ratify those agreements.[8]

The key to success, then, was working out a compromise acceptable to the NEA and other educational groups, the National Catholic Welfare Conference and other representatives of the Catholic Church, and the National Council of Churches and other Protestant groups.

The Johnson Administration plan was to emphasize "aid to children" rather than aid to schools, and particularly aid to children from low income families. It was hoped that by placing the emphasis on the child the church-state issue could be submerged. The President identified the program with his "war on poverty" rather than with earlier aid-to-education efforts. The greatest proportion of ESEA funds would be given under Title I to *public* school districts with children from low-income families. But as a concession to Catholic interests, the President's bill allowed parochial schools to receive funds along with public schools under Title II and Title III for libraries, textbooks, and instructional materials, and for supplementary educational centers and services. This money was only for peripheral items—not classroom construction or teachers' salaries—and specifically prohibited the use of federal funds for sectarian instruction or worship. Francis Keppel, Commissioner of Education in the Johnson Administration, was given the principal task of selling this compromise to the interested groups.

The NEA accepted the compromise despite its long-standing opposition to giving any public funds to church schools. Eidenberg and Morey explain the NEA decision as follows:

> Fear over possible exclusion from the policy making process helped persuade the NEA to go along in 1965 with an aid formula that would see some funds channeled into the hands of private and parochial schools. In 1965, to be on the side of a minority when education legislation got passed would have left the NEA without influence during the critical period after passage when the administrative regulations were being drawn up. . . . If for no other reason, the NEA could not afford to be with the losers the year federal aid finally got enacted. Since the NEA's principal reason for being was the passage of federal aid to

[8] Eidenberg and Morey, *An Act of Congress*, p. 77.

education legislation, the rival teacher organization's (the AFL-CIO-affiliated American Federation of Teachers) charges that the NEA had not been successful up to 1965 touched a sensitive chord.[9]

The National Council of Churches was not really enthusiastic about the Johnson Bill; they very much preferred President Kennedy's 1961 bill which would have completely excluded Catholic schools from federal aid programs. Yet responsible spokesmen for Protestant churches in America did not want to be charged with having hurt public education in America or blocked assistance for impoverished school children. Arthur Flemming, former Secretary of HEW during the Eisenhower Administration and later President of the University of Oregon, testified before the House Education Committee as Vice President of the National Council of Churches:

> The church and state issue . . . has been one of the principal roadblocks standing in the way of constructive federal legislation in the areas of elementary and secondary education. It has likewise been a divisive factor in the life of our nation.
> I hope that all concerned, both inside and outside of Congress, will analyze HR 2362 with the end in view of doing everything possible to make it an instrument of reconciliation. I believe that it can be. I believe that President Johnson and his associates should be commended for providing us with this opportunity of approaching an old unsolved problem with a new spirit.[10]

If this posture was not one of enthusiasm for the bill, at least it was not opposition.

Catholic education interests were defended on Capitol Hill by Speaker of the House John McCormick of Boston. Strong Catholic opposition to the bill might have meant failure. Catholic groups were also unenthusiastic about the bill. There was no guarantee that Catholic education would receive proportionately equal funding with public education under the legislation. Public school interests would be administering the grant money. It was not clear whether the bill was a victory for Catholics or whether it merely held out token support to Catholic education. But in the end the Catholic interests withheld their objections. In response to a direct question by a House Committee member as to whether or not the United States Catholic Conference (successor to the National Catholic Welfare Conference) endorsed the bill, director Monsignor Frederick G. Hochwalt said:

> It is a strong word (endorse), but it comes close to it. We look with favor upon those kinds of provisions and hope they can be worked out successfully. To say we endorse the whole thing line by line is a little too broad for us.[11]

[9] *Ibid.,* p. 63.
[10] Quoted in Eidenberg and Morey, *An Act of Congress,* p. 65-66.
[11] Quoted in Eidenberg and Morey, *An Act of Congress, p.* 68.

Liberal groups were aware of the fact that ESEA was *not* a general aid to education bill. But they too were willing to accept the bill as a compromise. Andrew Biemiller, chief lobbyist for the AFL–CIO, testified:

> I repeat . . . let's get started . . . and get a bill through here, and begin to get some money into our school systems where we now know it is badly needed, and then we can take another good look and get closer to the goal that both you and I want; and we make no bones about it; that we want a general education bill.[12]

Once support of the major interests was obtained, Congressional approval of ESEA was practically assured. Congressmen deliberately avoided any amendments which would upset the church-state compromise. The bill was introduced on January 12, 1965, and signed into law by the President on April 11, with very little change in the original wording. Most of the floor debate in the House and the Senate centered about minor variations in the aid formula. The ease and rapidity with which the bill passed Congress was a striking contrast to the bloody battles of earlier years. This turnabout in Congressional behavior would have mystified anyone who was not aware of the interest group compromise.

READING, WRITING, AND RELIGION IN THE COURTS

The First Amendment to the Constitution of the United States contains two important guarantees of religious freedom: (1) "Congress shall make no law respecting an establishment of religion . . . ," and (2) "or prohibiting the free exercise thereof." The Due Process Clause of the Fourteenth Amendment made these guarantees of religious liberty applicable to the states and their subdivisions as well as to Congress. Most of the debate over religion in the public schools centers around the "no establishment" clause of the First Amendment rather than the "free exercise" clause. However, it was respect for the "free exercise" clause that caused the Supreme Court in 1925 to declare unconstitutional an attempt on the part of a state to prohibit private and parochial schools and to force all children to attend public schools. In the words of the Supreme Court: "The fundamental theory of liberty upon which all governments in this Union repose excludes any general power of the state to standardize its children by forcing them to accept instruction from public teachers only. The child is not the mere creature of the state."[13] It is this decision that protects the entire structure of parochial schools in this nation.

---

[12] Quoted in Eidenberg and Morey, *An Act of Congress*, pp. 105-6.
[13] *Pierce* v. *The Society of Sisters*, 268 U.S. 510 (1925).

A great deal of religious conflict in America has centered around the meaning of the "no establishment" clause, and the public schools have been the principal scene of this conflict. One interpretation of the clause holds that it does not prevent government from aiding religious schools or encouraging religious beliefs in the public schools, so long as it does not discriminate against any particular religion. Another interpretation of the "no establishment" clause is that it creates a "wall of separation" between church and state in America to prevent government from directly aiding religious schools or encouraging religious beliefs in any way.

Those favoring government aid to parochial schools frequently refer to the language found in several cases decided by the Supreme Court, which appears to support the idea that government can *in a limited fashion* support the activities of church-related schools. In the case of *Pierce* v. *The Society of Sisters* (1925), the Court stated that the right to send one's children to parochial schools was a fundamental liberty guaranteed to all. In *Cochran* v. *the Board of Education* (1930), the Court upheld a state law providing free textbooks for children attending both public and parochial schools on the grounds that this aid benefited the *children* rather than the Catholic Church and hence did not constitute an "establishment" of religion within the meaning of the First Amendment.[14]

In *Everson* v. *Board of Education* (1947), the Supreme Court upheld bus transportation for parochial school children at public expense on the grounds that the "wall of separation between church and state" does not prohibit the state from adopting a general program which helps *all* children.[15] Interestingly, in this case even though the Supreme Court permitted the expenditure of public funds to assist children going to and from parochial schools, the Supreme Court voiced the opinion that the no establishment clause of the First Amendment should constitute a wall of separation between church and state. In the words of the Court:

> Neither a state nor the federal government can set up a church. Neither can pass laws which aid one religion, aid all religions, or prefer one religion over another. Neither can force nor influence a person to go to or to remain away from church against his will, or force him to profess a belief or disbelief in any religion. No person can be punished for entertaining or professing religious beliefs or disbeliefs, for church attendance or nonattendance. No tax in any amount, large or small, can be levied to support any religious activities or institutions, whatever they may be called, or whatever form they may adopt to teach or practice religion. Neither a state nor the federal government can, openly or secretly, participate in the affairs of any religious organizations or groups, and vice versa.[16]

[14] *Cochran* v. *Board of Education*, 281 U.S. 370 (1930).
[15] *Everson* v. *Board of Education*, 330 U.S. 1 (1947).
[16] *Ibid.*

So the Everson Case can be cited by those interests which support the allocation of public funds for assistance to children in parochial schools, as well as those interests which oppose any public support, direct or indirect, of religion.

The question of how much federal aid can go to church schools and for what purposes is still unresolved. Recently, in response to fiscal crises, Catholic church leaders have pressed hard for more aid from the federal government and the states. Many of these states have passed bills giving financial support to nonpublic schools for such purposes as textbooks, bus transportation, and remedial courses. Proponents of public aid for parochial schools argue that these schools render a valuable public service by instructing millions of children who would have to be instructed by the state, at great expense, if the parochial schools closed. There seemed to be many precedents for public support of religious institutions: church property has always been exempt from taxation; church contributions are deductible from federal income taxes; federal funds have been appropriated for the construction of religiously operated hospitals; chaplains are provided in the armed forces as well as in the Congress of the United States; veterans' programs permit veterans to use their educational subsidies to finance college educations in Catholic universities; federal grants and loans for college construction are available to Catholic as well as to public colleges, and so on. Of course, opponents of state aid to parochial schools challenge the idea that Catholic parents are being discriminated against when parochial schools are denied tax funds. They argue that free public schools are available to the parents of all children regardless of religious denomination. If Catholic parents are not content with the type of school that the state provides, they should expect to pay for the establishment and operation of special schools. The state is under no obligation to finance the religious preferences in education of Catholics or other religious groups. In fact, they contend that it is unfair to compel taxpayers to support religion directly or indirectly, and furthermore, the diversion of any substantial amount of public education funds to parochial schools would weaken the public school system. The public schools bring together children of different religious backgrounds and by so doing supposedly encourage tolerance and understanding. In contrast, church-related schools segregate children of different backgrounds, and it is not in the public interest to encourage such segregation. And so the dispute continues.

One of the most important Supreme Court decisions in the history of church-state relations in America came in 1971 in the case of *Lemon v. Kurtzman.*[17] The Supreme Court held that it was unconstitutional for a state to pay the costs of teachers' salaries or instructional materials in parochial schools. The Court acknowledged that it had previously approved the provision of state textbooks and bus trans-

[17] *Lemon* v. *Kurtzman*, 403 U.S. 602 (1971).

portation directly to parochial school children. But the Court held that state payments to parochial schools involved "excessive entanglement between government and religion" and violate both the Establishment and Free Exercise clauses of the First Amendment. State payments to religious schools, the Court said, would require excessive government controls and surveillance to insure that funds were used only for secular instruction. Moreover, the Court expressed the fear that state aid to parochial schools would create "political divisions along religious lines . . . one of the principal evils against which the First Amendment was intended to protect."

Religious conflict in public schools also centers around the question of prayer and Bible reading ceremonies conducted by public schools. A few years ago the practice of opening the school day with prayer and Bible reading ceremonies was widespread in American public schools. Usually the prayer was a Protestant rendition of the Lord's Prayer and Bible reading was from the King James version. In order to avoid the denominational aspects of these ceremonies, the New York State Board of Regents substituted a nondenominational prayer, which it required to be said aloud in each class in the presence of a teacher at the beginning of each school day.

> Almighty God, we acknowledge our dependence upon Thee, and we beg Thy blessings upon us, our parents, our teachers, and our country.

New York argued that this prayer ceremony did not violate the "no establishment" clause, because the prayer was denominationally neutral and because student participation in the prayer was voluntary. However, in *Engle* v. *Vitale* (1962), the Supreme Court stated that "The constitutional prohibition against laws respecting an establishment of a religion must at least mean in this country it is no part of the business of government to compose official prayers for any group of the American people to recite as part of a religious program carried on by government." [18] The Court pointed out that making prayer voluntary did not free it from the prohibitions of the no establishment clause; that clause prevented the establishment of a religious ceremony by a government agency, regardless of whether the ceremony was voluntary or not:

> Neither the fact that the prayer may be denominationally neutral, nor the fact that its observance on the part of the students is voluntary can serve to free it from the limitations of the establishment clause, as it might from the free exercise clause, of the First Amendment, both of which are operative against the states by virtue of the Fourteenth Amendment. . . . The establishment clause, unlike the free exercise clause, does not depend on any showing of direct governmental compulsion and is violated by the enactment of laws which establish an official religion

[18] *Engle* v. *Vitale*, 370 U.S. 421 (1962).

whether those laws operate directly to coerce nonobserving individuals or not.[19]

One year later in the case of *Abbington Township* v. *Schempp*, the Court considered the constitutionality of Bible reading ceremonies in the public schools.[20] Here again, even though the children were not required to participate, the Court found that Bible reading as an opening exercise in the schools was a religious ceremony. The Court went to some trouble in its opinion to point out that they were not "throwing the Bible out of the schools," for they specifically stated that the study of the Bible or of religion, when presented objectively as part of a secular program of education, did not violate the First Amendment, but religious *ceremonies* involving Bible reading or prayer, established by a state or school district, did so.

THE FORMAL STRUCTURE OF EDUCATIONAL DECISION MAKING

The formal responsibility for public education in America rests with the fifty state governments. State laws create local school boards and provide a means for choosing their members, usually, but not always, by popular election. State laws authorize boards to lay and collect taxes, to borrow money, to engage in school construction, to hire instructional personnel, and to make certain determinations about local school policy. Yet, in every state, the authority of local school districts is severely circumscribed by state legislation. State law determines the types and rates of taxes to be levied, the maximum debt which can be incurred, the number of years of compulsory school attendance, the minimum salaries to be paid to teachers, the types of schools to be operated by the local boards, the number of grades to be taught, the qualifications of teachers, and the general content of curricula. In addition, many states choose the textbooks, establish course outlines, fix styles of penmanship, recommend teaching methods, establish statewide examinations, fix minimum teacher-pupil ratios, and stipulate course content in great detail. Some states outlaw the mention of communism or the teaching of evolution in the classroom. In short, the responsibility for public education is firmly in the hands of our state governments.

State responsibility for public education is no mere paper arrangement. At one time there was no effective way that state governments could insure that local school districts conformed to state policies; there were no enforcement agencies or devices to guarantee enforcement of state regulations. But in recent years two devices have been utilized effectively by the states to help ensure that local districts

---

[19] *Ibid.*
[20] *Abbington Township* v. *Schempp*, 374 U.S. 203 (1963).

do not deviate from state standards. The first device is the statewide administrative agency sometimes called the state board of education, state department of education, or the superintendent of public instruction. The central task of these state administrative agencies is to oversee local school districts and ensure implementation of state policies. While there are some variations among the states in the power vested in these agencies, one trend is common to all of the states: State educational agencies are centralizing state control over education.

A second device for ensuring the implementation of state educational policies is state grants of money to local school districts. Every state provides grants in one form or another to local school districts to supplement locally derived school revenue. This places the superior taxing powers of the state in the service of public schools operated at the local level. In every state, an equalization formula in the distribution of state grants to local districts operates to help equalize educational opportunities in all parts of the state. Equalization formulas differ from state to state as do the amounts of state grants involved, but in every state, poorer school districts receive larger shares of state funds than wealthier districts. This enables the state to guarantee a minimum "foundation" program in education throughout the state. In addition, since state grants to local school districts are administered through state departments of education, state school officials are given an effective tool for implementing state policies, namely, withholding or threatening to withhold state funds from school districts that do not conform to state standards. The growth of state responsibility for school policy was accomplished largely by the use of money-state grants to local schools.

Increasing state participation in school finance, then, is an indication of increasing centralization of education in the states (see Table 7-2).

TABLE 7-2 FEDERAL, STATE, AND LOCAL CONTRIBUTIONS TO PUBLIC ELEMENTARY AND SECONDARY EDUCATION

	Percent of School Revenue Received from:		
	Federal Sources	*State Sources*	*Local Sources*
1970	7.3	40.7	52.0
1967	7.9	39.1	53.0
1963	4.4	39.3	56.4
1960	4.4	39.1	56.5
1957	4.0	39.4	56.6

Source: U.S. Bureau of the Census, *Statistical Abstract of the United States, 1970* (Washington, D.C.: Government Printing Office, 1971), p. 121.

One of the most dramatic reorganization and centralization movements in American government in this century has been the successful drive to reduce, through consolidation, the number of local school districts in the United States. Over the last thirty-year period, three out of every four school districts were eliminated through consolidation. Support for school district consolidation has come from state school officials in every state.

There is a slight tendency toward increased centralization in the poorer states and the states with lower adult education levels. It is in these states that the state governments have played a greater role in the financing of public schools and the school consolidation movement has made the greatest progress. State participation in school finance decreases among the more wealthy states and the states with educated adult populations. Apparently, the lack of economic resources is a stimulus toward state participation in school finance and school district consolidation. Affluence, on the other hand, enables smaller local school districts to function more effectively, reduces the need for state aid, and delays the movement toward school consolidation.

There are marked disparities between state educational programs. The decentralization of educational policy making in fifty separate state systems has meant a greater deal of variation in the character of public education from state to state. States differ in educational expenditures per pupil, average teacher salaries, teacher-pupil ratios, dropout rates, and many other educational measures. For example, New York spends two-and-one-half times more than Mississippi on the education of an average pupil. California teachers receive twice the salary of teachers in South Dakota. Teacher-pupil ratios in the states range from fifteen to near thirty. The dropout rate in Minnesota is less than 8 percent, while in Georgia it is over 30 percent. Most of the differences in state educational systems are related to economic resources in the states (see Chapter 11).

THE INFORMAL STRUCTURE OF
EDUCATIONAL GROUPS

The formal structure of local school districts often obscures the realities of educational politics in communities. School politics will differ from one community to another, but it is possible to identify a number of political groups who appear on the scene in school politics in almost every community.[21] There is, first of all, that small band of voters who turn out for school elections. It is estimated that, on the average, only about one-third of the eligible voters bother to cast ballots in school elections. Voter turnout at school bond and tax elections shows no ground swell of public interest in school affairs. Perhaps even more interesting is the finding that the larger the voter

[21] See Thomas H. Eliot, "Toward an Understanding of Public School Politics," *American Political Science Review*, Vol. 53 (December 1959), 1032-45.

turnout in a school bond referendum, the more likely the defeat of proeducational proposals.[22] In general, the best way to defeat a school bond referendum is to have a large turnout. Proponents of educational expenditures are better advised not to work for a large turnout, but for a better informed and more educationally oriented electorate.

School board members constitute another important group of actors in school politics. School board members are generally better educated than their constituents. They are selected largely from among business owners, proprietors, and managers. There is some evidence that people who are interested in education and have some knowledge of what the schools are doing tend to support education more than do the less informed citizens. However, the occupational background of school board members suggests that they are sensitive to tax burdens placed upon businessmen and property owners.

Professional educators are much less restrained in their enthusiasm for the public schools. Many professional educators are distrustful of the laymen who compose the school boards; they often feel that educational policy should be in the hands of professional educators. They may feel that important decisions about curriculum, facilities, personnel, and finances should be the special province of persons trained in education. They view the school board's role as one of defending the schools against public criticism and persuading the community to open its pocketbook. Professional educators often support the idea that "politics" should be kept out of education; to them, this means that laymen should not interfere with decisions that professional educators wish to make for themselves. School boards and voters (those who supply the money for public schools and therefore feel that it is their legitimate right to control them) believe that citizen control of education is a vital safeguard of democracy. But professional educators sometimes feel that school board members are uninformed about school problems and unwilling or unable to support the needs of education. As a case in point, school board members throughout the nation were much less likely to support federal aid to education than were professional educators. Many school board members felt that the federal government would strip them of their local power over the schools, while professional educators were less fearful of dictation from Washington.

The professional educators can be divided into at least three distinct groups. Numerically the largest group, yet politically the least significant, is the school teachers. The most powerful group is the professional school administrators, particularly the superintendents of schools. A third group consists of the faculties of teachers colleges and departments of education at universities. This latter group often

---

[22] See James Q. Wilson and Edward C. Banfield, "Public-Regardingness as a Value Premise in Voting Behavior," *American Political Science Review*, Vol. 58 (December 1964), 876-87.

has contacts with state departments of education, diffuses educational innovations and ideologies to generations of teachers, and influences requirements for teacher certification within the states.

State and local chapters of the National Education Association (NEA) represent both teachers and administrators, but often they are dominated by professional administrators. The participation of administrators in the National Education Association is one of the major criticisms of that organization made by the American Federation of Teachers (AFT).

The AFT has emerged as an important voice of teachers in the nation's largest cities. This labor union, representing classroom teachers, employs all the recognized techniques of labor organizations to achieve its goals. The AFT advocates collective bargaining for teachers and, whenever necessary, the strike. In the past, the much larger NEA viewed these techniques as unprofessional, and it criticized the AFT for its connection with other unions through the AFL–CIO. However, the growing membership of the AFT in large cities has brought about a greater degree of militancy by the NEA and its local and state chapters. The NEA has formed a Department of Classroom Teachers in order to blunt the charge that it is administrator dominated. While the NEA officially avoids going on "strike," it has invoked "professional sanctions" against states and school districts. Occasionally, "professional sanctions" have included a collective refraining from signing of teachers' contracts and a refusal to work.

EDUCATION IN THE GHETTO

The plight of the ghetto schools has become popular knowledge through the writings of Bel Kaufman (*Up the Down Staircase*) and Jonathan Kozol (*Death at an Early Age: The Destruction of the Hearts and Minds of Negro Children in the Boston Public Schools*). Disadvantaged black pupils are behind whites in standard achievement tests in the primary grades, and they fall further behind as they move through school. By the twelfth grade, the average black pupil is more than two years behind the average white on standardized tests of achievement, the black dropout rate in more than double the white rate, and black pupil self-esteem is lower. The validity of achievement and intelligence tests can be disputed, but there is little doubt that many ghetto blacks are educationally ill prepared for college, post–high school training, or the job market. The question of "equality of educational opportunity" is a serious one for urban schools and indeed for the entire nation (see Figure 7-2).

Government efforts at coping with ghetto educational deficiencies can be classified into three broad policy directions: (1) Ending de

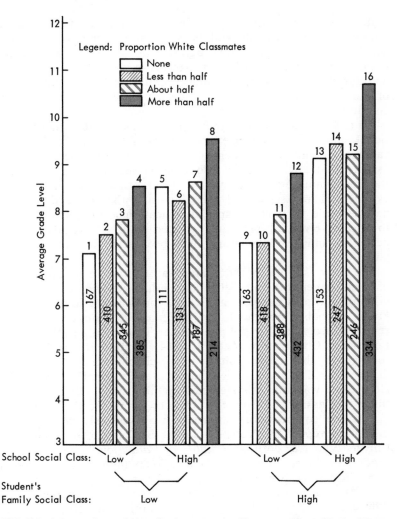

FIG. 7-2   Average Grade Level Performance of Twelfth Grade Negro Students by Individual Social Class Origin, Social Class Level of School and Proportion White Classmates, Metropolitan Northeast

Notes: The numbers used in the bars represent the number of cases. Data from the Coleman report is used by the U.S. Commission on Civil Rights to support the view that black pupils perform better academically in integrated schools. Note that performance of black children improves with the proportion of white classmates regardless of whether the black child's family social class is low or high, or whether the social class composition of the school is low or high. Note also that black children from higher family social class perform better academically than black children from lower family social class. Note also that black children from lower family social class perform better in schools with classmates of higher social class.

Source: U.S. Commission on Civil Rights, *Racial Isolation in the Public Schools,* Vol. 1 (Washington, D.C.: Government Printing Office, 1967), p. 90.

facto school segregation by racial balancing in the assignment of pupils to public schools and bussing pupils wherever necessary to achieve racial balance (this policy was discussed in Chapter 3); (2) Compensatory educational programs in ghetto schools to overcome learning difficulties of disadvantaged children; (3) Community control of ghetto schools in an effort to redesign public education to fit ghetto conditions.

To date the emphasis in public policy relative to equality of educational opportunity has been on compensatory programs for disadvantaged children. Compensatory educational programs generally assume that environmental problems create learning difficulties for the disadvantaged pupil—verbal retardation, lack of motivation, experiential and sensory deprivation—and that these difficulties can be overcome in part by special educational programs. In addition to special remedial programs grafted onto the regular school experience, compensatory efforts have been attempted at the preschool level.

The major thrust of the compensatory movement came in Title I of the Elementary and Secondary Education Act of 1965 with its billion-dollar-plus per year assistance for "poverty impacted" schools. Public schools throughout the nation were stimulated to upgrade remedial programs for the poor under Title I. In addition, under the Economic Opportunity Act of 1964, community action agencies throughout the nation initiated preschool remedial programs for disadvantaged children under the popular Project Head Start. Project Head Start was later transferred to public school administration with funds and assistance from the Office of Economic Opportunity.

But the compensatory approach was seriously challenged in an influential report by Professor James S. Coleman of Johns Hopkins University in 1967 entitled *Equality of Educational Opportunity*.[23] This report concluded that formal educational inputs, such as per pupil expenditure, teacher preparation, teacher-pupil ratios, libraries, laboratories, special programs and materials, etc., make relatively *little* difference in pupil achievement and motivation. However, children from disadvantaged backgrounds (regardless of race) benefit from integration with advantaged children (regardless of race). Moreover, advantaged children are not harmed by such integration, particularly if the disadvantaged are not a majority in the classroom. The startling implication of the Coleman Report was that schools make relatively little difference except as a place where kids learn from each other, and money spent improving ghetto schools is unlikely to produce any meaningful results. Later the U.S. Civil Rights Commission in its report *Racial Isolation in the Public Schools* used the Coleman data as ammunition to support its contention that integration, and not

[23] James S. Coleman, *Equality of Educational Opportunity* (Washington, D.C.: Government Printing Office, 1966).

Ghetto School. Photo by Dennis Brack, Black Star

compensatory education, was the key to the problem of equal educational opportunity.[24]

Earlier we discussed the feasibility—politically and otherwise—of ending de facto segregation. Neither Congress, nor the federal courts, nor urban school districts are enthusiastic about racial balancing or bussing to overcome de facto segregation. The prospects for widespread urban school integration are very dim. This situation, together with the findings of the Coleman Report that compensatory education has little value,[25] has stimulated the search for some other approach to equality of educational opportunity.

Decentralization of big city schools systems and "community control" of local schools as an approach to equality in urban education

[24] U.S. Commission on Civil Rights, *Racial Isolation in the Public Schools*, 2 vols. (Washington, D.C.: Government Printing Office, 1967).

[25] As one might expect, Coleman's explosive findings have been challenged. See Samuel Bowles and Henry M. Levin, "The Determinants of Scholastic Achievement—An Appraisal of Some Recent Evidence," *Journal of Human Resources*, Vol. 3 (Winter 1968), 3-24; Peter Schrag, "Why Our Schools Have Failed," *Commentary*, Vol. 45 (March 1968), 31-38.

has produced a great deal of controversy recently.[26] Proponents of "community control" have suggested that ghetto residents should be given control over ghetto schools in order to (1) shift from professional and administrative "dominance" of the schools to "a meaningful parental and community role in the education process," (2) deemphasize the acquisition of achievement skills (reading, writing, and arithmetic) in favor of "a humanistically oriented curriculum modifying the skill-performance standard by which educational quality is primarily measured," and (3) bring personnel into the schools who have "broader talents than the conventionally prepared career educator."

Support for the community control concept is found among black power advocates and black racial separatists, as well as educational reformers. Black militants have attacked desegregation because it implies that Negro pupils can learn well only by sitting next to white pupils. They want educational programs which emphasize black identity and self-awareness, and they reject programs designed to make black pupils "like" white pupils. More importantly, they want black political control of educational resources in the ghetto. Professor Marilyn Gittel explains:

> Community control implies a redistribution of power within the educational subsystem. It is directed toward achieving a modern mechanism for participatory democracy. It attempts to answer the political failure in education systems, and, as regards the educational failure, community control is intended to create an environment in which more meaningful educational policies can be developed and a wide variety of alternative solutions and techniques can be tested. It seems plausible to assume that a school system devoted to community needs and serving as an agent of community interests will provide an environment more conducive to learning.[27]

New York's unhappy experience with "community control" illustrates some of the problems involved in this concept.[28] In 1967 the Ford Foundation sponsored demonstration projects in community control in New York City, including a project in a ghetto area known as Ocean Hill–Brownsville. At the same time Mayor John V. Lindsay created an Advisory Panel on Decentralization of New York City Schools, headed by Ford Foundation President McGeorge Bundy. This Advisory Panel recommended a citywide program of school decentralization (the Bundy Plan).[29] An Ocean Hill–Brownsville Local

[26] See Marilyn Gittell and Alan G. Hevesi, eds., *The Politics of Urban Education* (New York: Praeger, 1969).
[27] *Ibid.*, pp. 365-66.
[28] *Ibid.*, pp. 305-77.
[29] Mayor's Advisory Panel on Decentralization of the New York City Schools, *Reconnection for Learning: A Community Control System for New York City* (New York: Office of the Mayor, 1967); reprinted in Gittell and Hevesi, *Politics of Urban Education.*

Governing Board was established and proceeded to act with considerable autonomy from the New York City Board of Education. When school opened in September 1967, the Board appointed five principals who were not on the Civil Service list and thereby incurred the opposition of the Council of Supervisory Associations representing school administrators. During a citywide school strike over pay increases and smaller classes, Ocean Hill–Brownsville schools stayed open, thereby incurring the opposition of the United Federation of Teachers representing the city's teachers. Throughout the 1967–68 school year there was a growing hostility and an exaltation of rhetoric between white teachers and administrators on the one hand and the Ocean Hill–Brownsville Governing Board on the other. The Board charged that certain white teachers were uncooperative and failed to understand ghetto problems. The teachers charged the Board with black racism and even anti-Semitism (many New York teachers and administrators are Jewish). In May 1968 the Board dismissed nineteen white teachers without notice or hearing, seven weeks before the end of the term, apparently because they were "out of tune with the political atmosphere in the community." The United Federation of Teachers called a citywide strike protesting the dismissals as violations of civil service regulations and due process of law. The strike seriously curtailed education in New York City during the 1968–69 school year. The issues of the strike were eventually mediated, but not without a tragic increase in distrust and suspicion between the races in the school system and the city at large.

Opponents of "community control"—particularly white teachers, teacher unions, and administrators—argue that decentralization creates administrative duplication, inefficiencies, and increased overhead costs. They contend that it results in wasted educational dollars, the destruction of the merit system, and the introduction of political and racial considerations in educational policies. Finally they contend that it promotes racial separatism and black militancy.

SUMMARY

Let us summarize educational policy with particular reference to the group interests involved:

1. Historically, educational policy has been decentralized in America, with states and communities carrying the major responsibility for public elementary and secondary and higher education. However, federal aid-to-education is nearly as old as the nation itself. Prior to 1865, federal aid was distributed for specific programs and services—vocational education; school lunch and milk; federally impacted schools; science, mathematics, and foreign language; higher education facilities—rather than general support of education.

2. The Elementary and Secondary Education Act of 1965 was the first large scale federal aid-to-education program. The long struggle over federal aid-to-education indicates the power of interest groups in blocking legislation which has widespread public support, and the necessity of accommodating specific interest groups in policy formation.

3. The difficulty in securing passage of a significant federal aid-to-education bill can be attributed to conflict between major racial and religious group interests over the character of such aid, rather than to opposition to the idea of federal aid.

4. For many years the question of whether federal aid should be withheld from racially segregated schools divided proponents of federal aid-to-education. Only after the passage of the Civil Rights Act of 1965, barring the use of federal funds in *any* segregated program or activity, was this divisive issue removed as a direct obstacle to federal aid-to-education.

5. Another divisive issue over federal aid-to-education was that of whether or not such aid should be withheld from private, church-related schools. Catholic interests would not support a bill which excluded such schools from assistance, and Protestant interests, as well as the National Education Association, opposed the idea of federal aid to church schools.

6. Congress stood ready to enact whatever compromise the various religious and educational groups could agree upon. Experience clearly indicated that no policy of federal aid-to-education was possible without prior group compromise. The final compromise—enacted as the Elementary and Secondary Education Act of 1965—focused on "aid to children" in poverty-impacted areas, and allowed church-related schools to receive federal funds for specific nonreligious educational services and facilities.

7. While educational decision making is still largely decentralized in America, state education departments are gradually centralizing policy making by means of state grants to local school boards, and gradually reducing by means of consolidation the number of local school boards.

8. Important groups in local school politics include taxpayers who vote in school board elections; school board members who are frequently owners of small businesses in the community; professional school administrators at the local level and from the state departments of education and faculties of teacher colleges; and school teachers. The American Federation of Teachers is a labor union representing many classroom teachers in large cities. The National Education Association, an older and

larger "professional group," represents school administrators and teachers; it has become more militant in recent years in protecting teacher interests.

9. Educational and community groups are divided over how to improve education in the nation's black ghettos. Integrationists advise against exclusive reliance on compensatory education programs in the ghettos, because these programs do not attack the problem of de facto segregation. However, bussing black students out of the ghetto to achieve racial balance in urban schools involves myriad problems—political, legal, administrative, and physical.

10. Decentralization of urban education and "community control" of ghetto schools has been supported by some reform groups as well as black militants. New York's experiment in community control has floundered in group conflict between white teachers and their union, black community activists, and educational administrators.

BIBLIOGRAPHY

COLEMAN, JAMES S., *Equality of Educational Opportunity*. Washington, D.C.: Government Printing Office, 1966.

EIDENBERG, EUGENE AND ROY D. MOREY, *An Act of Congress*. New York: Norton, 1969.

GITTELL, MARILYN AND ALAN G. HEVESI, eds. *The Politics of Urban Education*. New York: Praeger, 1969.

KIMBROUGH, RALPH B., *Political Power and Educational Decision-Making*. Chicago: Rand McNally, 1964.

ZEIGLER, HARMON, *The Political Life of American Teachers*. Englewood Cliffs, N.J.: Prentice-Hall, 1967.

URBAN AFFAIRS:
institutional forces and public policy

CHAPTER 8

DILEMMAS OF URBAN POLICY

In a special Presidential message to Congress proposing the Model Cities Program in 1966, the President summarized the nation's urban problems as follows:

- Some four million urban families living in homes of such disrepair as to violate decent housing standards.
- The need to provide over 30 percent more housing annually than we are currently building.
- Our chronic inability to provide sufficient low and moderate income housing, of adequate quality, at reasonable price.
- The special problem of the poor and the Negro, unable to move freely from their ghettoes, exploited in the quest for the necessities of life.
- Increasing pressures on municipal budgets, with large city per capita expenditures.
- The high human costs: crime, delinquency, welfare loads, disease, and health hazards. This is man's fate in those broken neighborhoods where he can "feel the enclosure of the flanking walls and see through the window the blackened reflection of the tenement across the street that blocks out the world beyond."
- The tragic waste, and indeed, the chaos, that threatens where children are born into the stifling air of overcrowded rooms, and destined for

a poor diet, inadequate schools, streets of fear and sordid temptation, joblessness, and the gray anxiety of the ill prepared.
• And the flight to the suburbs of more fortunate men and women who might have provided the leadership and the means for reversing this human decline.[1]

The urban "crisis" is really a series of interrelated problems which affect the nation as a whole. Poverty, poor housing, racial conflict, crime and delinquency, social dependency, ill health, overcrowding, joblessness, ignorance, white flight to the suburbs, and fiscal imbalance are national problems. Yet their impact is increasingly concentrated in the nation's large cities.

These problems are not a product of government organization or administration. However, we will observe in this chapter how institutional arrangements affect the ability of governments to deal effectively with urban problems. First, we will examine federal urban policy, with particular reference to the institutional arrangements which have affected federal programs in the nation's cities. Then we will examine the characteristics of city governments and the forces shaping the policies of cities.

The critical deficiency in federal urban policy is that there are no concrete goals or clear priorities in the hundreds of separate programs affecting cities. Unfortunately, neither the Model Cities Program, nor any other past or present federal program, has set any clear goals or priorities in dealing with the nation's urban ills. James Q. Wilson write about urban policy: *"We do not know what we are trying to accomplish* . . . Do we seek to raise standards of living, maximize housing choices, revitalize the commercial centers of our cities, and suburban sprawl, eliminate discrimination, reduce traffic congestion, improve the quality of urban design, check crime and delinquency, strengthen the effectiveness of local planning, increase citizen participation in local government? All these objectives sound attractive—in part, because they are rather vague—but unfortunately they are in many cases incompatible."[2]

The institutional arrangements of American government have proven remarkably well suited for pursuing different policies toward contradictory goals simultaneuosly. Government can maintain the support of competing groups in society by allowing different federal agencies to pursue incompatible goals and by permitting local communities to follow competing policies with federal money.

For example, the two federal program areas which account for the greatest expenditure of dollars for the physical improvement of cities are (1) the federal highway and transportation programs, (2) the

---

[1] Message from the President to the Congress, transmitting recommendations for City Demonstration Programs, January 26, 1966. 89th Congress, 2nd session. Reprinted in full in Thomas R. Dye and Brett W. Hawkins, eds., *Politics in the Metropolis*, 2nd ed. (Columbus: Charles E. Merrill, 1970).

[2] James Q. Wilson, "The War on Cities," *The Public Interest* (1966).

federal housing and urban renewal programs. The first is operated by the Department of Transportation (DOT) and the second by the Department of Housing and Urban Development (HUD). The urban portion of the interstate highway system is costing billions of federal dollars; the effect of these dollars is to enable people to drive in and out of the central city speedily, safely, and conveniently, and to open up suburban areas to business and residential expansion. Of course, these expressways also encourage middle-class (mostly white) families to move out of the central city and to enable commercial establishment to follow them. This leads to further racial segregation within the metropolitan region in housing and schools, and reduces the number of service jobs available to the poor living in the city. The encouragement of longer automobile trips from suburban residencies to downtown offices adds to pollution and congestion. While federal investment in mass transit facilities (subways, railways, busses) might reduce pollution and congestion, such investment would still encourage suburbanization, "white flight," and de factor segregation.

At the same time, the Federal Housing Administration (in HUD) and the Veterans' Administration are encouraging home ownership by insuring mortgages that are written on easy terms for millions of middleclass (mostly white) Americans. Most of these mortgages are for new homes because it is cheaper to build in vacant land and because so many prospective home owners want to move to the suburbs. So it turns out that these programs actually facilitate the movement of middle-class people out of the central city.

And meantime, the Urban Renewal Administration (in HUD) is helping cities tear down slum dwellings, often displacing the poor who live there at considerable hardship, in order to make way for office buildings, hotels, civic centers, industrial parks, and middle-class luxury apartments. In part, this effort is intended to lure suburbanites back to the central city. While urban renewal reduces the overall supply of housing to the poor in cities, the Housing Assistance Administration (in HUD) is assisting cities in building low-rent public housing units to add to the supply of housing for the poor.

Not only do different federal programs operate at cross-purposes, but the American system of federalism and the concern for local autonomy insures that different cities will use these programs in different ways. Wilson observes:

> Furthermore, the goals for most programs—especially urban renewal—were determined at the local level. This meant that urban renewal, in itself simply a tool, was used for very different purposes in different cities—in some places to get Negroes out of white neighborhoods, in others to bring middle-class people closer to downtown stores, in still other places to build dramatic civic monuments, and in a few places to rehabilitate declining neighborhoods and to add to the supply of moderately priced housing.[3]

[3] *Ibid.*

Despite the emphasis in federal urban programs on the *physical* characteristics of cities, most observers now acknowledge that "the urban crisis" is not primarily, nor even significantly, a physical problem. It is not really housing, or highways, or urban rebuilding that lie at the heart of urban discontent. Instead when we think of the challenges confronting cities, we think of racial tension, crime, poverty, poor schools, residential segregation, rising welfare rolls, fiscal crisis—in short, all of the major domestic problems facing the nation. In an urban society, *all* domestic problems become urban problems.

HUD—FEDERAL HOUSING AND URBAN DEVELOPMENT PROGRAMS

The Department of Housing and Urban Development (HUD) is the federal agency concerned primarily with public housing, mortgage insurance, urban renewal, community facilities, mass transit, and related programs, whose objectives are better houses and improved communities. HUD, the eleventh executive Department, was established in 1965 as a successor to the earlier independent agency, the Housing and Home Financial Administration. HUD administers federal housing and urban affairs' programs that were begun in the 1930s. The organization of HUD reflects the structure of these major federal programs:

> *Federal Housing Administration*
>   FHA programs of mortgage insurance
> *Federal National Mortgage Association*
>   FNMA ("Fanny Mae") secondary mortgage market operations for federally insured mortgages
> *Housing Assistance Administration*
>   Low rent public housing programs for low-income families
> *Urban Renewal Administration*
>   Federal programs for slum clearance, urban renewal, and planning assistance
> *Community Facilities Administration*
>   Federal grants and loans to municipalities for sewer, water, mass transit, and other public works

Each of these agencies reports to the Secretary of Housing and Urban Development.

The Federal Housing Administration was created in 1934 to guarantee private mortgages against default by the individual homebuyer, thereby enabling banks, savings and loan associations, and other lending agencies to provide long-term, low-interest, low-down-payment mortgages for Americans wishing to buy their own homes. After checking the credit rating of the prospective homebuyer, the FHA insures the private mortgage lender—bank, savings and loan company, insurance company, etc.—of repayment of the loan in case the homebuyer defaults. This reduces the risk and encourages mortgage lenders to make more loans at lower interest rates, lower down payments, and longer repayment periods. While these advantages in borrowing assist middle-class homebuyers, note that the *direct* beneficiaries of the FHA program are the banks and mortgage lending companies who are insured against losses. The FHA also establishes minimum building standards for homes it insures and thus has raised the general quality of middle-class housing. The FHA adds a small charge to each mortgage to finance a revolving fund to repay defaulted mortgages. However, the record of Americans in mortgage repayment is so good that FHA has consistently returned premium payments to the U.S. Treasury.

FHA has been extremely successful in promoting home ownership among millions of middle-class Americans. Millions of families have financed their homes through FHA-insured mortgages, and millions more have financed their houses through mortgages insured by the Veterans' Administration. A great many of these mortgages financed *suburban* homes. In fact the success of FHA and VA programs may have contributed to the deterioration of the nation's central cities by enabling so many middle-class white families to acquire their cherished homes in the suburbs, and leave the city behind.

The Federal National Mortgage Association, FNMA or "Fanny Mae," was created in the 1930s to further assist the mortgage market. FNMA can buy mortgages on the open market, particularly FHA and VA insured mortgages, when private mortgage money drys up. When mortgage money becomes more plentiful, it sells its mortgages. These market operations help to stabilize the mortgage market and insure a steady flow of money for home buying.

The Housing Act of 1937 established a federal public housing agency, later named the Housing Assistance Administration, to provide low-rent public housing for the poor who could not afford decent housing on the private market. The public housing program was designed for persons without jobs or incomes sufficient to enable them to afford homeownership even with the help of FHA. The Housing Assistance Administration does not build, own, or operate its own housing projects; rather it provides the necessary financial support to enable local communities to provide public housing for their poor if they chose to do so. The Housing Assistance Administration makes loans and grants to *local* housing authorities established by local governments to build, own, and operate low-cost public housing. Local housing authorities must keep rents low in relation to their tenants' ability to pay. This means that local housing authorities operate at a loss and the federal government reimburses them for this loss. No community is required to have a Public Housing Authority; they must apply to the Public Housing Administration and meet federal standards in order to receive federal financial support.

Public housing has always been involved in more political controversy than FHA. Real estate and building interests, which support

FHA because it expands their number of customers, have opposed public housing on the grounds that it is socialistic and wasteful. While, in theory, public housing serves individuals who cannot afford private housing, private real estate interests contend that public housing hurts the market for older homes and apartments. In addition, owners of dwellings seldom welcome competition from federally supported housing authorities. Also, political difficulties have been encountered in the location of public housing units. Many Americans will support public housing for low-income persons, so long as it is not located in their neighborhood. A large proportion of public housing occupants are Negroes, and thus public housing is automatically involved in the politics of race.

In recent years, many of the earlier supporters of public housing, including minority groups, labor, social workers, charitable organizations, and big-city political organizations, have expressed doubts about its effect. While providing improved living conditions, public housng has failed to eliminate poverty, ignorance, family disruption, juvenile delinquency, crime, and other characteristic troubles of slums. Very often, the concentration of large numbers of poor persons with a great variety of social problems into a single, mass housing project compounds their problems. Huge housing projects are impersonal and bureaucratic, and often fail to provide many of the stabilizing neighborhood influences of the old slums. Removing thousands of people from neighborhood environments and placing them in the institution-like setting of large public housing developments very often increases their alienation or separation from society and removes what few social controls exist in the slum neighborhood. Furthermore, Negro groups often complain that public housing is a new form of racial segregation, and indeed, the concentration of Negroes among public housing dwellers does lead to a great deal of de facto segregation in housing projects. Finally, it should be noted that rural interests are, at best, indifferent to public housing; although rural areas contain just as much substandard housing as city areas, the dispersal of rural dwellers over large land areas makes the public housing approach unfeasible.

Requests by communities for federal aid for public housing have far exceeded the amount of money appropriated by Congress. The result in most communities is a long waiting list of persons eligible for public housing for whom no space is available. To alleviate this shortage and to correct some of the problems involved in large-site housing projects, the Johnson administration obtained authorization from Congress for three programs to supplement public housing—a rent subsidy program, a dispersed public housing site program, and a new "turnkey" approach to the acquisition of public housing units. The rent subsidy program authorizes federal grants to local housing authorities to provide cash grants to families living in substandard housing, thus enabling them to rent decent private housing facilities. The dispersed public housing site program will provide federal grants to local housing authorities to enable them to purchase or lease existing single homes or apartment buildings throughout the community for operation as public housing units. The "turnkey" approach to the acquisition of public housing units encourages private builders to build public housing on their own sites and then sell it to local housing authorities. The purpose of all of these policies is to speed up the availability of public housing units and, perhaps more importantly, to eliminate dependence upon large, institutionlike public housing facilities and achieve more dispersal of public housing residents throughout the community. Opponents of these programs argue that the federal government is subsidizing "blockbusting" tactics in its attempt to disperse public housing dwellers; mostly Negroes, throughout the community. It is, they argue, a subtle form of open-housing legislation aimed at de facto housing segregation.

The Urban Renewal Administration was created to administer the federal program of slum clearance and urban renewal which was enacted in the Housing Act of 1949. After World War II, the suburban exodus had progressed to the point where central cities faced slow decay and death if large public efforts were not undertaken. Urban renewal could not be undertaken by private enterprise because it was not profitable; suburban property was usually cheaper than downtown property and it did not require large-scale clearance of obsolete buildings. Moreover, private enterprise did not possess the power of eminent domain that enabled the city to purchase many separately owned tracts of land and insure an economically feasible new investment.

To save the nation's central cities, the Urban Renewal Administration is authorized to match local monies to acquire blighted land, demolish or modernize obsolete or dilapidated structures, and make downtown sites available for new uses. The federal government does not engage in these activities directly, but makes available financial assistance to local urban renewal authorities for renewal projects. When the sites are physically cleared of the old structures by the local urban renewal authority, they can be resold to private developers for residential, commercial, or industrial use, and two-thirds of the difference between the costs of acquisition and clearance and the income from the private sale to the developers is paid for by the federal government. In other words, local urban renewal authorities sustain a loss in their renewal activities and two-thirds of this loss is made up by federal grants; the rest must come from local sources. However, the local share may include noncash contributions in the form of land donations, schools, streets, or parks.

No city is required to engage in urban renewal, but if it wishes federal financial backing, it must show in its application a "workable program" for redevelopment and the prevention of future blight. It must demonstrate that it has adequate building and health codes, good zoning and subdivision control regulations, proper administrative structures for renewal and other government services, sufficient local financing and public support, and a comprehensive plan of development with provision for relocating displaced persons. Failure to meet federal standards can halt federal urban assistance; for example, Houston, the largest city without any zoning, cannot get urban renewal funds.

Political support for urban renewal has come from mayors who wish to make their reputation as rigorous proponents of progress by engaging in large-scale renewal activities that produce impressive "before" and "after" pictures of the city. Businessmen wishing to preserve downtown investments and developers wishing to acquire land in urban centers have provided a solid base of support for downtown renewal. Mayors, planners, the press, and the good government forces have made urban renewal much more popular politically than public housing.

Originally, liberal reform groups and representatives of urban minorities supported urban renewal as an attack on the slum problem. However, recently they have become disenchanted with urban renewal, complaining that urban renewal has not dealt with the plight of the slum dweller. Too often, slum areas have been cleared and replaced with high-income residential developments or commercial or industrial developments that do not directly help the slum dwellers. Urban renewal authorities are required to pay landowners a just price for their land, but slum dwellers who rent their apartments are shoved about the city with only a minimal amount of support from the "relocation" division of urban renewal authority. Downtown areas have been improved in appearance, but usually at the price of considerable human dislocation. Thus, slum dwellers and the landlords who exploit them often join forces to oppose urban renewal.

The Community Facilities Administration was created in 1954 to provide technical and financial assistance to local governments in building community facilities—water and sewer systems, airports, mass transit, and other public works.

STRUCTURAL PROBLEMS IN FEDERAL URBAN POLICY

For over thirty years the federal government has been directly involved in housing and urban development programs. Yet today we continue to speak of the "urban crisis"—racial conflict, inadequate housing, air and water pollution, poor schools, crime and delinquency, crowded hospitals, traffic congestion, crippling city tax burdens, poorly paid policemen and other municipal workers, and so on. President Johnson summarized these problems as follows:

Some four million urban families living in homes of such disrepair to violate decent housing standards.

The need to provide over thirty percent more housing annually than we are currently building.

Our chronic inability to provide sufficient low- and moderate-income housing, of adequate quality, at a reasonable price.

The special problem of the poor and the Negro, unable to move freely from their ghettoes, exploited in the quest for the necessities of life.

Increasing pressures on municipal budgets, with large city per capita expenditures rising thirty-six percent in the three years after 1960.

The high human costs: crime, delinquency, welfare loads, disease, and health hazards. This is man's fate in those broken neighborhoods where he can "feel the enclosure of the flaking walls and see through the window the blackened reflection of the tenement across the street that blocks out the world beyond."

The tragic waste, and indeed, the chaos, that threatens where children are born into the stifling air of overcrowded rooms, and destined for a poor diet, inadequate schools, streets of fear and sordid temptation, joblessness, and the gray anxiety of the ill prepared.

And the flight to the suburbs of more fortunate men and women who might have provided the leadership and the means for reversing this human decline.[4]

The failure of federal urban policy to resolve these problems is *not* merely a product of structural or organizational defects in federal programs. Indeed, it is a serious difficulty of the institutional approach that it focuses on structural or organization problems when in fact the real issues are much more deeply rooted in social or economic dimensions of urban life. Poverty, racism, crime, pollution, overcrowding and other serious maladies afflicting mankind are not likely to be cured by tinkering with the organizational structure of government.

Yet it is possible to identify briefly a number of organizational and administrative problems which are serious obstacles to the development of an effective federal policy in housing and urban affairs: [5]

1. First of all, the major thrust of federal policy is now and always has been a commitment to the physical aspects of urban life— the provision of housing and transportation, the rebuilding of central cities, and development of community facilities, etc. It may be that the "urban crisis" is not primarily or even significantly a problem of housing or transit or facilities. It may be a problem of human conflict in crowded, high density, socially heterogenous areas.
2. Federal policy has frequently worked at cross-purposes, reflect-

[4] Message from President Johnson to Congress (see footnote 1).
[5] For a more detailed critique of federal urban policy, see James Q. Wilson, "The War on Cities"; and Edward C. Banfield, *The Unheavenly City* (Boston: Little, Brown, 1970).

ing organizational fragmentation of programs. For example, urban renewal tries to save central cities, while federal highway policy builds expressways making possible the suburban exodus and FHA has helped suburbanites to buy their own homes.

3. The Public Housing Program has tried to increase the supply of low-rent housing for the poor, while the urban renewal program, together with highway building, has torn down low-rent housing.

4. Federal civil rights policy is committed to desegregation but many large public housing projects concentrate blacks in de facto segregated neighborhoods and schools.

5. Federal policy has stressed *local* administration with local autonomy, flexibility, and participation in decision making. Yet this has meant that housing and urban renewal have been employed in different places for different purposes—in some places to help get blacks out of white neighborhoods, in others to subsidize white middle-class residents to come back to the central city, in others to restore business to downtown department stores, in others to build dramatic civic monuments or assist university expansion, in others to build sports palaces, and museums, or other middle-class centers, and in still others to improve the quality of life for urban blacks.

6. Direct federal-to-city grants for housing and urban renewal assist hard-pressed central cities, but generally overlook the possibilities for regional or metropolitan-wide housing and urban renewal programs. If it is true that segregation, slum housing, poverty, crime, and so on, are responsibilities of the entire metropolitan population, then grants to regional organizations for the implementation of housing and urban development policy would appear more appropriate than grants to cities.

7. Federal grant-in-aid programs provide money for specific purposes—frequently "new" or "innovative" or "demonstration" programs. Yet the real urban crisis may be occurring in the provision of traditional municipal services—policy protection, sewage disposal, sanitation—and what is required is the upgrading of existing services, not necessarily the initiation of "new" or "innovative" or "demonstration" programs.

8. The maze of federal grant-in-aid programs for cities (nearly 500 separate programs with separate purposes and guidelines) is uncoordinated and bureaucratic in character. Mayors and other municipal officials spend a great deal of time in "grantmanship"—learning where to find federal funds, how to apply, and how to write applications in such a way as to appear to meet the purposes and guidelines of the program.

9. The federal government has never set any meaningful priority among its hundreds of grant programs. The result is that too few dollars chase too many goals. Cities are sometimes pressured to apply for funds for projects they do not really need, simply be-

cause federal funds are available—while they may receive little or no federal assistance for more vital programs.

The reason for many of these administrative and organization problems is not merely incompetency on the part of government planners. Institutional analysis is misleading when it implies that these problems are strictly institutional. Frequently conflicting policies, incompatible goals, and competing government programs reflect underlying conflicts over public policy. Government institutions often accommodate conflict over public policy by enacting conflicting policies and establishing separate agencies to implement these policies. We can only admire a political system which so neatly accommodates conflicting demands!

The Model Cities Program, enacted in 1966, was an attempt to cope with some of the organizational and administrative problems in federal urban programs. Model Cities is not a new program or new approach to urban problems but rather an effort to reorganize old programs and approaches. The emphasis in Model Cities is upon "coordination" and "integrated planning" of federal programs in each participating city. The idea is to coordinate programs and grants in housing, urban renewal, and community facilities, with programs and grants in transportation, job training, education, economic opportunity, and related programs. A federal coordinator would be appointed for each participating city. Supplemental federal funds, in addition to existing federal grant programs, would be made available to participating cities as incentives for participation. The final verdict on the Model Cities Program is not in yet, but it is doubtful whether this reorganization and imposition of another layer of federal bureaucracy between urban needs and federal monetary resources will succeed in reducing existing organizational chaos, let alone solve any significant urban problems.

An alternative approach to the organizational and administrative problems in federal grant-in-aid programs is that of providing unrestricted *federal bloc grants* to states or cities with few or no strings attached. A related approach is that of *federal revenue sharing* where a certain percentage of federal tax collections would be turned back to states or cities for their own use. Bloc grants would be given by the federal government for stated purposes, such as education, health, welfare, transportation, or housing and urban development, and states or cities would spend the money for these purposes as they saw fit. Revenue sharing would give states and cities access to the fiscal resources of the federal government and ensure state and local control over the use of these funds.

The issue of bloc grants and revenue sharing extends well beyond the area of housing and urban development. Indeed, the structure of American federalism is vitally affected by the direction of federal grant-in-aid policy. Bloc grants and revenue sharing proposals are generally supported by those groups who fear centralization of power in federal bureaucracies. In addition, state and local officials welcome the notion of assigning the federal government the unhappy task of collecting money, while retaining for themselves the more agreeable task of deciding how the money should be spent. Many mayors support bloc grants and revenue sharing only on the guarantee that federal money will be given directly to cities and not allocated to state governments. Some urban groups—notably, blacks and poor people—are distrustful of state and local decision making, and would probably prefer the present arrangements, however chaotic, to any organizational shifts which would threaten their interests. The federal bureauracies themselves are less than enthusiastic about relinquishing too much control over policy making to state and local authorities.

URBAN ENVIRONMENT AND THE STRUCTURE OF CITY POLITICS

Let us examine the structure of city government, the social, economic and political forces shaping city politics, and the policies of city governments, and more importantly, the linkages between elements of urban life.

City politics come in a variety of structural packages. Cities vary in the form of government—*mayor-council, commission,* or *council-manager.* Municipal election systems vary as to whether they are *partisan* or *nonpartisan,* and whether or not council constituencies are *at-large* or *by ward.* Finally, urban governmental structures differ in the extent of *consolidation* or *fragmentation* in metropolitan regions.

These structural differences in city politics are frequently associated with the political success or failure of the municipal reform movement.[6] The municipal reform movement developed over the last century to fight "city machines" and "bosses." The reformers wanted to eliminate "politics" from local government, and they supported a variety of structural changes to do so. The reform movement put forward a program which included city manager government, nonpartisan elections, at-large constituencies, the elimination of many separately elected offices (the "short ballot"), the merit system of civil service, modern budget and planning practices, and the separation of the municipal government from state and national politics. Later the municipal reform movement also supported efforts to consolidate the many governmental units operating in metropolitan areas in the interests of economy, efficiency, and responsibility in metropolitan affairs.

The *council-manager* form of government was put forward as a

[6] See Edward C. Banfield and James Q. Wilson, *City Politics* (Cambridge, Mass.: Harvard University Press, 1963).

means of separating "politics" from "administration" in city government. Policy making would be vested in an elected council, but administration would be assigned to an appointed administrator known
as a manager. The reform ethos included a belief that there is a
"right" answer to public questions and that "politics" ought to be
divorced from city government. Municipal government is really a
technical and administrative problem rather than a political one.
City government should be placed in the hands of those who are best
qualified, by training, ability, and devotion to public service, to manage
public businesses. Popular control of government was to be guaranteed
by making the managers tenure completely dependent upon the will
of the elected council. In contrast to the council-manager form of
government, the mayor-council form is the more traditional and
"political" structure.

The *nonpartisan ballot* was the most widely adopted reform ever
put forward to curb the "machines" and ensure a "no party" style of
politics. Nearly two-thirds of America's cities use a nonpartisan ballot
to elect local officials. Reformers felt that nonpartisanship would take
the "politics" out of local government and raise the caliber of candidates for elected offices. They believed that nonpartisanship would
restrict local campaigning to local issues, and thereby remove extrane-
ous state-national issues from local elections. They also believed that,
by omitting party labels, local campaigns would emphasize the qualifications of the individual candidates rather than their party affiliations. Moreover, to eliminate traditional "ward politics" with its
emphasis on neighborhood affiliations, the reform movement proposed
that candidates for local office run in *at-large* rather than *ward* constituencies. This meant that all city councilmen would be elected by
a citywide constituency, rather than each councilman being elected by
a separate ward constitutency.

For many years reform movement also insisted that "the metropolitan problem" was essentially one of "fragmented" government—
that is, the proliferation of governments in metropolitan areas with
a lack of coordination of public programs. The objective of the metropolitan reform movement was to reorganize, consolidate, and enlarge
governmental jurisdictions; that is, to rid metropolitan areas of "ineffective multiple local jurisdictions" and "governments which do not
coincide with the boundaries of the metropolis."

From its beginning, reform politics were strongly supported by the
native middle-class, Anglo-Saxon, Protestant, old residents of the cities
whose political ethos was very different than that which the immigrants brought with them. The immigrant, and the "machine" and
"boss" that relied on his vote, fought in the late nineteenth century
to displace the native old family, Yankee elite that had traditionally
dominated Northern cities. The machine played an important role in
educating immigrants and assimilating them into American life. Ma-

GOVERNMENTAL FORM AND SIZE OF CITY

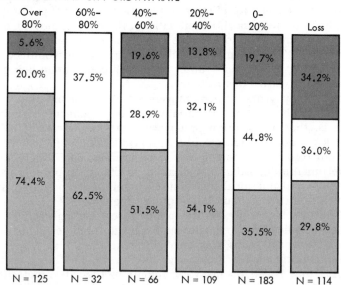

GOVERNMENTAL FORM AND CITY GROWTH RATE

FIG. 8-1

Source: John H. Kessel, "Governmental Structure and Political Environment," *American Political Science Review*, 56 (September 1962), 618. Reproduced by permission of the American Political Science Association.

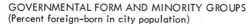

GOVERNMENTAL FORM AND MINORITY GROUPS
(Percent foreign–born in city population)

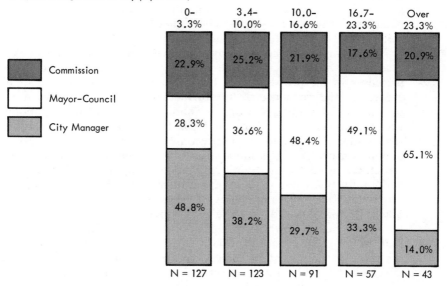

chine politics provided the means of upward social mobility for ethnic group members not open to them in businesses or professions. Machines did not keep out people with "funny" sounding names, but instead went out of its way to put these names on their ballot. Politics became a way "up" for the bright sons of Irish and Italian immigrants. In contrast, the twentieth century reform movement was largely a middle-class effort to recapture control of local government.

What characteristics of the urban environment are associated with reformed or unreformed structures of city government? First of all, city manager government is closely associated with the size of cities. Large cities show a distinct preference for the more "political" form of mayor-council government in contrast to the more "efficient" form of council-manager government (see Figure 8–1). Most of the nation's large cities have mayor-council governments; the council-manager and commission forms of government are most popular in the middle-size cities. The political environment of large cities is so complex that these cities require strong political leadership, which can arbitrate struggles for power, arrange compromises, and be directly responsible to the people for policy decisions. A large city requires a "political" form of government that can arbitrate the conflicting claims of diverse interests. On the other hand, smaller cities have fewer competing interests, more acceptance of a common public interest, and less division over community policy. A professional city manager would have less difficulty in recognizing cues about direct behavior in a small city than in a large city with a complex social and political structure. A single interest is more likely to dominate politics in a small city; therefore, such a city can use a professional administrator rather than a political negotiator. There is reason to believe that larger cities require political skills more than professional administration.

As one might expect, the mayor-council form of government is also associated with ethnicity in the population. When cities are compared, increases in the proportion of foreign born persons coincide with increases in the incidence of unreformed political institutions. A study by sociologist Daniel N. Gordon shows that foreign-born population was a correlate of that form in 1960.[7] Moreover this relationship persists under controls for region, economic base, population, size, and population change. It is interesting to note that unreformed political structures are associated with foreign-born populations but not necessarily with black populations. Apparently blacks have not allied themselves with machines and bosses to the extent that earlier Irish, Italian, Slavic immigrants did. Yet the most obvious explanation for the relationship between ethnicity and "politicized" institutions is the fact that ethnic groups were especially dependent upon political activities for their advancement in society. Since the early immigrants to the city lacked wealth and social standing they came to value access to government, public office holding, and patronage. They supported the "political" governmental forms in preference to forms that were intended to reduce the value of one of their few resources—their votes.

Reformed governmental structures are more common in middle-class cities with large proportions of well-educated, white-collar workers. Middle-class citizens are more likely to want government conducted in a businesslike fashion, with a council serving as a board of directors and a city manager as the president of a "municipal corporation." They are primarily concerned with efficiency, honesty, and saving their tax dollars. These values are not necessarily shared by labor and ethnic groups which may prefer a government which grants them small favors, dispenses patronage jobs, awards representation and "recognition" to groups, and can be held directly responsible by the voters at election time.

There is also a relationship between reformed institutions in city politics and the rate of population growth and mobility.[8] Growing cities face more administrative and technical problems than cities whose population is stable. There is a strong relationship between population growth and council-manager government. A rapidly growing city faces many administrative problems in providing streets,

---

[7] Daniel N. Gordon, "Immigrants and Urban Governmental Form in American Cities, 1933-1960," *American Journal of Sociology*, Vol. 74 (September 1968), 158-71.

[8] See also Robert R. Alford and Harry M. Scoble, "Political and Socioeconomic Characteristics of American Cities," *Municipal Year Book* (Chicago: International City Manager's Association, 1965), pp. 82-97.

sewers, and other services required by an expanding population. This creates a demand for a professional administrator. In contrast, the mayor-council form of government is associated with cities having relatively stable populations, in which the problems of growth are not quite so pressing but the problems of political conflict are well defined and persistent. Cities with a highly mobile population are also much more likely to have the manager form of government. Mobile middle-class populations are less likely to settle into stable political factions that compete with each other and require "political" institutions. Instead, more mobile populations seem to demand efficient, businesslike, service-producing governments—and a structure more convenient to these goals.

GOVERNMENTAL "FRAGMENTATION" IN METROPOLITAN AREAS

The reformers have also bemoaned governmental "fragmentation" in metropolitan areas. The "multiplicity" of governmental units in the metropolis is said to result in inefficient administration, duplicated governmental functions, and reduced ability to cope with problems across jurisdiction boundaries. Yet, despite the concern of reformers with "fragmentation," seldom has this concept been measured systematically. Recently the concept of metropolitan fragmentation was operationally measured in terms of the number of governmental units in a metropolitan area (an absolute measure of fragmentation), and the number of governmental units *per person* in a metropolitan area (a relative measure of fragmentation).[9] Individual metropolitan areas differ widely in these measures of fragmentation. It turns out that Chicago is the most fragmented metropolitan area in the nation with a total of 1,113 local governments operating in the metropolitan area. Several smaller metropolitan areas in the nation have fewer than ten governmental units.

Governmental fragmentation is closely related to size: the larger the metropolitan area, the more fragmented the governmental structure. The simple coefficients in Table 8–1 indicate that 50 percent of the variation in a number of governmental units in metropolitan areas can be attributed to size. Fragmentation is also related to age of settlement and the income levels in the metropolis, although these factors are less influential than size. Apparently the older the metropolitan area, the more fragmented its government becomes; and the more affluent its citizens, the more fragmentation, in the form of separate, relatively small units of government, can be afforded. Further analysis indicates that age and income are independently, although weakly,

---

[9] Brett W. Hawkins and Thomas R. Dye, "Metropolitan 'Fragmentation,' " *Midwest Review of Public Administration*, Vol. 4 (February 1970), 17-24.

TABLE 8-1 Conditions Associated with Metropolitan Governmental Fragmentation

| | Numbers of Governments | | | Governments per 100,000 | | |
	Total	School Districts	Munici- palities	Total	School Districts	Munici- palities
Size of metropolitan area	.71	.67	.74	—.15	—.11	.00
Age in decades	.48	.40	.49	—.19	—.14	.00
Percent nonwhite, central city	.06	.00	—.04	—.37	—.31	—.03
Metropolitan-wide SES						
Median family income	.28	.29	.24	.00	.00	—.05
White collar occupation	.15	.14	.15	.03	—.07	.07
High school graduates	.06	.08	.01	.12	.06	.08
City-suburban SES differences						
Nonwhite	.05	.01	.17	—.22	—.17	—.03
Median family income	.15	.07	.24	—.16	—.21	.00
White collar occupation	.17	.11	.26	—.26	—.25	—.04
High school graduates	.22	.16	.27	—.11	—.17	.00
Central city population as percent SMSA population	—.23	—.19	—.27	.14	.09	.05

Note: Figures are simple correlation coefficients for 212 Metropolitan areas.
Source: Brett W. Hawkins and Thomas R. Dye, "Metropolitan 'Fragmentation': A Research Note," *Midwest Review of Public Administration,* reproduced by permission.

related to fragmentation; these relationships are not a product of intervening effect of size. Interestingly, fragmentation is *not* related to city-suburban *differences* in class or racial composition. If fragmentation is measured in *relative* terms (governments per 100,000 people) it is much more difficult to observe environmental correlates. This measure of fragmentation is not related to size or age of income levels. Only percent nonwhite is significantly related to this measure of fragmentation.

URBAN GOVERNMENTAL STRUCTURES AND PUBLIC POLICY

Does it make any difference in the policies adopted by cities whether a city's governmental structure is "reformed" or "unreformed"? Do council-manager cities pursue notably different policies than mayor-council cities? Are there any consistent policy differences between cities with nonpartisan, at-large electoral systems and cities with partisan ward type electoral systems? Are metropolitan policies in areas of fragmented local government any different from metropolitan policies in areas with consolidated governmental structures? It is difficult to come to grips with these questions because, as we have seen, there are significant environmental differences between cities with different governmental structures. This makes it difficult to sort out the effect of governmental structure from the effect of urban environment. For example, if reformed cities pursue noticeably different policies than unreformed cities, we must be careful in attributing these policy differences to reformism, since we already know that reformed and unreformed cities differ in their size and socioeconomic composition. It may be that the environmental variables really account for the differences in policy in reformed and unreformed cities, just as they account for differences in structure.

In general the research described here suggests that *structural* characteristics of cities do have *some* independent effect on urban policy. It is also true that urban *environmental* variables have a *very important effect* on urban policies—an effect which is generally greater than structural characteristics. Nonetheless, there is evidence that the structure of government does affect the outcome of public policy, and this evidence lends validity to the structural approach.

In general, policies of reformed, manager governments are likely to be directed toward (1) promoting economic growth, and/or (2) providing life's amenities.[10] (Merely maintaining traditional services—care-taker government—is inconsistent with reformed, manager government.) Manager governments may be concerned with promoting economic growth through population expansion, industrial development, commercial activities, total wealth, and the like. This type of government is prepared to enact zoning regulations, reduce tax assessments, develop industrial parks, install utilities, and do whatever else may be required to attract business and industry and promote production. Another policy orientation of reform manager governments is that of providing and securing life's amenities. The policies of these governments accent the home environment rather than the working environment; laws stress safety, slowness, quiet, beauty, convenience, and restfulness. Neighborhoods are defended by rigid zoning laws and building codes, open spaces are guarded, traffic is routed around the city, and noise and smoke are curtailed. Reformed manager governments may assume either of these two policy orientations—promoting economic growth, or providing and securing life's amenities. The caretaker policy orientation is inconsistent with the reformed structure. A caretaker government is expected to provide minimum public services in the community and nothing more. Nothing new is ever tried and tax increases are steadfastly avoided. Pressing public problems are passed on to higher levels of government, given to private groups or charities, or ignored.

According to political scientists Oliver P. Williams and Charles R. Adrian it is contrary to the professional orientation of manager governments to be content with caretaker policies:

[10] Oliver P. Williams, "A Typology for Comparative Local Government," *Midwest Review of Political Science*, Vol. 5 (May, 1961), 150-64.

It is against his (the manager's) professional code of ethics to let the city's physical plant deteriorate for the sake of low taxes. The clash between the manager plan and care-taker government does not stop with professional values however. Career advancements for managers are based upon concrete achievements, not simply satisfied councilmen.[11]

There is some evidence that urban renewal policies may be effected by manager versus mayor government. Political scientist George S. Duggar reports that mayor cities were quicker to respond to the lure of federal money than manager cities and got a faster start on their urban renewal programs.[12] This finding would testify to the political awareness of mayors. On the other hand, Duggar reports that once urban renewal programs were begun, manager cities experienced slightly greater program achievement than mayor cities. Duggar admits that population size is a more influential variable in urban renewal achievement than governmental structure: greater achievement is associated with greater size. However, the author concludes that governmental structure does have some independent effect on urban renewal policies.

The structure of city governments has been found to be related to outcomes in water fluoridation battles. In a comparative study of several hundred cities sociologists Robert L. Crain and Donald B. Rosenthal found that fluoridation has a better chance of consideration and adoption in cities having a strong executive (a manager or a strong partisan mayor) and a relatively low level of direct citizen participation.[13] Broad popular participation, particularly in the absence of strong executive leadership, frequently spelled defeat for fluoridation. Moreover, a mayor's public endorsement is closely correlated with fluoridation adoption, even when a referendum is held. Another structural variable—partisanship—is also related to fluoridation outcomes. In both mayor and manager cities, partisan electoral systems are marked by the largest proportion of adoptions of fluoridation laws by city councils.

REFORM AND PUBLIC POLICY

What are the policy consequences of reform government? In a very important study of taxing and spending in two-hundred American cities with populations of 50,000 or more, political scientists Robert L. Lineberry and Edmund P. Fowler found that reformed cities tended to

---

[11] Oliver P. Williams and Charles R. Adrian, *Four Cities* (Philadelphia: University of Pennsylvania Press, 1963), p. 280.
[12] George S. Duggar, "The Relation of Local Government Structure to Urban Renewal," *Law and Contemporary Problem* (Winter 1961), pp. 55-65.
[13] Robert L. Crain and Donald B. Rosenthal, "Structure and Values in Local Political Systems: The Case of Fluoridation Decisions," *Journal of Politics*, Vol. 28 (February 1966), 169-95.

tax and spend *less* than unreformed cities.[14] Cities with manager governments and at-large council constituencies were *less* willing to spend money for public purposes than cities with mayor-council governments and ward constituencies. (However, cities with partisan elections did not actually spend any more than cities with nonpartisan elections.) In short, reformism *does* save tax money.

Lineberry and Fowler also found that environmental variables had an important impact on tax and spending policies. For example they concluded that:

1. The more middle class the city, measured by income, education, and occupation, the lower the general tax and spending levels.
2. The greater the home ownership in a city, the lower the tax and spending levels.
3. The larger the percentage of religious and ethnic minorities in the population, the higher the city's taxes and expenditures.

What turned out to be an even more important finding in the Lineberry and Fowler study was the difference in *responsiveness* of the two kinds of city governments—reformed and unreformed—to the socioeconomic composition of their populations. Reformed cities (cities with manager governments, at-large constituencies, and nonpartisan elections) appeared to be unresponsive in their tax and spending policies to differences in income, educational, occupational, religious, and ethnic characteristics of their populations. In contrast, unreformed cities (cities with mayor-council governments, ward constituencies, and partisan elections) reflected class, racial, and religious composition in their taxing and spending decisions.

Reformism tends to reduce the importance of class, home ownership, ethnicity, and religion in city politics. It tends to minimize the role which social conflicts play in public decision making. In contrast, mayor-council governments, ward constituencies, and partisan elections permit social cleavages to be reflected in city politics and public policy to be responsive to socioeconomic factors. These findings suggest that reformed cities have gone a long way toward accomplishing the reformist goal—that is, "to immunize city governments from 'artificial' social cleavages—race, religion, ethnicity, and so on." Thus, political institutions seem to play an important role in policy formation

> . . . a role substantially independent of a city's demography. . . . Nonpartisan elections, at-large constituencies, and manager governments are associated with a lessened responsiveness of cities to the enduring conflicts of political life.[15]

[14] Robert L. Lineberry and Edmund P. Fowler, "Reformism and Public Policy in Cities," *American Political Science Review*, Vol. 61 (September 1967), 701-16.
[15] *Ibid.*, p. 715.

TABLE 8-2   Environmental Characteristics and Tax and Spending Policy in Reformed and Unreformed Cities

Relationships Between	Correlations Between Environmental Characteristics and Taxing and Spending in:	
	Reformed Cities	Unreformed Cities
Taxes and		
Ethnicity	.62	.34
Private school attendance	.40	.25
Home ownership	—.70	—.44
Education	—.55	—.13
Expenditures and		
Ethnicity	.51	.05
Private school attendance	.46	.08
Home ownership	—.67	—.38
Education	—.49	—.37

Source: Adapted from figures in Robert L. Lineberry and Edmund P. Fowler, "Reformism and Public Policy in American Cities," *American Political Science Review*, Vol. 61 (September 1967), 701-16.

As Table 8-2 shows, the strength of the correlation between environment and taxing and spending, by categories of reform, decreases regularly with an increase in reform government.

SUMMARY

The urban crisis is not only, or even primarily, a problem of governmental organization or administration. The institutional approach is misleading to the extent that it implies that reforming governmental insitutions in the metropolis can solve problems of urban blight, inadequate housing, crime and delinquency, poverty and ill-health, pollution, racial tension, and other urban ills. Yet institutional arrangements are linked to the nature of the urban environment and even to the content of urban policy. Let us summarize our ideas about these linkages:

1. Federal housing and urban development policy centers about direct federal-to-city grants-in-aid for public housing, urban renewal, community facilities and related programs, together with mortgage insurance programs administered by the federal government itself. These programs are organized and administered separately from federal grants programs in education, welfare, economic opportunity, and transportation. These programs have emphasized the physical aspects of urban life.

2. Frequently federal programs in urban areas have worked at cross-purposes, reflecting organizational fragmentation. However, competing goals and conflicting policies reflect underlying conflicts over urban affairs, rather than merely organizational problems.

3. The question of federal control versus state or local autonomy in urban policy raises broad questions of centralization and de-centralization in the American federal system.

4. The municipal reform movement assumed that structural changes in city government would lead to a progressive middle-class policy orientation. The movement supported the city-manager form of government, nonpartisan elections, at-large constitu-encies, and metropolitan consolidation, in addition to other structural reforms.

5. The success of the reform movement in achieving these structural reforms is associated with characteristics of the urban environ-ment: reformed cities are more likely to be middle-sized cities, with native-born white populations and rapid population growth. The movement for metropolitan consolidation has had very few successes; governmental structure in older, larger metropolitan areas is particularly fragmented.

6. Reformed structural characteristics of government do have some independent effect on urban policy, although the effect of en-vironmental variables is generally greater. The policies of re-formed, manager governments are likely to be directed toward promoting economic growth and providing life's amenities, rather than resolving community conflict. Reformed city governments tax and spend less than unreformed governments.

7. There is some evidence that reformed governments are less re-sponsive in policy matters to the characteristics of their popula-tions. In contrast, the policies of unreformed cities (cities with mayor-council governments, ward constituencies, and partisan elections) tended to reflect the class, racial, and ethnic com-position of their populations.

8. The extent of metropolitan fragmentation was not related to any observable policy dimensions; fragmentation does not increase or decrease per capita government spending for education, high-ways, welfare, health, police, fire, sanitation, housing, or other urban services.

BIBLIOGRAPHY

BANFIELD, EDWARD C., *The Unheavenly City*. Boston: Little, Brown, 1970.

BANFIELD, EDWARD C. and JAMES Q. WILSON, *City Politics*. Cambridge, Mass.: Harvard University Press, 1963.

BOLLENS, JOHN C. and HENRY J. SCHMANDT, *The Metropolis*, 2nd ed. New York: Harper & Row, 1970.

HAWKINS, BRETT W., *Politics and Urban Policies*. New York: Bobbs-Merrill, 1971.

PRIORITIES AND PRICE TAGS:
an analysis of government spending

CHAPTER 9

DIMENSIONS OF GOVERNMENT SPENDING

Governments do some things which cannot be measured in dollars. Nevertheless, government expenditures are the best available measure of the overall dimensions of government policy. There are few public policies that do not require an expenditure of funds. Budgets represent government policies with price tags attached.

The expenditures of all governments in the United States—federal, state, and local—grew from 1.7 billion in 1902 to over 300 billion in 1970, an increase of nearly 5,000 percent (see Table 9–1). A great deal of the increase in government activity can be attributed to growth in the nation's population. And a great deal of the increase in dollar amounts spent by government is exaggerated by the diminishing value of the dollar, that is, by inflation. If we are to measure the growth of government activity accurately, we must examine government expenditures *per person*, and do so in *constant dollars*. This enables us to view past and present government activity in relation to the size of the population and the value of the dollar. It turns out that *per capita* expenditures of all governments *in constant dollars* increased over 1,000 percent from 1902 to 1970. Thus, we note that the increase in government spending cannot be attributed merely to increases in

TABLE 9-1   GROWTH IN POPULATION, WEALTH, AND GOVERNMENT ACTIVITIES
OVER SEVEN DECADES

	Population Millions	GNP Billions	GNP Per Capita Constant Dollars	All Government Spending Billions	All Government Spending Per Capita Constant Dollars	All Government Spending Percent of GNP
1902	79.2	21.6	1,089	1.7	84	7.7
1913	97.2	39.1	1,308	3.2	107	8.2
1922	110.1	74.0	1,380	9.3	174	12.5
1927	119.0	96.0	1,637	11.2	190	11.6
1932	124.9	58.5	1,196	12.4	254	21.3
1936	128.2	82.7	1,561	16.8	316	20.8
1940	132.6	100.6	1,782	20.4	353	20.3
1944	138.9	211.4	2,747	109.9	1,429	52.0
1946	141.9	210.7	2,288	79.7	866	37.8
1950	152.3	284.6	2,401	70.3	593	24.7
1952	157.6	347.0	2,609	99.8	751	28.8
1955	165.9	397.5	2,737	110.7	762	27.9
1960	180.7	502.6	2,815	151.3	848	30.1
1962	186.6	554.9	2,943	175.8	933	31.7
1967	199.1	789.7	3,380	257.8	1,102	32.6
1970	203.2	959.6	3,900	298.4	1,215	31.1

Source: U.S. Bureau of the Census, *Historical Statistics on Governmental Finances and Employment* (Washington Government Printing Office, 1967); updating from U.S. Bureau of the Census, *Statistical Abstract of the United States.*

population or the devaluation of the dollar, government activity has grown much faster than the population, and much faster than inflation.

An even more important yardstick of the growth of government activity is found in the relationship of government expenditures to the Gross National Product (GNP). The GNP is the dollar sum of all goods and services produced in the nation in a year, and it is a common measure of the size of the nation's economy. The growth of the GNP in the twentieth century reflects the expansion of the nation's economy: the GNP in dollar amounts grew from 21.6 billion dollars to over a trillion dollars in the early 1970s. Part of this growth, of course, was attributed to inflation and a growing population. But the GNP also increased in *per capita constant dollars* by more than 300 percent. Thus, the GNP has also grown much faster than the population, and much faster than inflation.

Government expenditures in relation to the Gross National Product have risen, somewhat bumpily, from 7.7 percent in 1902 to over 30 percent in the 1970s. If public programs financed by the government had grown at the same rate as private economic activities, this percentage figure would have remained at the same level over the years. But government activity over the long run has grown even *faster* than private enterprise. By any yardstick whatsoever, then, we find the growth of government activity in America has been substantial. Government activity now accounts for over one-third of all economic activity in the nation.

WARS, DEPRESSIONS, AND GOVERNMENT ACTIVITY

What accounts for the growth of government activity? Years ago, a European economist, Adolph Wagner, set forth a "law of increasing state activity" roughly to the effect that government activity increased faster than economic output in all developing societies.[1] He attributed his law to a variety of factors: increasing regulatory services required to control a more specialized, complex economy; increasing involvement of government in economic enterprise; increasing demands in a developed society for social services such as education, welfare, public health, etc. Thus the "law of increasing state activity" portrayed growth in government activity as an inevitable accompaniment of a developing society.

But the American experience raises serious doubts about the "law of increasing state activity." While it is true that governmental activity has grown in relation to the economy over the last seven decades, this growth has occurred in spurts during crisis periods rather than as a steady acceleration. Government expenditures in relation to the GNP have *not* increased predictably as if governed by a "law"; instead they have remained stable over long periods of time and spurted upward only in response to wars and depressions.

Wars and severe depressions bring about significant increases in government activity. National emergencies provide the opportunity for governments to increase the scope and magnitude of their activities, both in national defense and domestic service. When an emergency ends, government activities decline, but not to their old levels. Post-crisis expenditures level out on a higher plateau than precrisis expenditures. In the absence of crisis, government activity remains very stable *in relation to the economy*—total public spending as a proportion of the GNP stays about the same; government activity and the private economy grow at about the same rates. Thus, national emergencies provide the occasion for government activities to rise to successively higher plateaus (see Figure 9–1). Government expenditures have grown through a series of leaps associated with international crises, principally wars, and, to a lesser extent, in the Depression.

Scholars have summarized the American experience as follows:

> Whether the rule of "normal peacetime" stability would continue over large periods without crisis is unknown; unfortunately, such periods have in the past been of relatively short duration. The experience does, however, suggest a hypothesis that, over the short run at least, the political pressures in this democratic society are such as to prevent any sub-

[1] Adolph Wagner's major work is *Grundlegung der politischen oekonomie* (Leipzig, 1893). This work is discussed at length in Alan T. Peacock and Jack Wiseman, *The Growth of Public Expenditures in the United Kingdom* (Princeton: Princeton University Press, 1961).

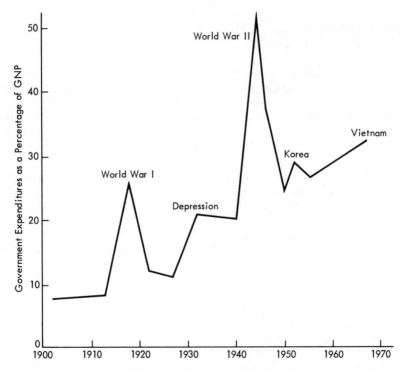

FIG. 9-1   Government Expenditures as a Percentage of the Gross National Product

stantial change in the total levels of expenditures upward or downward in relation to the economy as a whole. And it appears probable that the fixing of expenditure levels is a consequence of the stickiness of revenues, principally taxes, rather than of the shifting of expenditure needs. Crises, on the other hand, "unfreeze" revenue levels, permit them to rise and then, once the crises are past, they again congeal.

In sum, it is clear that expenditures of American governments have increased substantially by every measure, but that these increases have occurred spasmodically with the occurrences of international and domestic crises.[2]

There is greater stability in domestic affairs than in defense and international relations. *Defense* spending rises sharply during war, then declines after hostilities. During periods of peace, defense spending gradually declines as a proportion of the GNP. In contrast, *domestic* spending declines during wartime. During peacetime periods it tends to rise gradually. The only really dramatic increase in domestic spending occurred during the depression—a truly significant domestic crisis.

[2] Frederick C. Mosher and Orville F. Poland, *The Costs of American Governments* (New York: Dodd, Mead, 1964), pp. 28-29.

If we only consider *domestic* spending of governments, the stability of government activity in relation to the economy is striking. Today all governments in the United States are not spending much more for domestic services in relation to national resources than they spent in the 1930s (see Table 9–2)! Actually, were it not for the upward movement of social security payments as a percentage of the GNP, domestic spending would be lower today than in the 1930s! Social insurance payments have grown from next to nothing before the Depression, to nearly 4.5 percent of the GNP today.

TABLE 9-2 DEFENSE AND DOMESTIC SPENDING OF FEDERAL, STATE, AND LOCAL GOVERNMENTS AS A PERCENTAGE OF GNP

	All Government Spending	Defense [1]	Domestic [2]	Federal [3]	State-Local
1902	7.7	1.6	6.1	2.6	5.1
1913	8.2	1.2	7.0	2.5	5.7
1922	12.5	3.2	9.3	5.0	7.5
1927	11.6	2.1	9.5	3.6	8.0
1932	21.3	3.8	17.4	7.1	14.2
1936	20.8	2.4	17.4	10.2	10.6
1940	20.3	2.5	17.8	9.8	10.5
1944	52.0	41.6	10.4	47.2	4.8
1946	37.8	27.0	10.8	31.7	6.1
1950	24.7	10.0	14.7	15.7	9.0
1952	28.8	16.3	12.5	20.4	8.4
1955	27.9	13.1	14.8	18.4	9.5
1960	30.1	11.6	18.5	18.7	11.4
1962	31.7	11.7	19.9	18.9	12.8
1967	32.6	12.3	20.3	21.1	11.5
1970	31.1	11.9	19.2	20.5	10.6

[1] Defense, veterans, international relations, interest on war debt, atomic energy, space expenditures.
[2] All other, including social insurance.
[3] Including social insurance.

These trends indicate that defense and domestic spending move in different patterns, and sometimes compensate for each other. During World War II *defense* spending grew to over 40 percent of the entire economic product of the nation. In contrast, during World War II *domestic* spending dropped to 10 percent of the GNP, from highs of nearly 18 percent during the Depression. After World War II, domestic spending gradually regained momentum, with a brief drop-off during the Korean War. War tends to displace domestic spending with defense spending during the period of hostilities. But war also conditions citizens to tolerate major increases in government activity, and thus, after the war, government activity remains on a higher plateau than before the war. Domestic spending gradually displaces defense spending during peacetime periods.

During the Vietnam War, a deliberate effort was made by the John-

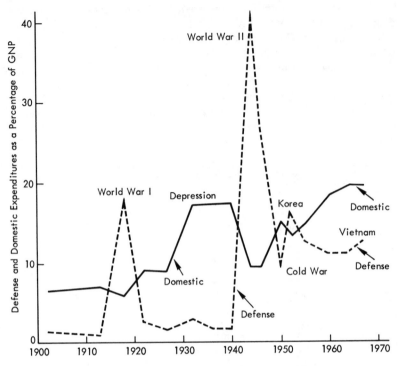

FIG. 9-2 DEFENSE AND DOMESTIC EXPENDITURES AS A PERCENTAGE OF THE GROSS NATIONAL PRODUCT

son and Nixon administrations to prevent the war from becoming a drain on domestic programs. National policy stressed "guns *and* butter." For the most part, the effort was successful. Domestic expenditures did *not* decline as percentage of the GNP, as had been the case in previous wars. Domestic expenditures remaind fairly stable in relation to the economy. The cost of the war in Vietnam (in so far as it is possible to separate the cost of this war from other defense expenditures) accounted for most of the increase in federal government spending as a percentage of the GNP in the 1960s; the war cost about 3 percent of the GNP.

IDENTIFYING NATIONAL PRIORITIES

A great deal of political rhetoric centers about national "priorities." The problem is to separate rhetoric from reality. We must distinguish between what is *said* to be a national priority, from what is actually given priority in the allocation of national resources. To identify actual priorities, we have determined the percentage of national income devoted to various government activties. The results are summarized

TABLE 9-3 GOVERNMENT EXPENDITURES BY FUNCTION IN RELATION TO
GROSS NATIONAL PRODUCT

Federal, State, & Local Government Expenditures	Percents of Gross National Product Devoted to Government Activity by Function			
	1950	*1955*	*1960*	*1968*
Total	24.7	27.8	30.0	32.7
National Defense and International Relations	6.5	10.9	9.4	9.6
Space Research	0.0	0.0	0.1	0.5
Postal Service	0.8	0.7	0.7	0.8
Education	3.4	3.2	3.9	5.0
Higher Education	0.4	0.4	0.6	1.2
Elementary and Secondary	2.1	2.5	3.0	3.4
Other	0.9	0.3	0.2	0.5
Highways	1.4	1.6	1.9	1.7
Public Welfare	1.1	0.8	0.9	1.3
Hospitals	0.7	0.7	0.8	0.9
Health	0.2	0.2	0.2	0.3
Police	0.3	0.4	0.4	0.4
Fire	0.2	0.2	0.2	0.2
Sanitation	0.3	0.3	0.3	0.3
Natural Resources	1.8	1.6	1.7	1.1
Parks and Recreation	0.1	0.1	0.1	0.2
Housing and Urban Renewal	0.2	0.2	0.2	0.3
Veterans Services	1.2	0.8	0.8	0.5
Financial Administration				0.3
General Control	0.6	0.5	0.6	0.3
Interest	1.7	1.4	1.8	1.7
Other	1.1	1.1	1.4	1.7
Social Security	2.4	2.3	2.3	4.4

in Table 9-3. Obivously all private needs are given priority over all public needs, since total public expenditures of federal, state, and national governments are less than one-third of the gross national product. This is what one might reasonably expect in a private enterprise, capitalist society.

The preference for private over public enterprise is not merely a myth. Americans have an abiding faith in private enterprise, and it is reflected in the allocation of national income in the public and private sectors of the economy. Over two-thirds of the GNP originates in the private sector. Traditionally expenditures in the *private* sector—whether for tobacco, alcohol, soda pop, automobiles, or housing—have been looked upon favorably in terms of economic growth. But expenditures in the *public* sector are generally supposed to be as low as possible. Most Americans approve of frugality in government spending, budgetary "austerity," and the elimination of "frills"; they prefer a government as small and as close to the people as possible. Yet there have been some who have challenged this balance of private over public allocation of resources. John Kenneth Galbraith wrote:

> The family which takes its mauve and cerise, air-conditioned, power-steered, and power-braked automobile out for a tour passes through

cities that are badly paved, made hideous by litter, blighted buildings, billboards, and posts for wires that should long since have been put underground. They pass into a countryside that has been rendered largely invisible by commercial art. . . . They picnic on exquisitely packaged food from a portable icebox by a polluted stream and go on to spend the night at a park which is a menace to public health and morals. Just before dozing off on an air mattress, beneath a nylon tent, amid the stench of decaying refuse, they may reflect vaguely on the curious unevenness of their blessings.[3]

Among public needs, national defense takes highest priority, especially if one considers veterans' benefits, space research, and interest on the national debt. America's *total* defense costs have recently run between 10 and 12 percent of the GNP; this is one of the highest defense efforts in the world. The only nations in the world which have placed any higher priority on defense in recent times are those which have been at war—Israel, the Arab states, and Vietnam.

Education is the nation's second largest public undertaking. Although education is a very small proportion of the federal government's budget, it is the largest spending item of state and local governments. Approximately 5 percent of the GNP is devoted to education.

Social security has been the fastest-growing large item of public spending. The Social Security Act was passed in 1935 providing for compulsory insurance against old age, death, dependency, disability,

[3] John K. Galbraith, *The Affluent Society* (Boston: Houghton Mifflin, 1958), p. 253.

Jeeps stand in field in Philadelphia awaiting shipment overseas. Wide World Photos

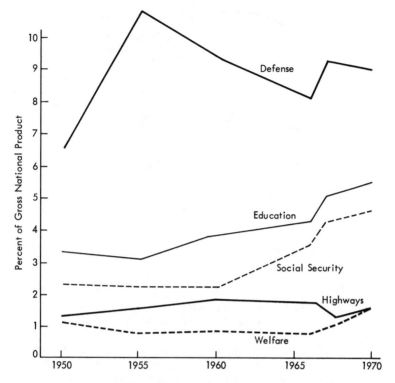

FIG. 9-3   NATIONAL PRIORITIES: EXPENDITURES OF ALL GOVERNMENTS BY FUNCTION AS A PROPORTION OF GROSS NATIONAL PRODUCT

and unemployment. In 1965, Medicare was added to the social security program to protect aged persons against costs of medical care. Today social insurance programs constitute over 4 percent of the GNP.

Welfare costs are also rising, not only in absolute dollars but also as a percentage of the Gross National Product. Today over 6 percent of the nation's population is on welfare rolls, and direct welfare costs exceed 1 percent of the GNP. If "welfare" is more broadly defined to include public health and hospital services, public housing, and social security, as well as direct welfare costs, the total is nearly 8 percent of the GNP.

Note that some items that are the object of a great deal of political rhetoric actually receive little priority in the allocation of national resources. Despite concerns over the quality of urban life, less than three-tenths of 1 percent of the GNP is devoted to government housing and urban renewal efforts. Regarding the popular issue of environmental control, it is interesting to note that only two-tenths of 1 percent of GNP is devoted to parks and recreation and 1.3 percent to na-

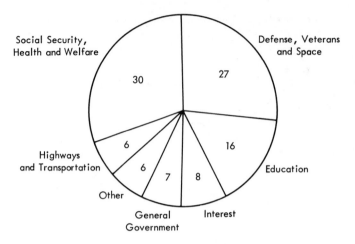

FIG. 9-4 TOTAL GOVERNMENT SPENDING BY MAJOR CATEGORY
(Figures show percentage of total)

tional resources (and this latter category is a very broad one including many expenditures that do not contribute to the quality of the environment).

If we merge broad categories of government spending, and again combine the spending of federal, state, and local government, we observe that the major objects of government spending are social security, health, and welfare; defense, veterans, and space; education; interest; general government; and highways and transportation (see Figure 9-4).

PUBLIC POLICY AND THE FEDERAL SYSTEM

At the beginning of the twentieth century, most government activity was carried on at the *local* level. The local tradition in American government rests on historical fact as well as cherished belief. Table 9-4 reveals that local governments once made about 59 percent of all government expenditures, compared to 35 percent for the federal government and 6 percent for state governments. Yet by the 1970s centralization in the American federal system had proceeded to the point where local governments were spending only 22 percent of all government expenditures, compared to 66 percent for the federal government and 12 percent for state governments.

Wars and the Depression had a great deal to do with the shift away from local reliance in American government. During national emergencies, both foreign and domestic, Americans have turned to the federal government for help. After the emergency, federal activity decreases somewhat in relation to state and local activity, but federal

TABLE 9-4 A Comparison of the Expenditures of Federal, State, and Local Governments Over Seven Decades

	Per Capita Public Expenditures [3]			Percentages of Total General Expenditures [3]		
	Federal [1]	State [2]	Local [2]	Federal [1]	State [2]	Local [2]
1902	$ 8	$ 1	$ 13	35%	6%	59%
1913	10	3	21	31	9	60
1922	33	9	41	40	11	49
1927	29	12	53	31	13	56
1932	32	16	50	34	16	50
1936	66	19	46	50	14	36
1940	75	23	57	48	15	37
1944	718	22	51	91	3	7
1946	472	27	62	82	6	12
1948	238	47	90	64	13	23
1950	294	57	110	64	12	24
1952	448	60	125	71	9	20
1955	440	72	155	66	11	23
1960	522	105	210	62	13	25
1962	584	114	236	63	12	25
1967	643	136	304	65	12	23
1970	968	170	323	66	12	22

[1] Figures include social security and trust fund expenditures.
[2] State payments to local governments are shown as local government expenditures; federal grants-in-aid are shown as federal expenditures.
[3] Figures may not total correctly because of rounding.

activity never returns to the precrisis level. Thus, during World War I and World War II, and the Korean and Vietnamese Wars, the federal government increased its percentage of total government activity, while local and state government percentages declined. Since the federal government has the primary responsibility for national defense, we would expect this to occur during wartime. But the federal government also expands its activities in response to domestic crisis—during the 1930s federal expenditures passed those of all local governments.

While foreign and domestic crises have brought about increasing centralization in American government, we noted that expanded federal activity has not come at the expense of state and local activity. Federal power and state-local power are not at the opposite ends of a seesaw; the growth of federal power has not necessarily curtailed the power of states and localities. National activity has expanded in the twentieth century but so has the activity of state and local governments.

The extent of centralization of government activity in the American federal system varies widely according to policy area (see Table 9-5). In the fields of national defense, space research, and postal service, the federal government assumes almost exclusive responsibility. In all other fields state and local governments share responsibility and costs with the federal government. State and local governments assume the major share of the costs of education, highways, health and hospitals,

TABLE 9-5   Federal and State-Local Shares of Expenditures
by Policy Areas, 1927-1967

	1927		1938		1967	
	Federal [1]	State and Local	Federal [1]	State and Local	Federal [1]	State and Local
National Defense	100	0	100	0	100	0
Space Research	100	0	100	0	100	0
Postal Service	100	0	100	0	100	0
Education	1	99	6	94	10	90
Highways	1	99	23	77	29	71
Welfare	6	94	13	87	58	42
Health and Hospitals	18	82	19	81	33	67
Natural Resources	31	69	81	19	80	20

[1] Federal grants-in-aid are shown as federal expenditures.

sanitation, fire and police protection. Welfare costs are being shifted to
the federal government. The federal government assumes the major
share of the costs of natural resource development and social security.

Over the years, the federal government has steadily increased its
share of responsibility in every important policy area of American
government. (See Figure 9-5.) Many feel that the date 1913, when the

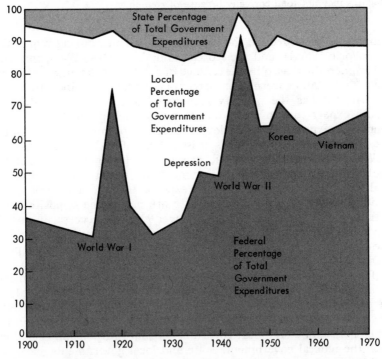

FIG. 9-5   Federal, State, and Local Proportions of Total Governmental Expenditures

Sixteenth Amendment gave the federal government the power to tax incomes directly, was the beginning of a new era in American federalism. Congress had been given the power to tax and spend for the general welfare in Article I of the Constitution. But the Sixteenth Amendment helped to shift the balance of financial power from the states to Washington when it gave Congress the power to tax the incomes of corporations and individuals on a progressive basis. The income tax gave the federal government the power to raise large sums of money, which it proceeded to spend for the general welfare as well as for defense. It is not coincidence that the first major grant-in-aid programs (agricultural extension in 1914, highways in 1916, vocational education in 1917, and public health in 1918) all came shortly after the inauguration of the federal income tax.

The federal "grant-in-aid" has become the principle instrument for the increased involvement of the federal government in domestic policy areas. The great depression of the 1930s put pressure on the national government to use its tax and spending powers in a wide variety of areas formerly reserved to states and communities. The federal government initiated grant-in-aid programs to states and communities for public assistance, unemployment compensation, employment services, public housing, urban renewal, and so on; it also expanded federal grants-in-aid programs in highways, vocational education, and rehabilitation. The inadequacy of state and local revenue systems to meet the financial crises created by the Depression contributed significantly to the development of cooperative federalism. States and communities called upon the superior taxing powers of the national government to assist them in many fields in which the federal government had not previously involved itself.

FEDERAL GRANTS-IN-AID

Today grant-in-aid programs are the single most important source of federal influence over state policy. Approximately one-sixth of all state and local government revenues are from federal grants. This money is paid out through a staggering number and variety of programs. There are probably 500 different federal grant programs in existence today. So numerous and diverse are federal aid programs that a substantial information gap surrounds the availability, purpose, and requirements of these programs. Learning about the availability of these programs and mastering the art of grant application places a serious burden on state and local officials. Moreover, the problem of program coordination, not only between levels of government, but also among federal agencies, is a truly difficult one.

Federal grants are available in nearly every major category of state and local government activity. Federal grants may be obtained to assist in everything from the celebration of the American Revolution Bicen-

TABLE 9-6 FEDERAL GRANTS-IN-AID AND STATE-LOCAL FINANCES

	Total Federal Grants-in-Aid in Millions of Dollars	Federal Grants as a Percentage of State-Local Revenue
1902	7	*
1913	12	*
1922	118	2.1%
1927	123	1.6
1932	232	2.9
1938	800	7.2
1940	945	8.1
1944	954	6.8
1948	1,861	8.6
1950	2,486	9.7
1955	3,131	8.3
1960	6,974	11.6
1962	7,871	11.3
1967	15,366	14.0
1970	25,029	18.0
1972 (est.)	34,288	20.0

* Less than 1 percent.

tennial to the drainage of abandoned mines, riot control, and school milk. However, federal aid for welfare and highways accounts for over two-thirds of total federal aid money.

Ira Sharkansky has observed that the history of federal grant-in-aid programs reflects in microcosm the contemporary policy orientations of American governments.[4]

Prior to World War I, federal grants reflected the concerns of a rural, agricultural society—the Smith-Level Act of 1914 establishing agricultural extension programs; the Smith-Hughes Act of 1917 supporting vocational education with an emphasis on agriculture and home economics; and the early Federal Aid Highway Act designed to assist in the construction of farm-to-market, rural roads. In the 1930s federal grant programs, particularly the public assistance sections of the Social Security Act of 1935, attempted to alleviate the hardships of the Depression. Public housing became an object of federal assistance in the Housing Act of 1937. In the 1940s and 1950s, federal aid programs assumed labels which made them appear to be part of the nation's defense effort; e.g., the National Defense Highway Act of 1956; the National Defense Education Act of 1957. In the 1960s the emphasis of grant-in-aid legislation was on poverty, education, and urban affairs: the Elementary and Secondary Education Act of 1965 with aid for "poverty impacted" schools; the Economic Opportunity Act of 1964 with federal money to assist communities in fighting poverty; and the Model Cities Program in 1966.

[4] Ira Sharkansky, *The Politics of Taxing and Spending* (New York: Bobbs-Merrill, 1969), pp. 155-56.

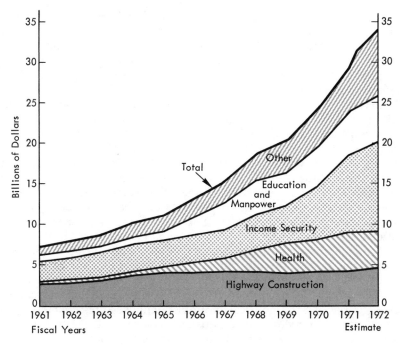

FIG. 9-6   FEDERAL AID TO STATE AND LOCAL GOVERNMENTS

Not only have federal grants-in-aid to the states expanded rapidly in terms of the numbers of programs and the dollar amounts involved, but states and communities have also come to *rely* on the national government for an ever-increasing share of their total revenues (see Table 9-6). Prior to the New Deal, federal grants amounted to only 2 or 3 percent of total state-local revenue. The New Deal itself, in spite of all of its innovations in federal aid programs, raised this proportion only to 7 or 8 percent. State-local reliance on federal aid has continued to increase over the last two decades, from 8 percent over total state-local revenues in 1946 to over 17 percent today. More than one-third of *state* revenues are derived from federal sources. Thus, no matter how it is measured—increased numbers of programs, increased dollar amounts, increased reliance by states and communities—federal aid has grown into a major influence over state and local governmental activity.

There are several reasons for this growth of federal aid.[5] First of all, these grants permit the federal government to single out and support those state and local government services in which it has a

[5] See George F. Break, *Intergovernmental Fiscal Relations in the United States* (Washington, D.C.: Brookings Institution, 1967); Deil S. Wright, *Federal Grants-in-Aid: Perspectives and Alternatives* (Washington, D.C.: American Enterprise Institute, 1968).

particular interest. Grants permit the national government to set national goals and priorities in all levels of government without formally altering the federal structure. Thus, as problems of public assistance, urban renewal, highway construction, education, poverty, and so on, acquire national significance, they can be dealt with by the application of national resources.

Second, the grant-in-aid system helps to overcome the inadequacies of state-local revenue resources. Contrary to the political rhetoric charging the states with fiscal conservatism, the states have actually demonstrated a great deal of fiscal courage, effort, and ingenuity in trying to cope with money problems. In the last two decades state-local expenditures have risen at a faster *rate* than federal expenditures. These fiscal efforts have meant increased income or sales tax rates in nearly every state in the past ten years as well as increased liquor and gasoline tax rates. Yet in spite of these near Herculean efforts by states, their fiscal problems continue to multiply.

States and communities must raise revenues and at the same time carry on interstate and inter-local competition for industry and wealth. While the influence of tax considerations on industrial locations decisions may be overstated by most law makers, this overstatement itself is part of the political lore at statehouses and courthouses that operates to impede revenue raising. Not only do competititve considerations inhibit state-local taxing efforts but they also tend to push them in regressive directions.

Debates over finances in state capitals invariably include references to the "pre-emption" of income taxes by the national government. There are no compelling economic reasons for the argument that the federal income tax pre-empts this source of revenue for the states (particularly since the federal government permits the deduction of state income taxes from total taxable income). Nonetheless in the minds of most state lawmakers and probably in the minds of their constituents as well, there is the belief that the federal government already takes all of the income taxes they wish to pay. This means states are stuck with sales taxes and localities with property taxes, and, in contrast to income taxes, these taxes respond sluggishly to rises in the GNP.

Another argument on behalf of federal grants-in-aid centers about the greater progessivity of the federal tax structure. If a particular government program is funded through state and local taxes, it is funded on a tax structure that is regressive or only mildly progressive; but if it is funded out of federal taxes, it is funded on a more progressive basis. This may help to explain the "liberal" predisposition for federal financial involvement.

Finally, grants-in-aid provide an opportunity for the national government to insure a uniform level of public service throughout the nation as a minimum or foundation program. For example, federal grants-in-aid to help achieve equality in educational opportunity in all parts of the nation, or help to insure a minimum level of existence for the poverty-stricken regardless of where they live.[6] This aspect of federal policy assumes that in some parts of the nation, state and local governments are unable, or perhaps unwilling to devote their resources to raising public service levels to minimum national standards.

Whenever the national government contributes financially to state or local programs, state and local officials have less freedom of choice than they would have without federal aid. They must adhere to federal standards or "guidelines," which invariably accompany federal grants-in-aid, if they are to receive their federal money. The national government gives money to states and communities only if they are willing to meet conditions specified by Congress. Often Congress delegates to federal agencies the power to establish the "conditions" that are attached to grants.

No state is required to accept a federal grant-in-aid. In other words, states are not required to meet federal standards or guidelines which are set forth as conditions for federal aid because they have the alternative of rejecting the federal money—and they have sometimes done so. But it is very difficult for states and communities to resist the pressure to accept federal money.

In short, through the power to tax and spend for the general welfare, and through "conditions" attached to federal grants-in-aid, the national government has come to exercise great powers in many areas orginally "reserved" to the states—highways, welfare, education, housing, natural resources, employment, health, and so on. Of course, federal grants-in-aid have enabled many states and communities to provide necessary and desirable services that they could not have afforded otherwise. Federal guidelines have often improved the standard of administration, personnel policies, and fiscal practices in states and communities. More importantly, federal guidelines have helped to insure that states and communities will not engage in racial discrimination in federally aided programs.

---

[6] The meaning of "equalization" in federal policy is more complex than it appears at first glance. Basically, equalization means some policy recognition of differences in the states' relative capacities to raise funds from their own resources, in order to achieve more uniform program standards throughout the nation. This means, first of all, equal federal grants per unit of need, whether the unit of need is defined as pupils, poverty-stricken families, ill-housed families, medically indigent, aged, etc. But exclusive reliance upon equal allocations per unit of need is likely to mean unequal program expenditures when state-local matching funds are required. This is because a grant offering Mississippi $2 per person which has to be matched on a 50-50 basis requires a larger state tax effort relative to personal income from Mississippi citizens than a similar $2 per person grant offered to New York's wealthier citizens. In view of unequal tax resources of the state, grants must take into account both program needs and fiscal resources. Equalization policy must also include a deliberate varying of the amount of federal funds directly with program needs and inversely with fiscal resources. Finally, equalization policy must also consider the minimum program level desired; then larger amounts of federal funds must go in support of minimum program levels and lesser amounts in support of programs exceeding minimum levels.

SOME CONCLUSIONS ABOUT
GOVERNMENT SPENDING

Government expenditures provide an overview of American public policy. Our analysis of government spending in this century suggests the following general propositions:

1. Government activity has grown in relation both to the size of the population and to the economy. Government activity now accounts for about one-third of all economic activity in the United States.
2. Government expenditures as a proportion of all economic activity in the nation remain stable over long periods of time, but they spurt upward in response to wars and depressions. When these crises subside, government expenditures associated with them decline somewhat, but stabilize at levels higher than before the crisis.
3. War conditions citizens to tolerate major increases in government activity. During war, government domestic spending declines; but after a war, domestic spending displaces defense spending and achieves a higher plateau than before the war.
4. Private expenditures exceed public expenditures in the United States by a two-to-three margin. The balance in favor of the private sector of American society reflects a preference for private over public enterprise.
5. Among public expenditures national defense takes highest priority. Education is the nation's second largest public undertaking. Social security and welfare costs are growing rapidly.
6. Wars and depressions have helped to shift responsibilities from local and state governments to the national government. However, national power and state-local power are not at opposite ends of a seesaw; national activity has expanded rapidly in the twentieth century, but so has the activity of state and local governments.
7. The national government assumes exclusive responsibility for national defense and related activity, international affairs, space research, social security, and the postal service. Welfare expenditures have been gradually shifted to the national government. States and local government retain the primary responsibility for education, highways, and health and hospital care, although national involvement in these fields is growing.
8. Federal grants-in-aid to state and local governments have been the principal instrument of the national government's involvement in domestic policy areas. These federal areas payments now make up nearly one-fifth of all state and local government revenue.

BIBLIOGRAPHY

BREAK, GEORGE F., *Intergovernmental Fiscal Relations in the United States.* Washington, D.C.: Brookings Institution, 1967.

MOSHER, FREDERICK C. and ORVILLE F. POLAND, *The Costs of American Governments.* New York: Dodd, Mead, 1964.

SHARKANSKY, IRA, *The Politics of Taxing and Spending.* New York: Bobbs-Merrill, 1969.

National Urban Coalition, *Counterbudget.* New York: Praeger, 1971.

BUDGETS AND TAXES:
incrementalism at work

Too often we think of budgeting as the dull province of clerks and statisticians. Nothing could be more mistaken. The budget is the single most important policy statement of any government. The expenditure side of the budget tells us "who gets what" in public funds, and the revenue side of the budget tells us "who pays the cost." There are few government activities or programs which do not require an expenditure of funds, and no public funds may be spent without budgetary authorization. Deciding what goes into a budget (the budgetary process) provides a mechanism for reviewing government programs, assessing their cost, relating them to financial resources, making choices among alternative expenditures, and determining the financial effort that a government will expend on these programs. Budgets determine what programs and policies are to be increased, decreased, lapsed, initiated, or renewed. The budget lies at the heart of public policy.[1]

INCREMENTALISM IN BUDGET-MAKING

The incremental model of public policy making is particularly well suited to assist in understanding the budgeting process. While the

[1] See Aaron Wildavsky, *The Politics of the Budgetary Process* (Boston: Little, Brown, 1964).

systems model helps to identify underlying environmental force affecting overall *levels* of public taxing and spending, the *process* by which decisions are reached on taxes and expenditures appears to conform to an incremental pattern. Budgetmaking is *conservative, fragmented, nonprogrammatic*, and *political.* Budgeting is conservative because decision makers generally consider last year's expenditures as a base. Active consideration of budget proposals is generally narrowed to new items or requested increases over last year's base. The attention of governors and legislators, and mayors and councils, is focused on a narrow range of increases or decreases in a budget. A budget is almost never reviewed as a whole every year, in the sense of reconsidering the value of existing programs. Departments are seldom required to defend or explain budget requests, which do *not* exceed current appropriations; but requested increases in appropriations require extensive explanation, and they are most subject to downward revision by higher political officials.

Budgeting is very *political.* As Aaron Wildavsky was told by a federal executive, "It's not what's in your estimates, but how good a politician you are that matters." [2] Being a good politician involves (1) the cultivation of a good base of support for your requests among the public at large and among people served by the agency; (2) the development of interest, enthusiasm, and support for your program among top political figures and legislative leaders, and (3) skill in following strategies that exploit your opportunities to the maximum. Informing the public and your clientele of the full benefit of the services they receive from the agency may increase the intensity with which they will support the agency's request. If possible, the agency should inspire its clientele to contact governors, mayors, legislators, and councilmen, and to help work for the agency's request. This is much more effective than the agency trying to promote for its own requests.

Budgeting is also quite *fragmented.* In theory, the budget office is supposed to bring together budget requests and fit them into a coherent whole, while at the same time relating them to revenue estimates. But often budget offices do little more than staple together the budget requests of individual departments, and it is very difficult for a governor or mayor, and almost impossible for a legislature or council, to view the total policy impact of a budget. Wildavsky explains that the fragmented character of the budgetary process helps to secure agreement to the budget as well as reduce the burden of calculation. Some budgets must be agreed upon by the executive and the legislature if the government is going to continue to function at all, and this pressure to agree often means that conflicts over programs must go unresolved in a budget. Calculations are made in small segments, often by legislative subcommittees, and must be accepted by the legislature

[2] *Ibid.*, p. 19.

as a whole. If each subcommittee challenged the result of the others, conflict might be so great that no budget would ever be passed. It is much easier to agree on a small addition or decrease to a single program than it is to compare the worth of one program to that of all others.

Finally, budgeting is *nonprogrammatic*. For reasons that accountants have so far kept to themselves, an agency budget typically lists expenditures under the ambiguous phrases: "personnel services," "contractual services," "travel," "supplies," "equipment." It is impossible to tell from such a listing exactly what programs the agency is spending its money on. Such a budget obscures policy decisions by hiding programs behind meaningless phrases. Even if these categories are broken down into line items (for example, under "personnel services," the line item budget might say, "John Doaks, Assistant Administrator, $15,000"), it is still next to impossible to identify the costs of various programs. Reform-oriented administrators have called for budgeting by programs for many years; this would present budgetary requests in terms of end products or program packages, like aid to dependent children, vocational rehabilitation, administration of fair employment practices laws, highway patroling, and so on. Chief executives generally favor program budgeting because it will give them greater control over the policy. But very often administrative agencies are hostile toward program budgeting—it certainly adds to the cost of bookkeeping, and many agencies feel insecure in describing precisely what it is they do. Wildavsky points out that there are some political functions served by *non*program budgeting. He notes that:

> Agreement comes much more readily when the items in dispute can be treated in dollars instead of basic differences in policy. Calculating budgets in monetary increments facilitates bargaining and logrolling. It becomes possible to swap an increase here for a decrease there or for an increase elsewhere without always having to consider the ultimate desirability of the programs blatantly in competition. . . . Party ties might be disruptive of agreement if they focused attention on policy differences between the two political persuasions. . . . Consider by contrast some likely consequences of program budgeting. The practice of focusing attention on programs means that policy implications can hardly be avoided. The gains and the losses for the interests involved become far more evident to all concerned. Conflict is heightened by the stress on the policy differences and increased still further by an inbuilt tendency to an all-or-nothing, "yes" or "no" response to the policy in dispute. The very concept of program packages suggests that the policy in dispute is indivisible, that the appropriate response is to be for or against rather than bargaining for a little more or a little less. Logrolling and bargaining are hindered because it is much easier to trade increments conceived in monetary terms than it is to give in on basic policy differences. Problems of calculation are vastly increased by the necessity, if program budgeting is to have meaning, of evaluating the

desirability of every program as compared to all others, instead of the traditional practice of considering budgeting in relatively independent segments.[3]

Program budgeting also provides the opportunity for the introduction of performance standards in the budgeting process. "Performance budgeting" usually involves the designation of some unit of service, for example, one pupil, one hosiptal patient, or one welfare recipient, and the establishment of standards of service and costs based upon a single unit of service. A common example of performance budgeting is found in school systems, where pupils are designated as a basic unit of service, and standards for numbers of teachers, supplies and materials, auxiliary personnel, building floor space, and many other cost items are calculated on the basis of the number of pupils to be served. Thus, standards may allocate teachers on the basis of one to 25 students, or a full time principal for every 250 students, or a psychologist for every 1,000 pupils, or $20 worth of supplies for every student, and so on. These formulas are used to determine the allocation of resources at budget time. One political consequence of the use of formulas in performance budgeting is the centralization of budgetary decision making. Departments are merely asked to provide the number of pupils, or patients, or recipients, or other units of service they expect to serve in the coming fiscal year. A central unit of budget analysis then determines allocations through the application of formulas to the service estimates provided by the departments. Many departments, accustomed to less bureaucratic procedures, feel that the use of formulas is mechanical and inflexible. But it is not surprising in a large and complex bureaucracy to understand the search for equitable patterns in the distribution of resources leading to the use of formulas applied throughout the system. Once a formula has been established, however, it is often difficult to change or adjust the formula from one year to the next. Performance budgeting places great power in the hands of the staff personnel budget officers who devise the formulas. Performance budgeting is generally favored by economy-minded groups, particularly businessmen who are familiar with the application of unit cost procedures to manufacturing enterprise.

THE FORMAL BUDGETARY PROCESS

It is difficult to imagine that, prior to 1921, the President played no direct role in the budget process. The Secretary of the Treasury compiled the estimates of the individual agencies, and these were sent, without revision, to Congress for its consideration. The Budget and Accounting Act of 1921 provided for an executive budget giving the President responsibility for budget formulation, and thereby giving

[3] *Ibid.*, p. 136-38.

him important means of controlling federal policy. The Bureau of the Budget, located in the Executive Office, has the key responsibility for budget preparation. In addition to this major task, the Bureau has related responsibilities for improving the organization and management of the executive agencies, for coordinating the extensive statistical services of the federal government, for analyzing and reviewing proposed legislation to determine its effect on administration and finance.

Preparation of the federal budget starts more than a year before the beginning of the fiscal year for which it is intended (see Figure 10-1). The Bureau of the Budget, after preliminary consultation with the executive agencies and in accord with presidential policy, develops targets or ceilings within which the agencies are encouraged to build their requests. This work begins a full sixteen to eighteen months before the beginning of the fiscal year for which the budget is being prepared. In other words, work will begin in January or March, 1974, on budget for the fiscal year beginning July 1, 1975, and ending June 30, 1976.

Budget materials and instructions go to the agencies with the request that the forms be completed and returned to the Bureau. This request is followed by about three months' arduous work by agency-employed budget officers, department heads, and the "grass roots" bureaucracy, in Washington and out in the field. Budget officials at the bureau level check requests from the smaller units, compare them with the previous year's estimates, hold conferences, and make adjustments. The process of checking, reviewing, modifying, and discussing is repeated on a larger scale at the department level.

The heads of agencies are expected to submit their completed requests to the Bureau of the Budget by mid-September or early October. Occasionally a schedule of "over ceiling" items (requests above the suggested ceilings) will be included.

With the requests of the spending agencies at hand, the Bureau begins its own budget review. Hearings are given each agency. Top agency officials support their requests as convincingly as possible. On rare occasions dissatisfied agencies may ask the budget director to bring their cases to the President.

In December the President, with his budget director, will devote time to the document which by now is approaching its final stages of assembly. They and their staffs will "blue pencil," revise, and make last minute changes, as well as prepare the President's message which accompanies the budget to Congress. After the budget is in legislative hands, the President may recommend further alterations as needs dictate.

Although the completed document includes a revenue plan with general estimates for taxes and other income, it is primarily an expenditure budget. Revenue and tax policy staff work centers in the Treasury Department and not in the Bureau of the Budget.

Preparation Stage

| Departments and Agencies | Bureau of the Budget | President |

March

Estimates revenues, forecasts expenditures

Sets forth general tax and spending policies

Issues instructions and guidelines for preparing agency

June

Preparation of agency requests

Compiles total expenditure requests and compares with revenue estimates; Makes recommendations regarding requests

Discusses major program areas with Budget Director and others. Establishes guidelines and planning figures

August

Advises agencies of reductions; allocates planned figures

Revises figures to meet planned figures; submits formal requests

October

Holds hearings, decides specific questions; prepares final budget message

Revises and approves budget message, transmits to Congress

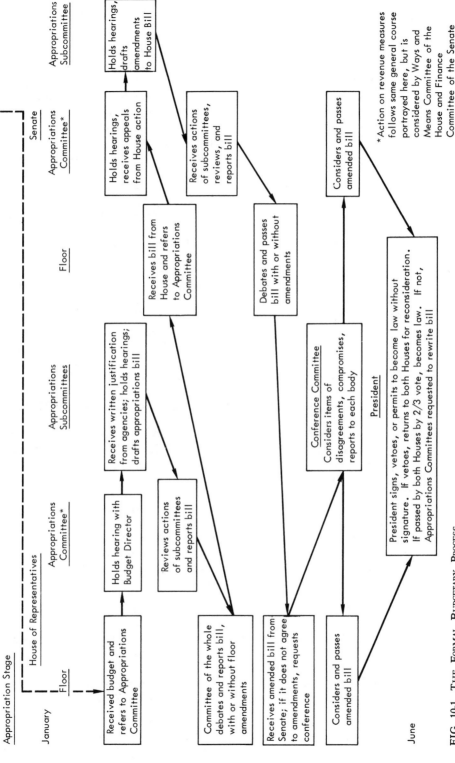

FIG. 10-1 THE FORMAL BUDGETARY PROCESS

Congress has two responsibilities in making money available for spending—authorization and appropriation. Authorization in a technical sense refers to the substantive legislation which establishes a program and enables an agency to spend money when appropriations are made. An appropriations measure, on the other hand, allows an agency to obligate the government to pay out funds and spend specified amounts. Before authorization legislation goes to the House or Senate floor, it is considered by appropriate program committees (for example, Aeronautical and Space Sciences, Education, and Labor, or Interior and Insular Affairs).

Consideration of and recommendations on appropriations measures are functions of the appropriations committees in both houses. Committee work in the House of Representatives is usually more thorough than it is in the Senate; the committee in the upper house tends to be a "court of appeal" for agencies against House action. Each committee, moreover, has about ten largely independent subcommittees to review the requests of a particular agency or a group of related functions. Specific appropriations bills are taken up by the subcommittees in hearings. Departmental officers are called to the Hill to answer questions on the conduct of their programs and to defend their requests for the next fiscal year. Lobbyists and other witnesses testify.

The subcommittees are of primary importance in congressional consideration of the budget. Since neither Congress nor the full committees have the time or understanding necessary to conduct adequate reviews, the subcommittee has become the locus of congressional budget analysis. Several factors contribute to its preeminent position. Each subcommittee specializes in a relatively small fraction of the total budget. It considers the same agencies and functions year after year. The long tenure characteristic of the membership of the prestigious appropriations committees guarantees decades of experience in dealing with particular programs. Although the work of the subcommittee is reviewed by the full committee, in practice it is routinely accepted with the expenditure of little time and debate.

The House Committee on Ways and Means and the Senate Finance Committee are the major instruments of Congress for consideration of *taxing* measures. Through long history and jealous pride they have maintained complete formal independence of the appropriations committees, further fragmenting legislative consideration of the budget.

In terms of aggregates, Congress does not regularly make great changes in the executive budget, rarely changing it more than 5 percent. The House normally cuts appropriations, the Senate restores a part, and the inevitable conference committee arrives at an amount close to what the President requested.

The budget is approved by Congress in the form of appropriations bills, from twelve to fifteen of them, each ordinarily providing for several departments and agencies. The number of revenue measures is smaller. As with other bills that pass Congress, the President has ten days to approve or veto appropriations legislation. He lacks the power to veto items in bills, and only rarely exercises his right to veto appropriations bills in their entirety.

Once the budgeted funds are authorized, controls over their expenditure shift to the executive establishment, although not immediately to the departments and agencies. The Bureau of the Budget may establish reserves against appropriations in order to provide for emergencies and to effect economies. The Bureau, after consultation with the agencies, apportions the appropriations, usually on a quarterly basis. A major purpose of apportionment is to prevent an agency from depleting its appropriation before the end of the fiscal year.

Allotment, a second step in federal budget execution, is a device by which the budget officer of each agency allocates funds to bureaus and the lesser units on a monthly or quarterly basis.

THE STABILITY OF PUBLIC POLICY

The most important influence over the size and content of this year's budget is last year's budget. One of the reasons for this is the continuing nature of most governmental programs and outlays. The greatest part of a government budget represents expenditures which are mandated by previous programs—for example, commitments to recipients of social security, commitments to veterans, interest which must be paid on the national debt, the maintenance of a defense establishment, and so on. Another reason for using last year's budget as a base is the cost that would be involved in generally reconsidering every government program and expenditure. There is not enough time and energy for the decision-making process required to do this, so past programs are assumed to be worthy of continuation at previous levels of expenditures. It is considered a waste of time to view every budget as a blank slate and to ignore past experience. Moreover, the political instability which would ensue if every program were reevaluated every year would be too much for the system; every political battle which has ever been fought over a program would have to be fought all over again every year. Obviously, it is much more practical and political to accept past decisions on programs and expenditures as a base, and concentrate attention on new programs and increases and decreases in expenditures. For all of these reasons, the range of decision making actually confronting legislative and executive officials is really quite small, generally within ten percent of the previous budget!

Political scientist Richard Fenno calculated the percentage change of appropriation to federal agencies over a twelve year period and found that: in one-third of all cases appropriations were within 5 percent of the previous year's appropriations; in one-half of all cases, appropriations were within 10 percent of the previous year; and in three-quarters of all cases appropriations were within 30 percent of the previous year.[4]

The federal budget is such a giant, complex document that no one is really able to view it in a comprehensive, holistic fashion. In such complicated situations we are likely to use simplified rules of thumb to enable us to find satisfactory solutions. Completely rational approaches are simply not possible when the problem is as complicated and multifaceted as the federal budget. Davis, Dempster, and Wildavsky were able to identify two simple rules of thumb which appeared to explain by far the greatest portion of budgetary allocations in any year:[5]

1. The agency request for a certain year is a fixed mean percentage of the Congressional appropriation for that agency in the previous year plus a random variable for that year.
2. The Congressional approximation for an agency in a certain year is a fixed mean percentage of the agency's request in that year plus a variable representing a deviation from the usual relationship between the Congress and the agency for the previous year.

Less than 15 percent of all of the budgetary decisions studied deviated significantly from these rules or from related propositions.

In a study of budgetary decisions at the state level (Illinois) Thomas Anton was able to identify several interesting informal practices which grow up among agency heads who understand the incremental nature of budgeting:[6]

1. Spend all of your appropriation. A failure to use up an appropriation indicates that the full amount was unnecessary in the first place, which in turn implies that your budget should be cut next year.
2. Never request a sum less than your current appropriation. It is easier to find ways to spend up to current appropriation levels than it is to explain why you want a reduction. Besides, a reduction indicates your program is not growing and this is an embarrassing admission to most government administrators.
3. Put top priority programs into the basic budget, that is, that part of the budget which is within current appropriation levels. Budget offices, governors and mayors, and legislative bodies will seldom challenge programs which appear to be part of existing operations.

[4] Richard F. Fenno, *The Power of the Purse: Appropriations Politics in Congress* (Boston: Little, Brown, 1966).
[5] Otto A. Davis, M. A. H. Dempster, and Aaron Wildavsky, "A Theory of the Budgetary Process," *American Political Science Review*, Vol. 60 (September 1966), 529-47.
[6] Thomas J. Anton, *The Politics of State Expenditures in Illinois* (Urbana: University of Illinois Press, 1966).

4. Increases that are desired should be made to appear small and should appear to grow out of existing operations. The appearance of a fundamental change in a budget should be avoided.
5. Give the budget office, chief executive, and the legislature something to cut. Normally it is desirable to submit requests for substantial increases in existing programs and many requests for new programs, in order to give higher political authorities something to cut. This enables them to "save" the public untold millions of dollars and justify their claim to promoting "economy" in government. Giving them something to cut also diverts attention away from the basic budget with its vital programs.

Anton also examined the respective roles of the governor, state agencies, the budgetary commission, and the legislature in budget making. Agency heads generally request much more than last year's appropriation. The executive budgetary commission makes heavy cuts into the agencies' requests. The governor makes additional requests to bring his budget into balance with revenues and avoid new taxes. But the general assembly restores many of the cuts in agency requests. The final budget is much higher than last year's appropriations, but much lower than agency requests.

THE FEDERAL BUDGET

The incremental nature of the federal government's budget is revealed in figures showing the percentage of federal expenditures going to various purposes over the years (see Table 10-1). These figures change, but they do not change much. The relative rankings of federal outlays by function remain the same. Despite a doubling of federal expenditures over a decade, the proportion of federal funds going to various purposes changes very little.

The major incremental changes over the decade have been the gradual drop off in defense spending as a proportion of the federal budget, and the steady increase in spending for health and welfare, including the social security program. The Vietnam War bolstered military spending from 1965 to 1969 but did not alter the long term decline in defense spending as a percentage of total federal outlays. Domestic spending has been increasing at a much faster pace than defense spending. The greatest increases have come in the area of health and welfare. Not only have public assistance payments and the costs of medical care for the poor skyrocketed, but the social security program has grown very rapidly. (Of course, social security taxes have been increased to cover the increased costs of social security; social security receipts were the fastest growing source of federal income over the decade.) The Elementary and Secondary Education Act of 1965 greatly increased federal outlays in education. The space program was important in the mid-1960s, but has been gradually cut back.

TABLE 10-1   Federal Expenditures Over a Decade

	1960	1965	1968	1970	1972 (est.)
	Billions of Dollars				
National Defense	45.9	49.6	80.5	79.4	77.5
International Affairs	3.0	4.3	4.6	4.1	4.0
Space Research	.4	5.1	4.7	3.9	3.1
Agriculture	3.3	4.8	5.9	6.3	5.8
Natural Resources	1.0	2.0	1.7	2.5	4.2
Commerce and Transportation	4.8	7.4	8.0	9.4	10.9
Community Develoment and Housing	1.0	.3	4.0	3.0	4.5
Health and Welfare	18.7	27.2	43.5	57.1	76.7
Education and Manpower	1.3	2.5	7.0	7.5	8.8
Veterans' Benefits	5.4	5.7	6.9	8.7	10.6
Interest	8.3	10.3	13.7	17.8	19.7
General Government	1.3	2.3	2.6	3.6	4.9
Total	92.2	118.4	178.8	197.9	230.7
	Percentage Distribution				
National Defense	48.8%	41.9%	45.0%	40.1%	33.8%
International Affairs	3.3	3.7	2.6	2.1	1.8
Space Research	0.4	4.3	2.6	2.0	1.4
Agriculture	3.6	4.1	3.3	3.2	2.5
Natural Resources	1.1	1.7	1.0	1.3	1.9
Commerce and Transportation	5.2	6.2	4.5	4.7	4.8
Community Development and Housing	1.1	0.2	2.3	1.5	2.0
Health and Welfare	20.3	23.0	24.3	28.8	33.5
Education and Manpower	1.4	2.1	3.9	3.8	3.8
Veterans' Benefits	5.9	4.8	3.8	4.4	4.6
Interest	9.0	8.7	7.7	9.0	8.6
General Government	1.4	1.9	1.5	1.8	2.2
Total	100.0	100.0	100.0	100.0	100.0

Source: Data derived from *The Budget of the United States Government, 1972* (Washington, D.C.: Government Printing Office, 1971).

TAX POLICY: WHO BEARS THE BURDENS OF GOVERNMENT?

The politics of taxation centers about the question of who actually bears the burden or "incidence" of a tax, that is, which income groups must devote the largest proportion of their income to taxes. Taxes that require high-income groups to pay a larger percentage of their incomes in taxes than low-income groups are said to be *progressive*, while taxes that take a larger share of the income of low-income groups are called *regressive*. Note that the *percentage of income* paid in taxes is the determining factor. Most taxes take more money from the rich than the poor, but a progressive or regressive tax is distinguished by the *percentages of income* taken from various income groups.

Progressive taxation is generally defended on the principle of ability to pay; that is, the assumption that high-income groups can afford to pay a larger percentage of their incomes into taxes at no more of a sacrifice than that required of lower-income groups to devote a smaller proportion of their income to taxation. This assumption is based on what economists call "marginal utility theory" as it applies to money: each additional dollar of income is slightly less valuable to an individual than preceding dollars (e.g., a $5,000 increase in the income of an individual already earning $100,000 is much less valuable to him than a $5,000 increase to an individual earning only $3,000 or an individual with no income). Hence, added dollars of income can be taxed at higher *rates* without violating equitable principles.

Opponents of progressive taxation generally assert that equity can only be achieved by taxing everyone at the *same* percentage of their income, regardless of the size of their income. Progressivity penalizes initiative, enterprise, and risk, and reduces incentives to expand and develop the nation's economy. Moreover, by taking incomes of high-income groups, governments are taking money that would otherwise go into business—investments, stocks, bonds, loans, etc.—and hence government is curtailing economic growth.

Regressive taxation is seldom defended as equitable in itself. However, some regressive taxes—notably the general sales tax—are such good revenue producers that they have many adherents. Sales taxes are less visible than income taxes; consumers generally consider them part of the price of an item. They can reach mobile populations whose income or property cannot be taxed by a state or local jurisdiction. When a major segment of the *national* tax structure is progressive, it is sometimes argued that some regressivity in state and local taxation is not inequitable in the light of the overall tax picture. It is also contended that inasmuch as low income groups benefit from many government services, they ought to share in their costs. Finally, opposition to sales taxation tends to reduce the overall amount of public funds available for public services. It can be argued that the benefits to low-income groups of increased government expenditures outweigh whatever burdens are imposed by the regressivity of sales taxation.

In considering the burden of incidence of a tax it is important not only to consider the *rate*, but also *economic behaviors* which affect burdens, and the problem of tax shifting. The *rate* simply states the percentage of the *base* (the object of the tax) which will go to taxes— for example, a 4 percent tax on all sales, or 10 percent tax on airline tickets, or a progressive sliding rate from 16 to 60 percent on income. A *rate* may appear to be neither progressive nor regressive, but economic behaviors may operate to make certain income groups more likely to bear the greater burden of the tax. For example, a 10 percent tax on jewelry or yachts does not have a progressive rate, but since high-income groups are presumed to spend a greater percentage of their income on these items than low-income groups, and therefore would spend a larger percentage on the tax on such items, the tax is presumed to be progressive. A 4 percent tax on all sales of consumer items is considered regressive because low-income groups devote a larger percentage, sometimes all, of their income to consumer items and hence bear the full brunt of the tax. High-income groups, which save or invest a sizeable proportion of their income and spend only part of it for consumer items, do not allocate the same proportion of their incomes to the payment of a sales tax as low-income groups. When the person taxed, such as a property-owner, can pass on the impact of the tax to other persons, such as renters, the burden of the tax is said to *shift*. Since poor people usually rent, and they must spend a large percentage of their income for housing, property taxes shifted onto them in the form of higher rents are generally considered regressive.

Over a decade ago, economist George Bishop calculated the burden by income class of various federal, state, and local taxes in America (see Table 10-2).[7] In general the federal tax structure is progressive, while state and local tax structures are regressive. The federal personal income tax is the only tax that is progressive throughout the entire range of incomes. This means that, in general, if a particular governmental function is financed through state and local revenue systems rather than federal revenues, it is being financed on a regressive rather than progressive revenue basis. Thus, much of the political debate over "federalism," that is, over which level of government, state or federal, should provide a particular governmental service, concerns the fact that the federal government tax structure is generally progressive, while the state and local tax structures are generally regressive. If the federal government pays for a particular governmental program, it is being paid for out of progressive taxes, whereas if state and local governments pay for a particular governmental program it is being paid for out of largely regressive taxes. There are many other factors to be considered in the allocation of responsibilities between states and the federal government, but the incidence of federal and state tax systems should not be overlooked. Bishop also estimates the incidence of the various types of state and local taxes. Property taxes are quite regressive. This conclusion is based on the assumption that the renter actually pays his property taxes through increased rentals levied by the landlord, and the further assumption that high income groups have more wealth in untaxed forms of property. Bishop has estimated that state and local taxes and excise taxes are generally regressive, but not as regressive as property taxes. The regressivity of sales taxation is based upon the assumption that low income groups must devote most, if not all, of their income to purchases, while high income groups devote larger shares of their income to savings. Many states exclude some of the necessities of life from sales taxation, such as packaged food bought in supermarkets, in order to reduce the burden of sales taxation on the poor. Yet, on the whole, sales taxation remains more regressive than income taxation.

[7] See George A. Bishop, "The Tax Burden by Income Class, 1958," *National Tax Journal*, 14 (March 1961).

TABLE 10-2 TAXES AS A PERCENTAGE OF TOTAL INCOME BY INCOME CLASS

Source	Under $2,000	$2,000– 3,999	$4,000– 5,999	$6,000– 7,999	$8,000– 9,999	$10,000– 14,999	$15,000 and Over	Total
			Family Personal-Income Class					
TOTAL TAXES	28.3%	26.3%	25.9%	25.7%	23.9%	24.0%	35.9%	27.4%
Federal Taxes:								
Individual Income	1.8	4.5	6.0	7.9	7.5	8.9	16.3	8.7
Corporation Income	3.8	3.2	3.0	3.0	3.0	3.6	8.8	4.3
Excises and Customs	4.0	3.3	3.1	3.0	2.9	2.7	1.8	2.8
Estate and Gift	.0	.0	.0	.0	.0	.0	1.7	.3
Social Insurance	6.1	4.9	4.3	3.3	2.7	2.0	1.2	3.1
Total	15.7	15.9	16.4	17.2	16.2	17.2	29.8	19.2
State and Local Taxes:								
Individual Income	.5	.8	.6	.2	.2	.3	.7	.5
Corporation Income	.2	.2	.1	.1	.2	.2	.4	.2
Excises and Sales	4.8	3.9	3.7	3.6	3.5	3.2	2.1	3.3
Estate and Gift	.0	.0	.0	.0	.0	.0	.5	.1
Property	5.9	4.6	4.1	3.7	3.4	2.8	2.1	3.5
Social Insurance	1.3	1.0	.9	.8	.6	.4	.2	.7
Total	12.6	10.4	9.5	8.5	7.8	6.9	6.1	8.2

Source: George A. Bishop, "The Tax Burden by Income Class, 1958," *National Tax Journal*, 14 (March 1961), 54. Reprinted by permission of *The National Tax Journal* and George A. Bishop.

FEDERAL TAX SOURCES

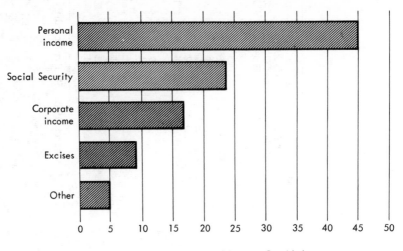

STATE AND LOCAL TAX SOURCES

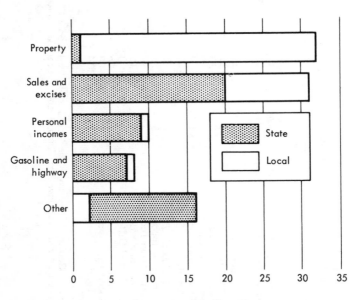

FIG. 10-2   FEDERAL, STATE, AND LOCAL TAX SOURCES

Finally, it should be noted that the social security system is financed on a regressive revenue structure. Social security payments are made only on wage and salary income, not on profits, capital gains, interest, and dividends, which provide a large share of the income of upper-income groups. More importantly, the social security payments are only collected on the *first* $7,800 of wage income; thus persons earning *more* than this amount pay a *lower* percentage of their total income into social security than persons earning less than this amount. Of course, this financing system was established on the principle that social security is an "insurance" program in which participants only received what they paid for; it was not established as an income redistribution system.

While there is no constitutional requirement that assigns different types of taxes to federal, state, and local governments in America, over the years, these three levels of government have come to rely on separate tax bases. (See Figure 10-2.) The federal government's principal reliance is on personal and corporate *income* taxes. State governments also rely on income taxes to some extent (two-thirds of the states levy income taxes), but the principal source of state tax revenues is *sales taxation*. Consumers are a notoriously weak pressure group. And it seems easy for taxpayers to dribble pennies away two or three at a time. Sales tax does not require obvious payroll deductions as income taxation or year-end tax bills as property taxation. It is a steady producer of large amounts of revenue. Local governments rely primarily on *property* taxes. Real estate is relatively easy to find for tax purposes, and it cannot be easily moved out of the local jurisdiction. A local sales tax can result in merchants moving beyond city boundaries, and a city income tax can speed the population exodus to suburbia.

INCREMENTALISM IN TAXATION

Incrementalism is a characteristic of tax policy just as it is a characteristic of expenditure policy. A review of major tax decisions of the federal government over the last decade clearly indicates the obstacles to significant change in the tax structure.

Since the adoption of the Sixteenth Amendment in 1913, the income tax has been the chief producer of revenue for the federal government and the chief object of political conflict. Yet despite many efforts at tax "reform"—efforts which, if successful, would result in a reallocation of burdens among income groups—Congress has never undertaken any comprehensive rewriting of federal tax laws. Instead, tax policy has been characterized by a gradual accretion of decisions, most which have resulted in a reduction in progressivity.

The actual incidence of the federal income tax is a matter of great controversy. While nominal rates are very progressive, the actual effective tax rate on income—the rate that income is taxed after

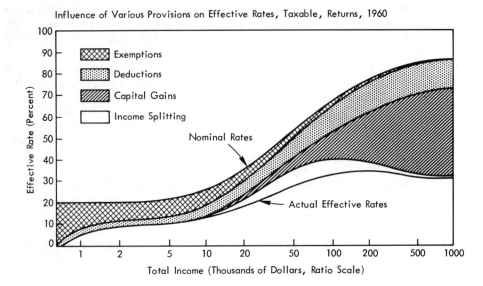

Influence of Various Provisions on Effective Rates, Taxable, Returns, 1960

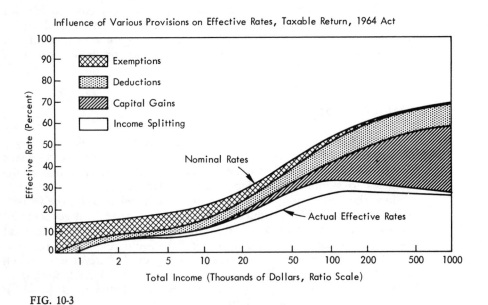

Influence of Various Provisions on Effective Rates, Taxable Return, 1964 Act

FIG. 10-3

Source: Joseph A. Pechman, "Individual Income Tax Provisions of the Revenue Act of 1964." *Studies in Government Finance* (Washington, D.C.: Brookings Institution, 1965). Used by permission.

exemptions, deductions, capital gains, and income-splitting provisions are considered—is much less progressive than generally believed. The Internal Revenue Code is hundreds of pages long, and it contains a long list of exemptions, deductions, and special treatments; these have been expanded by administrative and court decisions. Almost ritualistically, Congressmen and Presidents have pledged to eliminate "loopholes" and "reform" the tax structure. Yet every major effort to do so has failed.

In 1964, Congress passed the Revenue Act of 1964 which was supposed to achieve tax reform as well as tax reduction. Yet the political controversies engendered by the reform proposals was so great that reform provisions had to be jettisoned from the tax bill in order to obtain any tax reduction. The final Act *reduced* the progressivity of nominal rates—from the previous 20 to 87 percent to a range of 14 to 68 percent (see Figure 10-3). It failed to have any significant impact on actual effective tax rates since it retained nearly all of the traditional exemptions, deductions, and special treatments, particularly capital gains. Economist Joseph A. Pechman contends that the actual effective tax rate of the individual income tax never exceeds 30 percent for even the highest income groups.

In 1968, the costs of the Vietnam War and the resulting inflation moved the President and Congress to consider an increase in the personal income tax. Again there was considerable controversy over "loopholes"—particularly the capital gains treatment, the oil depletion allowance, allowances for business expenses, and tax-free status of municipal bond income. But the device finally settled upon was a "surtax" of 10 percent—a uniform 10 percent increase over whatever tax the individual was already paying. This device again left the basic tax structure untouched. Two years later the surtax was removed —again with no significant change in tax laws.

SPENDING POLICY: WHO ENJOYS THE BENEFITS OF GOVERNMENT?

Expenditures as well as taxes can be progressive or regressive in their impact. Obviously public assistance payments are *progressive* expenditures since they are of greater benefits to low-income families than high-income families. In contrast, interest payments—interest on government bonds and notes paid out to investors—are *regressive* expenditures since they are likely to go to high-income rather than low-income groups. In determining the distributional impact of expenditures, assumptions must be made about the use of government services by various income classes, and the relationship of this use to their total income. We must consider education, health, public assistance, recreation, police and fire, etc., and the use which is made of these governmental services by various income groups.

The estimated benefits of governmental expenditures for various

TABLE 10-3 DISTRIBUTION OF EXPENDITURE BENEFITS BY INCOME CLASS

Expenditure Category	Under $2,000	$2,000–2,999	$3,000–3,999	$4,000–4,999	$5,000–5,999	$6,000–7,999	$8,000–9,999	$10,000–14,999	$15,000 and Over	Total [1]
Direct										
Elem. & Sec. Education	5.0%	8.0%	10.1%	14.3%	15.6%	19.9%	17.1%	8.1%	1.9%	100.0%
Higher & Other Education	1.4	2.1	3.4	6.6	10.0	15.7	20.6	25.3	14.7	99.8
Highways	3.2	5.1	8.2	11.4	13.7	19.4	20.5	13.5	4.9	99.9
Public Welfare	49.7	24.8	8.1	5.3	5.1	2.8	1.8	2.2	...	99.8
Agriculture	5.5	8.6	11.6	11.1	12.6	14.5	15.1	11.5	9.4	99.9
Liquor Store	2.4	3.7	8.0	9.8	11.6	18.8	22.3	17.0	6.3	99.9
Insurance Trust	21.4	20.0	17.2	9.7	9.2	9.3	7.8	4.7	0.6	99.9
Interest	4.8	9.9	10.1	8.9	8.2	11.5	16.4	14.9	15.1	99.8
Other—General	8.6	7.8	9.1	11.2	12.4	16.6	17.4	11.3	5.5	99.9
Intergovernmental										
Education	4.5	7.1	9.1	13.1	14.7	19.3	17.6	10.7	3.9	100.0
Highways	3.3	5.1	8.2	11.4	13.8	19.4	20.5	13.4	4.9	100.0
Public Welfare	49.8	24.8	8.1	5.3	5.1	2.8	1.7	2.2	...	99.8
Other—General	8.6	7.8	9.1	11.2	12.4	16.6	17.4	11.3	5.5	99.9

[1] Rows may not total 100.0% due to rounding.
Source: Tax Foundation, Inc., *Tax Burdens and Benefits of Government Expenditures by Income Class, 1961 and 1965.* New York, Tax Foundation, Inc., 1967, pp. 48-51.

types of public service are presented in Table 10-3. As we might expect, the most progressive of all government services in its distributional impact is welfare. Three-quarters of all welfare expenditures go to the two lowest income classes. Social security benefits are also very progressive. Expenditures for public schools and highways tend to benefit middle-income groups more than the poor or the rich. Apparently the poor do not get as much out of public education as the middle class; neither do the wealthy who limit the size of their family and make greater use of private schools. Public expenditures for higher education are generally regressive, since it is the middle and upper-middle classes who are most likely to send their children to college. Only in the very highest income categories are the benefits of public higher education expenditures diminished, probably because this group relies more on private colleges and universities.

In general, the distributional impact of government expenditures is moderately progressive.

THE POLITICS OF INCOME REDISTRIBUTION

What factors shape the distribution of government burdens and benefits among classes of people? Let us attempt to identify political systems that distribute burdens and benefits progressively, and systematically distinguish them from political systems that distribute burdens and benefits regressively. Then let us try to observe the environmental and political correlates of progressivity and regressivity and the distributional impact of public policy.

Once again the fifty states provide an excellent opportunity to examine systematically variation in an important policy output and to observe the conditions associated with this variation. Brian R. Fry and Richard F. Winters (of Stanford University) calculated the *net* distributional impact among income classes of state government revenues and expenditures for each of the fifty states.[8] They did so by: (a) calculating the amounts paid in revenue and amounts received in benefits by each state government for each income class in their state (they did this by using the assumptions about incidence presented in Tables 10-2 and 10-3); (b) calculating the ratio of revenues paid to benefits received, for each income class in each state; and (c) summing the ratios for the three lowest income classes in each state. The result is a measure of the *net* distributional impact of state revenues and expenditures. The higher the ratio, the greater the distributional impact in a progressive direction, that is, in the direction of providing greater benefits for low-income groups while collecting less revenue from these groups.

The net distributional impact of state revenues and expenditures is progressive in every state. According to Fry and Winters, the ratio

[8] Brian R. Fry and Richard F. Winters, "The Politics of Redistribution," *American Political Science Review*, Vol. 64 (June 1970), 508-22.

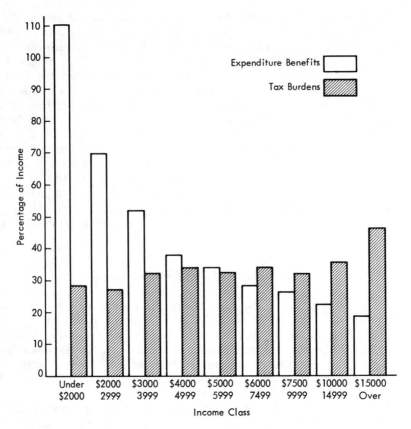

FIG. 10-4   Total Tax Burden and Expenditure Benefit as Percent of Income by Income Class

Source: Tax Foundation, Inc., *Tax Burdens and Benefits of Government Expenditures by Income Class* (New York: The Tax Foundation, 1967).

of benefits to taxes for low-income groups in the most progressive states—Missouri and Massachusetts—was better than ten to one. The ratio in the least progressive states—Wyoming and Virginia—was better than five to one. This variation among the states in the distributional impact of their taxing and spending—the fact that the progressivity of some states is twice as great as that of other states—provides an opportunity to observe systematically the correlates of progressivity in political systems.

Progressivity in the distributional impact of state taxes and expenditures is more closely related to urbanization than any other socioeconomic condition. The findings presented in Table 10-4, derived from the Fry and Winters' study, indicate a positive relationship between progressivity and urbanization: the more urban states have somewhat higher ratios of benefits to taxes for low-income groups

TABLE 10-4 THE LINKAGES BETWEEN ENVIRONMENTAL RESOURCES, POLITICAL SYSTEM CHARACTERISTICS, AND THE DISTRIBUTIONAL IMPACT OF STATE TAXING AND SPENDING

	Correlation Coefficients with Progressivity in Distributional Ratios of State Taxing and Spending	
	Simple	*Partial*
Level of Environmental Resources		
Income	.17	—.27
Urbanization	.33	.15
Education	—.01	.17
Distribution of Environmental Resources		
Income inequality (Gini)	.00	.22
Political System Characteristics		
Voter participation	.14	.37
Party competition	—.21	—.14
Malapportionment	.06	.01
Governor power	.25	.12
Civil service coverage	.31	.34
Legislative professionalism	.52	.28

than the less urban states. However, this relationship is not a very close one; there are several urban states such as Michigan with less progressive distributional ratios, and some more rural states such as Oklahoma with fairly high ratios. Moreover, progressivity is unrelated to wealth and education. Wealthy states with well-educated adult populations are no more progressive in their tax and expenditures impact than poorer states with less-educated adult populations.

What is perhaps even more noteworthy is the fact that tax and revenue policy is not any more progressive in states with greater inequality in the distribution of wealth than in states with less inequality. One might assume that the greater the inequality of income (as measured by the Gini index), the greater the need or demand for redistribution through state revenue and expenditure policies. But progressivity does *not* increase with increases in the Gini index, or with increases in the proportion of poor people in the states.

What about the effect of political variables on distributional policy? The traditional myths about the progressive impact of party competition, voter participation, and reapportionment are unsupported by systematic evidence. *Pluralism* has no discernible effect on distributional policy. Progressivity in distributional impact of state taxing and spending does *not* increase with increases in party competition, voter participation, or fair apportionment. Again we find little reason to attribute any policy impact to these characteristics of political systems. The same is true for executive organization.

However, it appears that reformism in state politics—as reflected in the extension of civil service coverage and legislative professionalism—is indeed associated with progressivity in distributional policy. Civil service coverage, and especially legislative professionalism, are positively correlated with progressivity. The causal linkage in this case is probably not directly from civil service coverage or legislative professionalism to progressive redistribution in state taxing and spending. It is more likely that civil service coverage and legislative professionalism are part of a broader political ethic of reformism, and it is this ethic that produces a tax and revenue system that is more progressive in its distributional impact.

SUMMARY

Incrementalism is particularly descriptive of the budget-making process. Since budgets are the most important policy statements of governments, incrementalism heavily impacts the entire range of policy-making.

1. Budgeting is conservative, because decision makers generally consider last year's expenditures as a base and focus their attention on a narrow range of increases or decreases in expenditures.
2. Budgeting is fragmented, because agencies and legislative committees generally deal with specific segments of the budget; seldom is there much consideration given to the total policy impact of a budget.
3. Budget is non-programmatic, because careful consideration of the policy implications of each expenditure might create irresoluble conflicts. Evaluating the desirability of every program as compared to all other programs would be politically infeasible.
4. The formal budgetary process illustrates the fragmented character of budgetary decision making and the diffusion of responsibility for expenditure policy.
5. The range of decisions actually available to policy makers in the development of a budget is really quite small, generally within 10 percent of the previous budget.
6. Realizing the incremental nature of budget making, agency heads devise a series of informal budgetary practices designed to minimize the appearance of change and guarantee the gradual expansion of agency activities.
7. Despite a doubling of federal expenditures over a decade, the proportion of federal funds going to various purposes has not changed very much. Defense expenditures have declined somewhat as a proportion of all federal expenditures while welfare and education expenditures have risen.
8. Tax policy is also characterized by incrementalism. Despite rhetoric about eliminating tax "loopholes" and "reforming" the tax structure, Congress has preferred to make minor changes in tax laws rather than undertake their major restructuring.
9. An analysis of the two major federal tax decisions of the last decade reveal that Congress and the President: (1) reduced

the progressivity of federal taxes (1964), and (2) increased revenues through a surtax on existing taxes (1968) rather than undertake tax reform or impose new taxes.

10. Policies which distribute government burdens and benefits among income groups can be identified by calculating the progressivity and regressivity of both taxes and expenditures. Progressivity means that the tax burden is a higher percentage of income of high-income groups than of low-income groups, or that the expenditure benefit is a higher percentage of the income of low-income groups than of high-income groups. Regressivity in tax burdens and expenditure benefits means just the opposite.

11. The burden of all federal taxes is progressive, although not steeply so. The most progressive of all taxes is the federal personal income tax. In contrast, state and local taxes are regressive, owing to the reliance of state and local governments on sales and property taxation.

12. The distributional impact of most government expenditures is moderately progressive. Welfare and social security expenditures are very progressive. Expenditures for schools and highways tend to benefit middle-income groups more than the rich or poor. Expenditures for public higher education are generally regressive since more middle- and upper-class families send their children to college.

13. The distributional character of public policy in the American states is *not* closely related to environmental forces. While urbanization bears some relationship to progressivity, neither income, nor education, nor income inequality are related to the net distributional effect of government taxing and spending in the states. Pluralism has no discernible impact on distribution policy; neither party competition, voter participation, malapportionment, nor executive power have any relationship to distribution policy. In contrast, reformism—as reflected in civil service coverage and legislative professionalism—*is* associated with progressivity in net distributional policy.

BIBLIOGRAPHY

ANTON, THOMAS J., *The Politics of State Expenditures in Illinois.* Urbana, Ill.: University of Illinois Press, 1966.

FENNO, RICHARD, *The Power of the Purse: Appropriations Politics in Congress.* Boston: Little, Brown, 1966.

LINDBLOM, CHARLES E. and DAVID BRAYBROOKE, *The Strategy of Decision.* New York: Free Press, 1963.

WILDAVSKY, AARON, *The Politics of the Budgetary Process.* Boston: Little, Brown, 1964.

INPUTS, OUTPUTS, AND BLACK BOXES:
a systems analysis of state policies

CHAPTER II

EXTENDING THE BOUNDARIES OF POLICY ANALYSIS

Political science has been so preoccupied with describing political institutions, behaviors, and processes, that it has frequently overlooked the overriding importance of environmental forces in shaping public policy. Of course, political scientists generally recognize that environmental variables affect politics and public policy, but these variables are often slighted, and occasionally ignored, in specific policy explanations. The problem seems to be that the concepts and methods of political science predispose scholars to account for public policy largely in terms of the *internal* activities of political systems. Political science never lacked descriptions of what goes on within political systems; what it has lacked is a clear picture of the *linkages* between environmental conditions, political activity, and public policy.

What is the environment? By the environment we mean anything that lies outside of the boundaries of the political system yet within the same society. Needless to say, this takes in a great deal of territory. Environmental variables include such things as the level of technological development, the extent of urbanization, the literacy rate, the level of adult education, the character of the economic system and its level of development, the degree of modernization of the society, the occupational structure, the class system, racial composition and ethnic diversity, mobility patterns, prevailing myths and beliefs, and so on. Any variable which is distinguishable from the political system itself yet lies within the same society is part of the environment.

From the almost unlimited number of environmental conditions which might influence public policy outcomes, we must choose only a limited number for inclusion in our research. Although we are fortunate today that computer technology enables us to handle far more environmental variables than would ever be possible without such technology, we are still obliged to reduce our studies to manageable proportions by making some selection among environmental variables. Let us begin our analysis of environmental determinants of public policy by reviewing the research literature on the impact of economic development on public policy.

ENVIRONMENTAL RESOURCES AND PUBLIC POLICY: PREVIOUS RESEARCH

Economists have contributed a great deal to the systematic analysis of public policy. Economic research very early suggested that government activity was closely related to the level of economic development in a society.[1] Economic development was broadly defined to include levels of wealth, industrialization, urbanization, and adult education. Economic theory linked all of these environmental variables to public policy through the following chain of reasonings:

> Industrialization, whether in a planned or unplanned society, is said to result in increased specialization and demands for coordination. Coordination in a free enterprise economy is provided by the market mechanism and by corporate bureaucracies, but a great deal is also provided by the government. Industrial development mandates the growth of public regulatory activities. The coordination demanded in our industrial society also involves certain inescapable difficulties; the expansion of some industries and the contraction of others, overestimates and underestimates of economic conditions, and errors of judgment resulting in economic imbalances. In response to these dislocations, collective remedial action tends to increase, and added responsibilities are placed upon government. In addition, urbanization is understood to lead to a variety of social problems which are presumed to be amenable to collective action. This too implies added government responsibilities. Migration from rural to urban areas in response to the development of in-

[1] See, for example, Bruce R. Morris, *Problems of American Economic Growth* (New York: Oxford, 1961); Walter Krause, *Economic Development* (Belmonth: Wadsworth, 1961); W. W. Rostow, *The Process of Economic Growth*, 2nd ed. (New York: Norton, 1962).

dustry, the decline of agriculture, and the general search for economic opportunity by individuals in business also create government responsibilities. Economic development also involves expansion, at the state and local levels, of education, transportation, and welfare services which are largely the responsibility of governments, as a result of dislocations and as an integral part of economic growth. Such expansion involves not only adjustments of state policies in these areas but also adjustment of the government tax and revenue systems which must finance all of these new responsibilities.[2]

Thus, there are good theoretical reasons for believing that economic development is an important environmental determinant of the level of governmental taxing, spending, and service.

These linkages in economic theory appear to be well supported in the research literature. Systematic analysis of the economic determinants of *state and local* government expenditures began with the publication of Solomon Fabricant's *The Trend of Government Activity in the United States Since 1900*.[3] Fabricant employed the comparative analysis of state and local spending in the fifty states to define the relationships between three socioeconomic measures (per capita income, population density, and urbanization) and per capita expenditures of state and local governments. Using data for 1942, Fabricant found that variations in these environmental variables in the states accounted for more than 72 percent of the variation among the states in total state and local spending. Of these three environmental variables, he found that per capita *income* shows the strongest relationship to expenditures.

Another economist, Glenn F. Fisher continued Fabricant's analysis of the economic determinants of state and local government spending into the 1960s.[4] He found that Fabricant's original three socioeconomic variables (per capita income, population density, and urbanization) were somewhat *less* influential in determining levels of state and local government spending than they had been two decades before. The three variables which had explained 72 percent of the variation in state and local spending in 1942 explained only 53 percent variation in spending in 1962. However, by adding other economic variables (e.g., percentage of families with less than $2,000 annual income, percentage increase in population, percentage of adult education with less than five years schooling) Fisher was able to explain even *more* of the interstate differences in state and local per capita

[2] Thomas R. Dye, *Politics, Economics and the Public* (Chicago: Rand McNally, 1966), p. 8.
[3] Solomon Fabricant, *Trend of Government Activity in the United States Since 1900* (New York: National Bureau of Economic Research, 1952).
[4] Glenn W. Fisher, "Interstate Variation in State and Local Government Expenditures," *National Tax Journal*, Vol. 17 (March 1964), 57-74.

spending than Fabricant's original analysis. And, like Fabricant, Fisher found that per capita *income* was the strongest single environmental variable associated with state and local expenditures.

Economists Seymour Sachs and Robert Harris added to this research literature by considering the effect of federal grants-in-aid on state and local government expenditures.[5] By 1960 it appeared that environmental resources were losing some of their explanatory power in relation to state-local spending, particularly in the areas of welfare and health. Sachs and Harris also noted that the ability of income, population density, and urbanization to explain interstate variation in total state-local spending had declined from 72 percent in 1942 to 55 percent in 1960 (see Table 11-1). They particularly noted the decline in the explanatory power of these three variables in the areas of welfare (from 45 percent in 1942 to 11 percent in 1960) and health (from 72 percent in 1942 to 44 percent in 1960).

They suggested that the decline in the explanatory power of economic resources could be attributed to the intervening effect of federal grants-in-aid, particularly in the welfare and health fields. They reasoned that federal grants were freeing the states from the constraints of their own economic resources. Federal grants were "outside money" to state and local government officials which permitted them to fund programs at levels beyond their own resources. Hence the decline in the closeness of the relationship between economic resources and state-local spending, particularly in the fields with the heaviest federal involvement: welfare and health.

Table 11-1 is adapted from the Sachs and Harris study. It shows the declines over time in the importance of economic resources in explaining state-local spending. It also shows what happens when federal grants-in-aid are included among the explanatory variables: federal grants add considerably to the explanation of state-local spending. The proportion of total state-local spending explained by economic resources alone is 53 percent; but by considering federal grants-in-aid in addition to economic resources, 81 percent of total state-local spending can be explained. Note that in the welfare field the proposition of explained variables leaps from 11 percent to 83 percent by the inclusion of federal aid. This means that a state's economic resources have relatively little to do with its welfare spending; federal policy is the primary determinant of state-local spending in this field. It should be noted, however, that income remains the single most important determinant of state-local spending for all other functions. Sachs and Harris, on the basis of regression analysis, conclude "Per capita income remains the most important determinant of expenditures even after the federal aid variables are added."

[5] Seymour Sachs and Robert Harris, "The Determinants of State and Local Government Expenditures and Intergovernmental Flow of Funds," *National Tax Journal*, Vol. 17 (March 1964), 78-85.

TABLE 11-1 THE LINKAGES BETWEEN ENVIRONMENTAL RESOURCES, FEDERAL AID, AND STATE-LOCAL SPENDING

State-Local Expenditures	*Percent of State-Local Spending Determined By:*			
	Economic Development [1]			*Environmental Resources plus Federal Aid* [2]
	1942	*1957*	*1960*	*1960*
Total Expenditures	72	53	53	81
Higher Education	—	37	45	—
Local Schools	59	62	60	81
Highways	29	34	37	83
Public Welfare	45	14	11	83
Health and Hospitals	72	46	44	47
Police	81	74	79	⎫
Fire Protection	85	67	74	⎬ 63
General Control	59	45	52	⎭

Note: Figures are coefficients of multiple determination (R^2) for 48 states.
[1] Economic development is defined as per capita income, population density, and percent urbanization.
[2] Three economic development variables plus per capita federal aid.
Source: Adapted from Seymour Sachs and Robert Harris, "The Determinants of State and Local Government Expenditures and Intergovernmental Flow of Funds," *National Tax Journal*, Vol. 17 (March, 1964), 78-85.

ENVIRONMENTAL RESOURCES AND LEVELS OF PUBLIC SPENDING AND SERVICE

There is little doubt that levels of government revenue, expenditures, and services are closely linked to environmental resources. While there are some notable exceptions, virtually all of the systematic evidence points to this fact: environmental resources (particularly wealth) are the most important determinants of *levels* of government taxing, spending, and service. Socioeconomic measures such as per capita income, adult education, and urbanization, consistently turn out to be the most influential variables in systematic analysis of public policies, when public policies are defined as levels or amounts or averages of taxes, expenditures, or services.

Table 11-2 presents a typical selection of public policy outcomes in the American states defined in terms of levels of taxing, spending, and service. These are important policy outcomes in education, health and welfare, highways, public regulation, and taxing and spending. Let us summarize the environmental-policy linkages revealed in this table. First of all, differences in educational expenditures among the fifty states are closely related to differences in wealth. (Figure 11-1 is a graphic portrayal of this relationship.) Wealth also explains most of the differences among the states in measures reflecting the level of educational service, such as average teacher salaries and pupil-teacher ratios. In contrast, environmental resources are not as influential in explaining health and welfare expenditures as they are in explaining

TABLE 11-2 THE RELATIONSHIP BETWEEN ENVIRONMENTAL RESOURCES AND LEVELS OF SPENDING AND SERVICE IN THE FIFTY STATES

| Levels of Spending and Service | Simple Correlation Coefficients | | | Total | |
	Income	Education	Urban	Multiple Coefficients	Percent Explained
Education					
Per Pupil Expend.	.83	.59	.51	.74	70
Average Teacher Salary	.88	.57	.69	.90	81
Teacher-Pupil Ratio	—.43	—.50	—.13	.54	29
Per Capita Educ. Expend.	.61	.75	.20	.78	61
Welfare					
Per Capita Welfare Expend.	.01	.07	.19	.31	09
Per Capita Health Expend.	.42	.45	.53	.57	32
Unemploy. Benefits	.80	.67	.55	.81	66
OAA Benefits	.63	.61	.49	.68	46
ADC Benefits	.74	.55	.51	.74	55
Gen. Assist. Benefits	.79	.43	.58	.76	62
OAA Recipients	—.55	—.35	—.22	.59	35
ADC Recipients	—.30	—.42	—.15	.42	18
Unemploy. Recipients	.58	.23	.39	.64	42
Gen. Assist. Recipients	.47	.30	.41	.49	24
Highway					
Per Capita Highway Expend.	.01	.36	—.37	.68	46
Public Regulation					
Numbers of Laws	.47	.30	.41	.47	22
Public Employes Per Popul.	.26	.61	.07	.67	45
Public Employee Salary	.49	.19	.40	.55	30
Per Capita Corrections Expend.	.69	.58	.32	.72	52
Police Protection	.64	.32	.75	.78	62
Finance					
Per Capita Total Expend.	.78	.74	.54	.78	62
Per Capita Total Revenue	.64	.75	.29	.77	60
Per Capita Tax Revenue	.76	.74	.59	.82	67
Per Capita Debt	.59	.30	.61	.67	45

education expenditures. Per capita welfare expenditures do not correlate with measures of environmental resources, and this can be attributed to the effect of federal participation in welfare financing. (The federal government provides half of the funds spent on public assistance, and federal percentages of total public assistance expenditures declined with increases in state income levels. This means that federal policy offsets the effect of wealth so that per capita welfare expenditures do not reflect income levels in the states.) However, the impact of environmental resourcs on benefit levels in health and welfare programs is quite obvious. Benefits per recipient for unemployment, old age assistance, aid to families with dependent children, and general assistance are quite closely related to income levels in the states. In these programs receiving federal aid—old age assistance, aid to families with dependent children, and unemployment—poorer states provide assistance to more recipients per population than richer states. But in general assistance programs, which are not federally aided, richer states provide assistance to more recipients than poorer states.

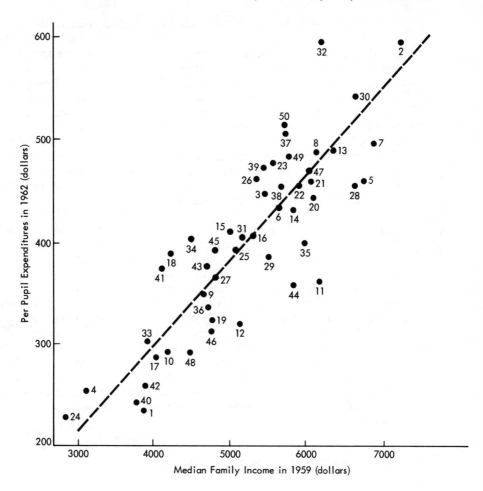

1 Ala.	11 Hawaii	21 Mass.	31 N.M.	41 S.D.
2 Alaska	12 Idaho	22 Mich.	32 N.Y.	42 Tenn.
3 Ariz.	13 Ill.	23 Minn.	33 N.C.	43 Tex.
4 Ark.	14 Ind.	24 Miss.	34 N.D.	44 Utah
5 Calif.	15 Iowa	25 Mo.	35 Ohio	45 Vt.
6 Colo.	16 Kan.	26 Mont.	36 Okla.	46 Va.
7 Conn.	17 Ky.	27 Neb.	37 Ore.	47 Wash.
8 Del.	18 La.	28 Nev.	38 Pa.	48 W.Va.
9 Fla.	19 Me.	29 N.H.	39 R.I.	49 Wis.
10 Ga.	20 Md.	30 N.J.	40 S.C.	50 Wyo.

FIG. 11-1 THE FIFTY STATES ARRANGED ACCORDING TO MEDIAN FAMILY INCOME AND PER PUPIL EXPENDITURES FOR EDUCATION

Source: Thomas R. Dye, *Politics, Economics, and the Public* (Chicago: Rand McNally & Co., © 1966), p. 126. Reproduced by permission.

Highway expenditures in the states are also related to environmental conditions, although in a somewhat different fashion than health, welfare, and education expenditures. Rural states spend *more* per capita on highways than urban states.

The legislatures of wealthy, urban states introduce and enact more laws than the legislatures of poor rural states. Moreover, there are more public employees per population in wealthy urban states than in poor rural states. Finally, the average monthly salaries of public employees in wealthy, urban states is greater than in poor rural states. All of this suggests that the level of government activity and public service is a function of the availability of resources. Police protection (as well as crime rates) is related to urbanization, and per capita correctional expenditures are related to wealth.

There is little doubt that the overall ability of states to raise revenue and spend money is a function of their level of economic resources. Both per capita expenditures and per capita revenues are closely related to wealth. Per capita tax levels are also related to wealth, as is the ability to carry larger per capita debt levels.

In short, there are many significant linkages between environmental resources and policy outcomes in the states. The level of government taxing, spending, and service can largely be explained with reference to wealth, urbanization, education. In fact, the only measures of the level of government activity and service which are *not* closely related to environmental resources are those measures which are directly impacted by federal policy. Only where federal policy offsets the impact of economic resources on state policy outcome do we find any reduction in the coefficients between government activity and economic resources.

FEDERAL GRANTS AS "OUTSIDE MONEY"

Federal grant-in-aid money is now a very important resource of state and local governments in America. Federal grants now account for one-third of all state government revenues and one-sixth of all local government revenues. State and local government officials tend to view federal grants as "outside money" to help support programs in education, welfare, health, highways, housing, urban renewal, and a myriad of other programs. This "outside money" tends to free states and communities from some of the constraints of their own limited economic resources, and, therefore, reduce somewhat the impact of state and local economic resources on levels of public spending and service. Thus, in explaining levels of public spending and service, we must consider federal grant money as well as environmental resources.

Our own analysis of the effect of federal grant money on public policy in the states confirms the ideas of economists Sachs and Harris.

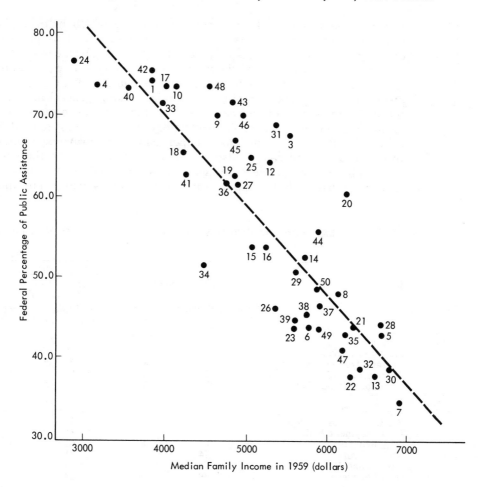

1 Ala.	11 Hawaii	21 Mass.	31 N.M.	41 S.D.
2 Alaska	12 Idaho	22 Mich.	32 N.Y.	42 Tenn.
3 Ariz.	13 Ill.	23 Minn.	33 N.C.	43 Tex.
4 Ark.	14 Ind.	24 Miss.	34 N.D.	44 Utah
5 Calif.	15 Iowa	25 Mo.	35 Ohio	45 Vt.
6 Colo.	16 Kan.	26 Mont.	36 Okla.	46 Va.
7 Conn.	17 Ky.	27 Neb.	37 Ore.	47 Wash.
8 Del.	18 La.	28 Nev.	38 Pa.	48 W.Va.
9 Fla.	19 Me.	29 N.H.	39 R.I.	49 Wis.
10 Ga.	20 Md.	30 N.J.	40 S.C.	50 Wyo.

FIG. 11-2 THE FIFTY STATES ARRANGED ACCORDING TO MEDIAN FAMILY INCOME AND
FEDERAL CONTRIBUTIONS TO PUBLIC ASSISTANCE

Source: Thomas R. Dye, *Politics, Economics, and the Public* (Chicago: Rand
McNally & Co., © 1966), p. 126. Reproduced by permission.

Federal money is indeed an important resource which helps explain interstate variation in levels of spending and service. This is particularly true in the two areas of greatest federal involvement—welfare and highways. Table 11-3 shows the explanatory value of adding federal aid to income, education, and urbanization in regression problems on levels of spending and service. Adding federal aid raises the multiple coefficient for per capita welfare expenditures from .31 to .81, a dramatic increase in explanatory power. Adding federal aid raises the multiple coefficient for per capita highway expenditives from .68 to .84. Federal aid also explains differences among the states in the number of recipients of welfare benefits. (It is very possible that the causal relationship is the reverse: states which put more

TABLE 11-3 ENVIRONMENTAL RESOURCES, FEDERAL AID, AND LEVELS OF SPENDING AND SERVICE IN THE FIFTY STATES

Levels of Spending and Service	Environmental Resources		Environmental Resources and Federal Aid	
	Multiple Coefficients	Percent Explained	Multiple Coefficients	Percent Explained
Education				
Per Pupil Expend.	.85	70	.84	70
Average Teacher Salary	.90	81	.90	81
Teacher-Pupil Ratio	.54	29	.55	30
Per Capita Educ. Expend.	.78	61	.81	66*
Welfare				
Per Capita Welfare Expend.	.31	09	.81	66*
Per Capita Health Expend.	.57	32	.57	32
Unemployment Benefits	.81	66	.81	66
OAA Benefits	.68	46	.68	47
ADC Benefits	.74	55	.74	55
Gen. Assist. Benefits	.76	62	.79	63
OAA Recipients	.59	35	.82	68*
ADC Recipients	.42	18	.62	39*
Unemployment Recipients	.64	42	.64	42
Gen. Assist. Recipients	.49	24	.49	24
Highways				
Per Capita Highway Expend.	.68	46	.84	70*
Public Regulation				
Numbers of Laws	.47	22	.47	22
Public Employes Per Population	.67	45	.69	48
Public Employee Salaries	.55	30	.57	32
Per Capita Corrections Expend.	.72	52	.72	52
Police Protection	.78	62	.78	62
Finance				
Per Capita Total Expend.	.78	62	.81	66*
Per Capita Total Revenue	.77	60	.81	66*
Per Capita Tax Revenue	.82	67	.82	67
Per Capita Debt	.67	45	.67	45

* An asterisk indicates a significant increase in explained variance by the addition of federal aid to multiple regression problem.

recipients on welfare rolls get more federal aid.) Federal aid also makes a significant contribution to explaining expenditures, per capita total expenditures, and per capita revenues.

STABILITY AND CHANGE IN INPUT-OUTPUT RELATIONSHIPS

Do relationships between environment and public policy persist over time? Most of the linkages described so far are based on data from the last decade. Can these same linkages be observed in other time periods? Are there any changes over time in the nature of the relationships between environment and public policy?

To explore these questions, we traced the relationships between several environmental variables and levels of public spending in the states over a period of seven decades—1890 to 1960. The results are shown in Figure 11-3. Each of the three diagrams traces the strength of the relationships (measured in terms of the size of the simple correlation coefficients) between environmental variables and total state-local spending, spending for education, and spending for welfare, in the fifty states.

Wealth has *always* been an important determinant of levels of total spending for public services in the American states. A half century ago, states and communities relied primarily on property taxes, and hence the value of property for revenue. Property value was the principle determinant of total state-local spending. In more recent decades personal income has been an even more influential determinant of public spending and services. There is no indication of any weakening over time in the relationships between wealth and government spending.

In contrast, urbanization, and particularly industrialization, are clearly losing their influence over time as determinants of public spending. At one time, differences in the degree of industrialization among the fifty states helped to account for differences in spending policies. But in recent years, as all states became more or less industrialized, differences in the degree of industrialization ceased to be a determinant of public policy. The same decline in influence of public policy can be observed in urbanization, although this variable has not yet lost all of its influence. But certainly urbanization is not as important today as it was a few decades ago.

Education has a strong and persistent impact on public policy. The educational level of the adult population has an impact on spending equal to that of wealth, and an impact on spending for education which is even greater than wealth. There is no evidence that this relationship is weakening.

In general, then, we can say that income and education are persistent determinants of levels of government spending in the states. However,

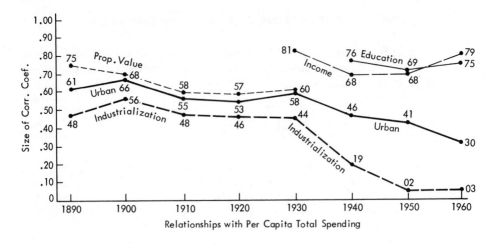

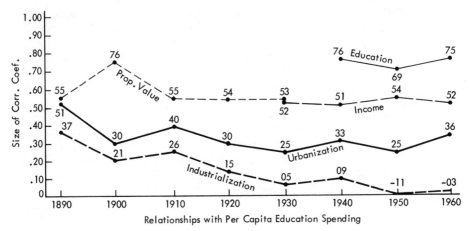

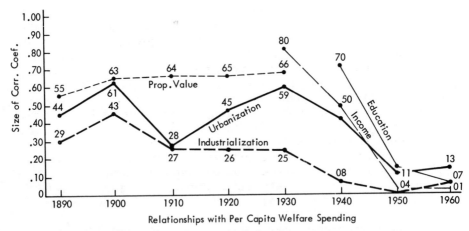

FIG. 11-3 STABILITY AND CHANGE IN RELATIONSHIPS BETWEEN ENVIRONMENTAL RE-
SOURCES AND LEVELS OF PUBLIC SPENDING OVER TIME

one important exception must be noted: environmental inputs have completely lost their influence over state-local welfare spending over the last few decades. The reason for this seems clear: when the federal government stepped into the welfare field during the New Deal, federal funds relieved the states of dependence on their own resources. Thus, ever since the 1930s the relationship between environmental resources and welfare spending in the states has been declining. The obvious effect of federal intervention in the welfare field on input-output relationships suggests once again that federal money must be viewed as an important input variable determining state-local policy.[6]

POLITICS, ENVIRONMENT, AND POLICY: PREVIOUS RESEARCH

The political system functions to transform demands generated in the environment into public policy. The traditional literature in American politics instructed students that characteristics of the political system, particularly two-party competition, voter participation, and apportionment, did have direct bearing on public policy.[7] Since political scientists devoted most of their time to studying what happened *within* the political system, it was natural for them to believe that the political processes and institutions which they studied were important in terms of public policy outcomes. Moreover, the belief that competition, participation, and equality in representation had important consequences for public policy squared with the value placed upon these variables in the prevailing pluralist ideology.

The assertion that political variables, such as party competition, voter participation, and malapportionment, affected public policy rested more upon *a priori* reasoning than upon systematic research. It seemed reasonable to *believe* that an increase in party competition would increase educational spending, welfare benefits, numbers of welfare recipients, highway spending, health and hospital care, and so on, because competitive parties would try to outbid each other for public favor by offering such inducements, and the overall affect of such competition would be to raise levels of spending and service. It also seemed reasonable to believe that increased voter participation

---

[6] See also Richard I. Hofferbert, "Ecological Development and Policy Change in the American States," *Midwest Journal of Political Science*, Vol. 10 (November 1966), 481-92; and Richard I. Hofferbert, "Socioeconomic Dimensions of the American States: 1890-1960," *Midwest Journal of Political Science*, Vol. 12 (August 1968), 401-18.

[7] V. O. Key, Jr., *American State Politics: An Introduction* (New York: Knopf, 1956); V. O. Key, Jr., *Southern Politics in State and Nation* (New York: Knopf, 1951); Duane Lockard, *New England State Politics* (Princeton: Princeton University Press, 1959); Malcolm Jewell, *The State Legislature* (New York: Random House, 1962); Duane Lockard, *The Politics of State and Local Government* (New York: Macmillan, 1963); John H. Fenton, *People and Parties in Politics* (Glenview, Ill.: Scott, Foresman, 1966).

would influence public policy, presumably in a more liberal direction. Finally, it seemed reasonable to believe that malapportionment also affected public policy.

However, in order to assess the *independent* effect of politics on public policy, it was important to control for the intervening effects of environmental variables. Early research in state politics demonstrated conclusively that party competition and voter participation were themselves heavily impacted by environmental variables. A number of scholars—Ranney and Kendall, Key, Schlesinger and Golembiewski, for example—indicated that economic development affects the level of interparty competition; they reported statistically significant associations between urbanism, income, and industrialization, and classifications of party competition among the states.[8] Knowledge of this linkage between the environment and the political system, coupled with knowledge about the linkage between the environment and public policy, clearly suggested that scholars should test to see if party competition *independently* affected public policy, or whether both party competition and public policy were products of economic development. For example, if it was shown that, in general, wealthy states have more party competition than poor states, it might be that differences in the level of welfare benefits of competitive and noncompetitive states are really a product of the fact that the former are wealthy and the latter are poor. If this was the case, policy differences between the states might be attributable to wealth rather than to party competition. In order to isolate the effect of party competition on education and welfare policies from the effect of environmental variables, it is necessary to control for these variables.

The first hint that political variables might not be as influential in determining levels of public taxing, spending, and service as commonly supposed, came in an important research effort by Richard E. Dawson and James A. Robinson in 1963.[9] These political scientists examined the linkages between socioeconomic variables (income, urbanization, industrialization), the level of interparty competition, and nine public *welfare* policies. They concluded that: "High levels of interparty competition are highly interrelated both to socioeconomic factors and to social welfare legislation, but the degree of interparty competition does not seem to possess the important intervening influence between socioeconomic factors and liberal welfare programs that our original hypothesis and theoretical schemes suggested." These

[8] Austin Ranney and Wilmoore Kendall, "The American Party System," *American Political Science Review*, Vol. 48 (1954), 477-85; V. O. Key, Jr., *American State Politics* (New York: Knopf, 1956), p. 99; Joseph A. Schlesinger, "A Two-Dimensional Scheme for Classifying States According to the Degree of Inter-Party Competition," *American Political Science Review*, Vol. 49 (1955), 1120-28; Robert T. Golembiewski, "A Taxonomic Approach to State Political Party Strength," *Western Political Quarterly*, Vol. 11 (1958), 494-513.
[9] Richard E. Dawson and James A. Robinson, "Inter-Party Competition, Economic Variables, and Welfare Policies in the American States," *Journal of Politics*, Vol. 25 (May 1963), 265-89.

researchers failed to uncover any evidence that a competitive political system devoted any more resources to welfare functions than a noncompetitive system *at the same level of economic development.* Thus, Dawson and Robinson raised serious doubts about the relevance of a political variable—party competition—which most political scientists had believed to be an influential determinant of public policy. Perhaps more importantly, the Dawson–Robinson article inspired political scientists to undertake comparative systematic research into the determinants of public policy.

In 1965 Thomas R. Dye published a comprehensive analysis of public policy in the American States, *Politics, Economics, and the Public.*[10] Employing Easton's systems model, Dye described the linkages between the four economic development variables, four political system characteristics, and over ninety separated policy output measures in education, health, welfare, highways, corrections, taxation, and public regulation. This research produced some findings that were very unsettling for many political scientists. Four of the most commonly described characteristics of political systems—(1) Democratic or Republican control of state government, (2) the degree of interparty competition, (3) the level of voter turnout, and (4) the extent of malapportionment—were found to have *less* affect on public policy *than* environmental variables reflecting the level of economic development—urbanization, industrialization, wealth, and education. According to the author, "the evidence seems conclusive: economic development variables are more influential than political system characteristics in shaping public policy in the states." Like Dawson and Robinson, Dye reasoned that most of the associations which occur between political variables and policy outcomes are really a product of the fact that economic development influences *both* political system characteristics *and* policy outcomes. When political factors are controlled, economic development continues to have a significant impact on public policy. But when the effects of economic development are controlled, political factors turn out to have little influence on policy outcomes. Of course, the author pointed out several policy areas where political factors remained important (notably the division of state versus local responsibilities for public services), and he also identified certain policy areas where federal programs tended to offset the impact of economic development levels on state policies. Yet, in an attempt to generalize about the determinants of public policy, he concluded that, *on the whole*, economic development was *more* influential in shaping state policies *than* any of the political variables previously thought to be important in policy determination.

Several additional studies in the mid–1960s appeared to confirm the idea that political variables were less influential than the economic environment in determining levels of government taxing, spend-

---

[10] Thomas R. Dye, *Politics, Economics, and the Public* (Chicago: Rand McNally, 1966).

ing, and service. Several articles employed systematic comparative analysis to assess the impact of apportionment practices on policy outcomes in the fifty states while controlling for the effects of environmental factors.[11] It turned out that there were few measurable policy differences between states which were well apportioned and states which were malapportioned, and that economic variables were *more* influential in determining policy outcomes than apportionment practices. Another study reported that the organizational structure of state executive branches and formal powers of governors were not *as* influential as economic measures in determining the level of government activity in the states.[12] A comprehensive study by Richard I. Hofferbert examined the relationships between environmental variables, malapportionment, party competition, and welfare policies. He concluded: "Structural characteristics and, if one prefers to give partisan variables a separate berth, the nature of the party system and its operation do not seem to go very far toward explaining the kinds of policies produced in the states. . . . We see by the data presented here and elsewhere, however, clear indication that there is a relationship between the environment and policy." [13]

Most of these systematic policy studies were based upon comparative observations made at one point in time. To confirm that linkages between environment, system, and policy persisted *over time*, Richard I. Hofferbert studied the relationships between environmental forces, political conditions, and public policy in the American states from 1890 through 1960. He detected a slight *decline* in the strength of the relationships between environmental forces and policy outcome over this time period. He reasoned that a generally high level of economic development provides political decision makers with greater latitude in policy choices, and tends to free them from the restraints imposed by limited resources. While environmental forces continue to be the major determinant of public policy, the implication of Hofferbert's study is that in the future *the attitudes of political leaders* may be increasingly important in determining levels of public spending and service.

A partial challenge to the general direction of these findings is found in a recent factor analytic exercise by Ira Sharkansky and Richard I. Hofferbert. Sharkansky and Hofferbert factor analyze twenty-one specific socioeconomic variables, fifty-three specific political system variables, and thirty-four specific expenditure and service

[11] Thomas R. Dye, "Malapportionment and Public Policy in the States," *Journal of Politics*, Vol. 65 (August 1965), 586-601; Herbert Jacob, "The Consequences of Malapportionment: A Note of Caution," *Social Forces*, Vol. 43 (December 1964), 256-61.

[12] Thomas R. Dye, "Executive Power and Public Policy in the States," *Western Political Quarterly*, Vol. 22 (December, 1969), 926-39.

[13] Richard I. Hofferbert, "The Relation Between Public Policy and Some Structural and Environmental Variables in the American States," *American Political Science Review*, Vol. 60 (March 1966), 73-82.

measures for the American states. These efforts give birth to two *environmental* factors: "industrialization" and "cultural enrichment"; two political *system* factors: "turnout-competition" and "professionalism-local reliance"; and three *policy outcome* factors: "welfare-education," "highways-natural resources," and "public safety." Their next step is an examination of the correlations between these factors. "Cultural enrichment" correlates with "turnout-competition" and "industrialization" correlates with "professionalism-local reliance." Among the policy outcome factors, "public safety" correlates most closely with "cultural enrichment" and "highway-natural resources" correlates most closely with "industrialization." However, "welfare education" correlates more closely with "turnout-competition" than with "industrialization" or "cultural enrichment." In other words, one policy outcome factor is more closely associated with a political system factor than with either environmental factor. "We shall conclude that systemic linkages exist between dimensions of state politics and public services that are independent of socioeconomic characteristics." [14]

The importance of all of this research was that political scientists were using comparative systematic research methods to explain public policy, and they were looking beyond the confines of the political system itself to the social, economic, and cultural environment in their search for the forces shaping public policy. Their most important and controversial set of findings was that certain political variables which had previously claimed a great deal of attention from political scientists—notably party competition, voter participation, and malapportionment—were not *as* influential in determining levels of government taxing, spending and service *as* environmental variables reflecting a level of economic development. Some scholars reacted to these findings as if political science had a vested interest in finding that traditional political variables were the most important factors in explaining public policy, and as if the discovery that economic or other environmental variables are more important than traditional political variables in explaining public policy is somehow damaging to the discipline.[15] A more balanced view, of course, is that political science derives its importance from what it seeks to explain—public policy.[16] The important thing to achieve is the most effective and

[14] Ira Sharkansky and Richard I. Hofferbert, "Dimension of State Politics, Economics, and Public Policy," *American Political Science Review*, Vol. 63 (September 1969), 867-79.

[15] See John H. Fenton, *People and Parties in Politics* (Glenview, Ill.: Scott, Foresman, 1966), pp. 31-49; and Duane Lockard, "State Party Systems and Policy Outputs," in Oliver Garceau, ed., *Political Research and Political Theory* (Cambridge, Mass.: Harvard University Press, 1968), pp. 190-220.

[16] William Keech and James W. Prothro set forth a truly professional view of the relationships between research findings, professional interests, and ideological commitments. In referring to *Politics, Economics, and the Public* these scholars stated:

This research has produced some findings that have been unsettling for

efficient explanation of policy outcomes. If economic or other environmental variables explain public policy more clearly than political variables, so much the better. The object is to explain public policy, and not to assert the primacy of politics or economics in determining policy outcomes.[17]

PLURALISM AND PUBLIC POLICY

The political system includes *all* of the institutions, structures, processes, and behaviors which function to transform demands into governmental decisions. This includes political party activity, voting behavior, the structure and behavior of executive and legislative bodies, interest group activity, and lobbying, formal constitutional arrangements, the political attitudes of both elites and masses, political customs and traditions, the apportionment system, the structure and behavior of courts, the formal and informal power of governors, etc., etc., etc. The list of political system characteristics which might conceivably affect public policy is boundless!

A review of the traditional literature on American politics reveals an especially intense interest among political scientists in three electoral system variables—party competition, voter participation, and equity in representation. All of these variables are highly valued in pluralist political ideology. There are good *a priori* reasons for believing that these three variables may directly affect the outcome of public policy, and there are many assertions in the state politics literature that they do.

Certainly these three manifestations of pluralism—party competition, voter participation, and malapportionment—are incomplete representations of political systems. But at least we can *begin* our search for policy determinants by looking at these variables, and testing some widely held notions about their impact on public policy. These

---

many political scientists. Dye concludes that "the evidence seems conclusive: economic development variables are more influential than political system characteristics in shaping public policy in the states." Some have reacted to these and earlier findings as if political science had a vested interest in political phenomena, and as if the discovery that economic or other variables are more important than political variables in explaining policy is somehow to damage the discipline. A more balanced view is that political science derives its importance from its dependent variables, the phenomena it seeks to explain. Thus the important thing to achieve is the most effective and efficient explanation of political variables. If economic or other independent variables explain policy more clearly than political variables, so much the better. The point is that we must seek out the best explanations, not that they must be political.

See William Keech and James W. Prothro, "American Government," *Journal of Politics* (May 1968), pp. 438-39.

[17] The best critical review of this literature is Herbert Jacob and Michael Lipsky, "Outputs, Structure, and Power: An Assessment of Changes in the Study of State and Local Politics," *Journal of Politics*, Vol. 30 (May 1968), 510-38.

three variables considered together suggest an ideal model of pluralist democracy. High voter participation, intense party competition, and fair apportionment suggest a normative model of pluralist democracy which is current in the literature of American political science. In contrast, low voter participation, an absence of party competition,[18] and unfair apportionment suggest a type of political system which has been widely deplored by American political scientists. Hence, it is very important that we inquire about the impact of these particular system variables on public policy.

Let us examine the relationship between party competition, voter participation, and malapportionment, and policy outcomes reflecting levels of government taxing, spending, benefits, and services in the American states.

In Table 11-4 party competition appears closely related to a number of important policy outcomes. States with a high degree of party competition tend (1) to spend more money per pupil per public schools, (2) to pay higher teacher salaries, (3) to enjoy lower pupil-teacher ratios, (4) to pay more liberal welfare benefits, (5) to grant unemployment compensation and several assistances to more persons, (6) to pay higher salaries to their public employees, (7) to spend more total public monies, and (8) to raise more total revenue and tax revenue, than states with less competitive party systems. Political participation also appears closely associated with levels of government activity. In the field of education, higher voter participation in the states is associated with higher per pupil expenditures, higher teachers' salaries, lower pupil-teacher ratios. Better participation is also associated with increased welfare benefits. There is also a tendency for states with higher particpation rates to spend more money on highways, have more public employees per population, pay higher salaries for public employees, and have higher correctional expenditures. Finally, political participation is associated with increased total government spending, and increased revenues and taxes.

Malapportionment is not as closely associated with policy outcomes as competition and participation. There are slight associations between malapportionment, expressed in terms of urban under-representation, and per pupil expenditure, average teacher salaries, pupil-teacher ratios, and welfare benefits. There are no relationships between malapportionment and overall government taxing and spending or the number of public employees.

[18] Competition, participation, and equity in representation are conceptually linked in pluralist political thought. Statistic analysis reveals that competition and participation are also linked empirically; states with competitive parties are also states with high voter turnouts. The coefficient for this relationship in the fifty states is .72. Even after controlling for the effects of the environment (income, urbanization, and education) competition and participation are still significantly, and independently, associated; the partial coefficient for the relationship between competition and participation controlling for three environmental variables is .45. In contrast, malapportionment is unrelated to either a competitive party system or voter turnout in the fifty states.

TABLE 11-4 PLURALISM AND LEVELS OF GOVERNMENT ACTIVITY IN THE FIFTY STATES

Levels of Government Activity	Party Competition	Pluralism Voter Participation	Mal-apportionment
Education			
Per Pupil Expenditures	.59*	.48*	.10
Average Teachers Salaries	.49*	.34*	.00
Teacher-Pupil Ratio	.64*	.62*	—.15
Per Capita Educ. Expend.	.46*	.38*	—.05
Welfare and Health			
Unemployment Benefits	.52*	.42*	.13
OAA Benefits	.55*	.54*	.02
ADC Benefits	.69*	.63*	.14
Gen. Assist. Benefits	.52*	.46*	.17
OAA Recipients	—.48*	—.38*	—.19
ADC Recipients	—.17	—.09	—.07
Unemployment Benefits	.35*	.29	.29
Gen. Asst. Benefits	.38*	.44*	.13
Per Capita Welfare Expend.	.03	.06	—.17
Per Capita Health Expend.	—.20	.06	—.08
Highways			
Per Capita Highway Expend.	.25	.27	.04
Public Regulation			
Numbers of Laws	—.17	—.19	—.24
Public Employees per Population	.24	.21	—.01
Per Capita Corrections Expend.	.42*	.31*	.02
Policemen per Population	.25	.13	—.03
Taxing and Spending			
Total Per Capita Expend.	.61*	.53*	.02
Total Per Capita Revenue	.47*	.38*	—.04
Total Per Capita Taxes	.59*	.51*	.01
Total Per Capita Debt	.21	.11	.05
Environmental Resources			
Income	.66*	.52*	.14
Education	.62*	.49*	.14
Urbanization	.29	.18	.01

* An asterisk indicates a significant relationship.

Finally, it should be noted that pluralism in the American states—as measured by party competition, and voter participation—is also related to environmental resources—income, education, and urbanization. High levels of income, education, and urbanization tend to foster party competition. Voter participation is notably higher in states with higher incomes and well-educated adult populations. In contrast, malapportionment is *not* as closely related to enviromental resources as party competition and voter turnout. The legislatures of poor rural states with less-educated adult populations were just as likely to be malapportioned as the legislatures of wealthy urban states with well-educated adult populations.

The relationships in the American states between environmental resources and political participation and competition may be of significance to the study of political systems generally. There is reason to believe that environmental resources, such as wealth, urbanization, and education, are prerequisite to the development of liberal pluralist democracy, including voter participation and party competition, in any political system. Students of comparative government have identified the relationship between economic development variables and the political systems of nation-states. Seymour Lipset found that economic development variables and rates of change in these variables were related to stable democratic government as opposed to unstable democratic government or dictatorship.[19]

The importance of these environmental system linkages for policy analysis are clear: since competitive, participatory political systems stand higher on measures of wealth, and education, and urbanization than noncompetitive, nonparticipatory systems, policy differences between these types of political systems may not necessarily be the product of competition or participation itself. Policy differences between competitive, participatory states and noncompetitive, nonparticipatory states may *really* be a product of their differing levels of wealth, urbanization, and education rather than a direct product of competition or participation. Later we will control for the effects of environmental resources in order to observe the independent effect of competition and participation on policy outcomes.

REFORMISM AND PUBLIC POLICY

Another set of political system characteristics which have interested both scholars and statesmen over the years center about reform, professionalism, and innovation in government. Reformism has been an important political movement in American state and local government for over a century.[20] The reform style of politics emphasizes among other things, the replacement of political patronage practices with a civil service system; the professionalization of government service; the reorganization of government to promote efficiency and responsibility; and a preference for an antiseptic, "no politics" atmosphere in government.[21] At the *municipal* level reformism has promoted the manager form of government, nonpartisan elections, home rule, at-large constituencies, and comprehensive planning; it is fairly easy to distinguish between "reformed" and "unreformed" cities by looking at these structural characteristics. It is somewhat more difficult to identify *states* where reform has had an identifiable impact. However, we have selected three variables which are conceptually linked to reformism at the state level—civil service coverage

[19] Seymour Martin Lipset *Political Man* (New York: Doubleday, 1960); and "Some Social Requisites of Democracy: Economic Development and Political Legitimacy," *American Political Science Review*, Vol. 53 (1959), 69-105.
[20] See Richard Hofstadter, *The Age of Reform* (New York: Knopf, 1955).
[21] See Thomas R. Dye, *Politics in States and Communities* (Englewood Cliffs, N.J.: Prentice-Hall, 1969), Chapter 10.

of state employees, professionalism in the state legislature, and administrative innovation.

The percentage of state employees covered by civil service is directly related to one of the primary objectives of the reform movement in state and local government. It is reasonable to assume that this variable taps the broader political ethic of reformism and progressivism in state politics. It is not so much that civil service itself would affect the content of public policy, but that civil service is an indicator of reformism, and reformism may influence the level of public taxing, spending, benefits, and services.

Some state legislatures are highly "professional" while others are not. By "professional" we mean that in some legislatures the members are well-paid and tend to think of their jobs as full-time ones; members and committees are well staffed and have good informational services available to them; and legislative assistance, such as bill drafting and statutory revision, is available. In other legislatures, members are poorly paid and regard their legislative work as part-time; there is little in the way of staff for members or committees; and little or nothing is provided in the way of legislative assistance and services. In the 1960s John Grumm constructed a "professionalism index" based upon (1) the compensation of legislators, (2) total length of legislative sessions in a biennial, (3) expenditures for legislative services, and (4) a legislative services' score awarded each state by the Citizens Conference on State Legislatures.[22] Again, we should note: it is not likely that professionalism itself has any great influence on the content of public policy, but rather that professionalism is an indicator of a progressive style of politics which might affect public policy.

Reformism may also be measured by the relative speed with which state governments adopt new programs. Wisconsin's reputation as a progressive state was gained early in the twentieth century when it pioneered in the adoption of the direct primary, the state income tax, workman's compensation, and legislative bureau. Reputations of this kind are usually based upon random impressions which may or may not be accurate, but it is true that some states have been more innovative than others and more ready to adopt new programs and policies. Jack Walker constructed an "innovation score" based on the speed displayed by the states in the twentieth century in adopting eighty-eight new programs in welfare, health, education, planning, administration, highways, civil rights, corrections, labor, taxes, and public regulation.[23] The score was derived for each state by calculating percentage of total time elapsing between the first and last adop-

---

[22] John G. Grumm, "Structural Determinants of Legislative Output," paper delivered at the Conference on the Measurement of Public Policy, Ann Arbor, Michigan, 1968.
[23] Jack L. Walker, "The Diffusion of Innovations Among the American States," *American Political Science Review*, Vol. 63 (September 1969), 885-87.

tion of a program that elapsed between the first adoption and the particular state's own aceptance of the program. For example, if the total time elapsing between the first and last adoption of a program was twenty years, and Massachusetts enacted a program ten years after the first adoption, then Massachusetts received a score of .50 on that particular program. The innovation score is the average of a state's scores on all programs.

The indicators of reformism in state politics are related to a number of measures of public benefits and services in the fifty states (see Table 11-5). States with comprehensive civil service programs tend to (1) spend more money per pupil for public schools, (2) pay higher teachers' salaries, (3) spend more for health services, (4) pay more liberal welfare benefits, (5) enjoy better police protection, (6)

TABLE 11-5 REFORMISM AND THE LEVELS OF GOVERNMENT ACTIVITY
IN THE FIFTY STATES

Levels of Government Activity	Civil Service Coverage	Reformism Legislative Professionalism	Innovation Score
EDUCATION			
Per Pupil Expenditures	.41*	.32*	.60*
Average Teachers Salaries	.50*	.48*	.62*
Teacher-Pupil Ratio	—.10	.05	—.32*
Per Capita Educ. Expend.	.09	—.10	.18
WELFARE AND HEALTH			
Unemployment Benefits	.19	.16	.18
OAA Benefits	.50*	.30*	.33*
ADC Benefits	.36*	.31*	.56*
Gen. Assist. Benefits	.41*	.16	.63*
OAA Recipients	.43*	.24	.70*
ADC Recipients	.42*	.41*	.68*
Unemployment Recipients	—.17	—.26	—.29
Gen. Assist. Recipients	—.10	.08	—.19
Per Capita Welfare Expend.	.53*	.38*	.49*
Per Capita Health Expend.	.10	.32*	.38*
HIGHWAYS			
Per Capita Highway Expend.	—.10	—.62*	—.30*
PUBLIC REGULATION			
Numbers of Laws	.29	.51*	.32*
Public Employees per Popul.	.03	—.24	—.05
Per Capita Corrections Exp.	.42*	.17	.43*
Policemen per Population	.45*	.52*	.45*
TAXING AND SPENDING			
Total Per Capita Exp.	.31*	.32*	.46*
Total Per Capita Revenue	.25	—.02	.24
Total Per Capita Taxes	.32*	.33*	.55*
Total Per Capita Debt	.39*	.53*	.53*
ENVIRONMENTAL RESOURCES			
Income	.49*	.36*	.63*
Education	.19	—.01	.29
Urbanization	.40*	.61	.59

* An asterisk indicates a significant relationship.

and tax and spend more than states with less comprehensive civil service coverage. States with more "professional" legislatures also provide somewhat higher levels of benefits and services than states wtih less professional legislatures. Moreover, it is interesting to note that (1) professional legislatures pass more laws than nonprofessional legislatures, and (2) professional legislatures spend *less* money on highways (frequently the pork barrel of state government) than nonprofessional legislatures. Finally, innovative states generally (1) tax and spend more than noninnovative states, (2) provide higher benefit and services levels in education, health, welfare, and corrections, and (3) have a generally higher level of government activity.

Of course, we must remember that relationships which are shown in simple correlation coefficients do not necessarily mean that reformism *causes* particular policy outcomes. Relationships between reformism and public policy may occur because both reformism and public policy are affected by environmental forces. Note in Table 11-5 that civil service coverage, legislative professionalism, and innovation are closely related to income and urbanization. Since we know that these environmental forces are linked to the same policies, we must consider the possibility that environment is shaping both reformism and public policy.

THE RELATIVE IMPORTANCE OF ENVIRONMENTAL AND POLITICAL FORCES IN SHAPING PUBLIC POLICY

So far we have talked only about the relationships between (a) environmental resources and political system characteristics; (b) political system characteristics and public policy, and (c) environmental resources and public policy.

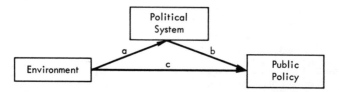

We have established linkages between levels of government taxing, spending, benefits, and services, and both the level of environment resources and the character of the political system; and we also know that levels of environmental resources are closely linked to the character of political systems.

But we have not yet examined the *relative importance* of environmental resources and political system characteristics in the determination of public policy. Are public policies determined primarily by environmental resources, with political system variables having only a marginal impact on policy? (Linkage c). Or are political system variables really more influential in determining the content of public policy than environmental resources? (Linkage b).

In order to assess the relative influence of environmental and political variables in shaping public policy we have constructed a series of multiple regression problems using various combinations of independent (environmental and political) variables. The multiple correlation coefficients tell how much of the total variation in a policy outcome can be explained by *all* of the environmental and political variables entered into the multiple regression problem. More importantly, partial correlation coefficients tell us the policy impact of each environmental and political variable while controlling for the effects of all other environmental and political variables in the problem. In other words, the partial coefficients give us a very good idea of the relative influences of each of our environmental and political variables in producing variation in levels of public taxing, spending, benefits, and service.

A series of multiple regression problems were performed on all of the measures of levels of government activity in the American states. The results obtained with per pupil expenditures for education, per capita expenditures for welfare, per capita expenditures for highways, per capita total revenues, average weekly unemployment benefits, average monthly ADC payments, and police protection per population are representative of the results obtained with our other policy measures. These are presented in Table 11-6.

The first set of multiple regressions in Table 11-6, under the label "Problem 1: Environment," shows the combined effects of our environmental variables—income, education, urbanization, and federal aid—on each of our policy measures. Note the size of the multiple correlation coefficients obtained by using only these four environmental variables: a significant proportion of the variation in all of our policy measures can be attributed to environmental forces alone. An asterisk indicates the single most influential independent variable in each of the problems. Income is the single most influential variable in determining per pupil expenditures for education, unemployment benefits, and ADC benefits; education is the single most influential variable in determining per capita total revenues; urbanization is the single most influential variable in determining police protection; and federal aid is the single most influential variable in determining per capita expenditures for welfare and highways.

Now let us combine our environmental variables with measures reflecting pluralism in the political systems of the fifty states as in our second set of regressions "Problem 2: Environment and Pluralism." When measures of pluralism—party competition, voter participation, and equality of apportionment—are added to our environ-

TABLE 11-6 MULTIVARIATE ANALYSIS: THE RELATIVE IMPORTANCE OF ENVIRONMENTAL AND POLITICAL FORCES IN EXPLAINING LEVELS OF SPENDING AND BENEFITS IN THE FIFTY STATES

| Independent Variables | | Partial Coefficients in Regression Problems on: | | | | | |
	Per Pupil Expenditures	Per Capita Welfare Expend.	Unemployment Benefits	ADC Benefits	Per Capita Highways	Police Protection	Per Capita Total Revenue
Problem 1: Environment							
Income	.68*	—.02	.51*	.50*	—.21	.35	.38
Education	—.09	.21	.20	.01	.35	—.24	.55*
Urbanization	—.10	.42	.06	.04	—.10	.55*	—.21
Federal Aid	.09	.79*	.05	—.04	.67*	—.00	.40
Multiple Coefficient	.84	.81	.81	.74	.84	.78	.81
Problem 2: Environment and Pluralism							
Income	.64*	—.13	.50*	.36*	—.22	.38	.37
Education	—.11	.18	.21	—.10	.34	—.21	.55*
Urbanization	—.08	.53	.06	.18	—.12	.51*	—.22
Federal Aid	.10	.83*	.06	.05	.68*	—.06	.35
Party Competition	—.05	.12	.09	—.14	—.18	.03	.04
Voter Participation	—.05	.00	.06	—.04	—.14	—.09	—.17
Malapportionment	.05	.04	.05	.23	.21	—.07	.05
Multiple Coefficient	.84	.86	.81	.81	.85	.79	.82
Problem 3: Environment and Reformism							
Income	.60*	—.37	.43*	.35	.00	.37	.23
Education	—.05	.27	.23	.00	.38	—.17	.48*
Urbanization	—.12	.18	—.00	.19	—.30	.46*	—.14
Federal Aid	.10	.83*	.07	.05	.68*	—.15	.20
Civil Service	—.07	.21	—.06	—.10	.06	.22	.12
Legislative Professionalism	—.04	.04	.04	—.42	—.37	.24	—.01
Innovation	.19	.14	.14	.60*	.03	—.34	—.08
Multiple Coefficient	.85	.86	.82	.85	.86	.84	.82

* An asterisk indicates the strangest independent variable in each problem.

mental variables, there is *no really significant increase* in explanatory power. The multiple coefficients for Problem 2 are not significantly higher than those for Problem 1. A knowledge of the extent of pluralism in a political system does *not* enable us to predict levels of government activity with any more accuracy than merely knowing the level of environmental resources. Moreover, in every case, the single most influential independent variable remains an environmental variable even after the addition of our pluralist measures to the regression problems. In no case does party competition, voter participation, or malapportionment emerge as more influential *than* the most influential environmental variable in determining policy.

If we combine environmental variables with measures reflecting reformism in political systems, "Problem 3: Environment and Reformism," the relative strength of the environmental variables is undiminished. The only exception noted is in welfare benefits, particularly average ADC payments, where reformism does indeed increase the size of the multile coefficient over coefficient obtained with environmental variables alone. Moreover, when reformism is added to the analysis of welfare benefits, the most influential independent variable is no longer income, but innovation. Thus, although the earlier reasoning of V. O. Key and others about the policy impact of *pluralism* on welfare benefits remains unproven, political *reformism* does turn out to be a significant factor in raising the level of welfare benefits. On the whole, however, reformism as a political system characteristic is *less* influential *than* environmental resources in determining levels of public spending and services.

A CLOSER LOOK: ALTERNATIVE
CAUSAL MODELS IN POLICY DETERMINATION

What are the *causal* implications of the research on public policy? So far we have examined the *relative importance* of environmental resources and political variables in the determination of levels of government spending and service. But we really have not yet specified the *causal* linkages between environment, system, and policy. Let us try to conceive of some alternative causal models and then test these models against our data from American state politics.[24]

The causal model suggested in the early state politics literature for public policy determination conceived of a developmental sequence from environment to political system to public policy. The environment shaped the character of political system and the character of the political system shaped public policy:

[24] An earlier attempt at testing causal model in state policy analysis is Charles F. Cnudde and Donald J. McCrone, "Party Competition and Welfare Policies in the American States," *American Political Science Review*, Vol. 63 (September 1969), 858-66.

Model 1: Sequential – Environmental

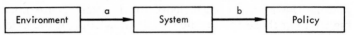

For example, it was argued that states with well-developed complex economies would be more likely to have competitive parties since the diversity of economic interests would provide a context for the emergence of political competition. Party competition, in turn, will lead to political appeals for support to wider publics including the "have nots." Competition and party labels also made it easier for "have nots" to sort out political actors and issues, and thereby enable them to promote their own interests in public policy. Hence, competition led to move "liberal" public policy, particularly in the welfare field.

A second causal model conceives of public policy as directly shaped by environmental forces, with the political system functioning as a more or less neutral mechanism transferring demands generated by the environment into public policy. The character of the political system is shaped by the environment, but the character of the political system itself has little direct impact on public policy. Whatever association there is between the political system variables and public policy is merely a product of the fact that both are shaped by environmental forces. Thus:

Model 2: Environmental

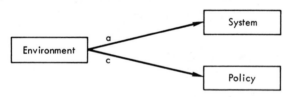

For example, it can be argued that wealthy, urban, industrial states spend more per pupil for education for the very simple reason that they can easily afford to do so. Tax revenues and the ability to spend money on education are closely tied to economic resources. It is also true that party competition is tied to economic development and diversity and therefore to higher per pupil expenditures for education. But party competition does not itself really have an independent impact on educational expenditures. Higher per pupil expenditures are a direct product of economic revenues, not of party competition.

A third causal model views public policy as shaped by *both* environmental forces and political system characteristics. The environment shapes the character of the political system which in turn shapes public policy, *and* the environment also directly affects public policy. This is a hybrid of our developmental and environmental models. Thus:

Model 3:   Hybrid – Environmental

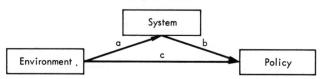

This model has a certain charm in that it recognizes multiple causal paths. An added advantage is that it is easier to establish statistically: all that is required is *some* evidence that political system variables independently influence public policy, whether or not they are more or less influential than environmental variables.

There are three additional models which are *possible*; but in the light of the evidence already presented about the relative impact of environmental resources compared to political variables these models are very *improbable*. These possibilities emphasize the primacy of political system characteristics in shaping the environmental resources and public policy. One might be labeled the "sequential-political" model:

Model 4:   Sequential – Political

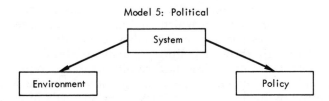

where the degree of pluralism, competition, participation, reformism, etc., in the political system is viewed as causing environmental resources to develop, which in turn leads to changes in public policy.

Another causal possibility is the purely "political model":

Model 5:   Political

where the character of the political system determines both the level of environmental resources and public policy, and the environment has no independent effect upon public policy. Finally, a hybrid model emphasizing the primacy of politics is possible:

Model 6:   Hybrid – Political

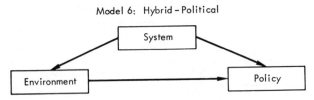

where the political system shapes policy directly and also does so through affecting environmental resources.

These alternative causal models can be subjected to formal testing. To do so we control first for environmental resources while observing the relationship between political variables and public policy, and then control for political variables while observing the relationship between environmental resources and public policy. If controlling for environmental resources completely "washes out" the relationships between political variables and public policy, then we must reject the idea that political variables are the primary determinants of public policy. This means, first of all, rejecting Models 4 and 5 which give little weight to environmental resources in explaining public policy; and second rejecting the notion in Model 1 that political variables are crucial independent variables which must be affected before environmental resources will affect public policy.

If controlling for political variables completely washes out the relationships between environmental resources and public policy, then we must reject the idea that environmental resources are primary in determining public policy. This would mean rejecting Models 1 and 2, and also rejecting Model 4 which assumes a change in the environment must precede a change in public policy. Finally, various combinations of test outcomes are possible where some relationships are completely washed out while others are not, and some relationships are reduced in their strength under controlled conditions but not completely washed out. These combinations of tests allow us to select from among the hybrid models.

The results of causal analysis lead us to reject causal models which designate political system characteristics as primary causes of variation in public policy. The only causal models which prove acceptable are those in which environmental resources are viewed as primary forces shaping public policy, either directly or both directly and indirectly through political system variables.

Table 11-7 summarizes test results on seven representative measures of levels of public spending and service in the American states. Controlling for political variables never succeeds in completely washing out relationships between environmental resources and public policy. In contrast controlling for economic resources frequently succeeds in washing out relationships between political variables and public policy, and always succeeds in reducing these relationships. The fact that controlling for environmental resources always reduces

TABLE 11-7 CAUSAL MODELS IN POLICY DETERMINATION

	Model 1 *Sequential-* *Environmental*	*Model 2* *Environmental*	*Model 3* *Hybrid-* *Environmental*
Per Pupil Expenditures	No	Yes	No
Per Capita Welfare Expend.	No	Yes	No
Unemployment Benefits	No	Yes	No
ADC Benefits	No	No	Yes
Per Capita Highway Expend.	No	Yes	No
Police Protection	No	No	Yes
Per Capita Total Revenue	No	Yes	No

	Model 4 *Sequential-* *Political*	*Model 5* *Political*	*Model 6* *Hybrid-* *Political*
Per Pupil Expenditures	No	No	No
Per Capita Welfare Expend.	No	No	No
Unemployment Benefits	No	No	No
ADC Benefits	No	No	No
Per Capita Highway Expend.	No	No	No
Police Protection	No	No	No
Per Capita Total Revenue	No	No	No

relationships between the political variables and public policy leads us to reject in every case the propositions set forth in early political science literature that environment shapes public policy only through changes which are made in the political system. Environmental resources can affect public policy directly. However, the fact that controlling for political variables sometimes reduces the relationship between environmental resources and public policy obliges us to accept the idea that environmental resources can affect public policy both directly and indirectly through political variables; this hybrid model can be observed with regard to welfare benefits and police protection. In short, we can rule out all of our causal models except Model 2 Environmental

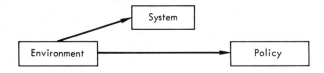

and Model 3 Hybrid Environmental.

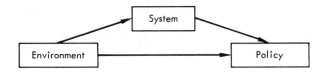

SUMMARY

The policies dealt with in this analysis reflected *levels* of taxing, spending, benefits, and services in education, health, welfare, highways, police, and government finance. It is important to remember that the results obtained in analyzing *levels* of government activity may not be the same as those obtained in analyzing *distributional* policies or qualitative policies. Moreover, we investigated only a limited number of political system characteristics—pluralism and reformism. It is possible that other political system characteristics might be related to some policy outcomes in a different fashion. However, let us set forth some general propositions about public policy which are suggested by our analysis:

1. Economic development is an important determinant of overall levels of government taxing, spending, and service. Wealth, as measured by per capita personal income, is the single most important environmental variable associated with levels of government taxing, spending, and service.

2. Federal grants-in-aid, considered "outside" money to state and local governments, help to release these governments from their dependence upon economic conditions within their jurisdictions and permit them to spend at higher levels than they would otherwise be able to do. Federal grants reduce the impact of a state's own economic resources on its level of spending and service. Thus, in explaining levels of public spending and service in the states, one must consider federal grants as well as environmental resources.

3. Wealth and education have been consistent determinants of the level of government spending and service over time. In contrast, industrialization has been losing influence as a determinant of government spending. Only where the federal government has intervened and offset disparities among the states has the influence of environmental variables been significantly reduced.

4. The traditional literature in American politics asserted that characteristics of political systems—particularly party competition, voter participation, and malapportionment—had an important impact on the content of public policy. But recent systematic research suggests that the characteristics of political systems are not *as* important *as* environmental conditions in shaping public policy. Most of the correlations between political system variables and public policy measures are a product of the fact that environmental forces shape *both* the political system and public policy.

5. Pluralism implies that factors such as party competition and voter participation are important determinants of public policy. And it is true that states with competitive parties and high voter turnouts have generally higher levels of taxing, spending, benefits, and service in a variety of policy areas. But these same states also tend to be wealthy urban states with well-educated adult populations.

6. Reformism—as measured by civil service coverage, professionalism in legislatures, and administrative innovation—is associated with higher levels of taxing, spending, benefits, and service in the states. However, reformism is also associated with environmental conditions—income, urbanization, and education.

7. Multivariable analysis indicates that, in general, environmental variables—income, urbanization, education, and federal aid— are more influential in determining levels of taxing, spending, benefits, and service, *than* either pluralism or reformism in the political system. Reformism is somewhat *more* influential *than* pluralism in determining some policy outcomes, but in most cases the single strongest determinant of government activity is an environmental variable.

8. The testing of alternative causal models in policy determination leads us to reject the proposition that environmental forces shape public policy *only* through changes which are made in the political system. We must also reject the idea that the character of the political system must be changed in order to change public policy. Environmental resources can affect public policy directly regardless of the character of the political system. However, in some policy areas environmental forces shape public policy both directly and indirectly through political variables.

BIBLIOGRAPHY

DYE, THOMAS R., *Politics, Economics, and the Public: Policy Outcomes in the American States.* Chicago: Rand McNally, 1966.

FRANCIS, WAYNE, *Legislative Issues in the Fifty States: A Comparative Analysis.* Chicago: Rand McNally, 1969.

HOFFERBERT, RICHARD I. and IRA SHARKANSKY, eds., *State and Urban Politics.* Boston: Little, Brown, 1971.

JACOB, HERBERT and KENNETH VINES, eds., *Politics in the American States,* 2nd ed. Boston: Little, Brown, 1971.

SHARKANSKY, IRA, *Spending in the American States.* Chicago: Rand McNally, 1968.

THE POLICY-MAKING PROCESS:
getting inside the system

CHAPTER 12

THE BLACK BOX PROBLEM

It is vitally important that we understand what goes on in the little black box labeled "political system." The systems approach employed in the previous chapter deals with aggregate characteristics of *whole* political systems; this model does not say much about what goes on *within* political systems. Our comparative analysis focused attention on the linkages between environmental resources, system characteristics, and public policy, and dealt with numbers of whole political systems. But we also want to know what happens *within* political systems. We want to know how public policy is generated within the political system, how institutions and processes function to handle demands generated in the environment, and how parties, interest groups, voters, governors, legislators, and other political actors behave in the policy-making process.

Let us try to illustrate the differences between a *comparative systems* approach and a *within-system* approach. Finding a high correlation between cigarette smoking and the incidence of cancer among human systems is important. But this correlation does not in itself reveal the functioning of cells within the human body: we still want to know *how* cancers are formed and how they behave. So

265

also finding a high correlation between urbanization and police protection does not in itself reveal the functioning of political systems; we will want to know *how* a political system goes about transferring demands arising from the socioeconomic environment into public policy.

Traditionally political science concerned itself with describing political institutions, processes, and behaviors. But, as we noted earlier, most studies did not carefully examine the impact of institutions, processes, and behavior *on public policy.* Most studies simply described the functioning of the political system itself, and did not investigate the impact of its functioning on the content of public policy. So in spite of a great body of literature on American politics, we do not have very many studies which systematically examine the linkages between specific institutions, processes, and behaviors and the *content of public policy.*

In describing the political process, however, it is important to remember that the acitivities of voters, interest groups, parties, legislators, executives, and other political actors are greatly constrained by environmental conditions. We have already described the great influence environmental resources have on the character of the political system and the content of public policy. It is true that not *all* of the variance in public policy can be explained by environmental resources. However, the activities of parties, groups, and individuals *within* the political system are heavily impacted by the nature of the environment. So our initial systems approach has warned us not to expect the activities of individuals, groups, parties, or decision makers to produce policies at variance with environmental resources and constraints.

MASS OPINION AND PUBLIC POLICY

The influence of public opinion over government policy has been the subject of great philosophical controversies in the classic literature on democracy. Edmund Burke believed democratic representatives should serve the *interest* of the people but not necessarily conform to their *will* in deciding questions of public policy. In contrast, some democratic theorists have evaluated the success of democratic institutions by whether or not they facilitate popular control over public policy.

The philosophical question of whether public opinion *should* be an important independent influence over public policy may never be resolved. But the empirical question of whether public opinion *does* constitute an important independent influence over public policy can be tackled by systematic research. However, even this empirical question has proven very difficult to answer.

The problem in assessing the independent effect of mass opinion on the actions of decision makers is that the actions of decision makers help to mold mass opinion. Public policy may accord with mass opinion but we can never be sure whether mass opinion shaped public policy or public policy shaped mass opinion.

In V. O. Key's most important book, *Public Opinion and American Democracy*, he wrote:

> Government, as we have seen, attempts to mold public opinion toward support of the programs and policies it espouses. Given that endeavor, perfect congruence between public policy and public opinion could be government *of* public opinion rather than government *by* public opinion.[1]

While V. O. Key himself was convinced that public opinion did have some independent effect on public policy, he was never able to demonstrate this in any systematic fashion. He lamented:

> Discussion of public opinion often loses persuasiveness as it deals with the critical question of how public opinion and governmental action are linked. The democratic theorist founds his doctrines on the assumption that an interplay occurs between mass opinion and government. When he seeks to delineate that interaction and to demonstrate the precise bearing of the opinions of private citizens on official decision, he encounters almost insurmountable obstacles. In despair he may conclude that the supposition that public opinion enjoys weight in public decision is a myth and nothing more, albeit a myth that strengthens a regime so long as people believe it.[2]

Yet V. O. Key compiled a great deal of circumstantial evidence supporting the notion that elections, parties, interest groups, and other representative procedures do institutionalize channels of communication from citizens to decision makers.

But there is very little *direct* evidence in the existing research literature to support the notion that public opinion is an important influence over public policy. Many surveys reveal the absence of any knowledge or opinion about public policy on the part of masses of citizens. This suggests that mass opinion has little influence over the content of public policy. How can mass opinion be said to affect public policy when there *is* no mass opinion on a great many policy questions? Studies suggesting that the masses of people have little knowledge of, or interest in, or opinion about a great many policy questions clearly imply that public opinion has little impact on the content of public policy. Likewise studies which indicate that public opinion is unstable and inconsistent also imply that public opinion has little policy impact.

Yet, in order to test systematically the *independent* effect of mass

[1] V. O. Key, Jr., *Public Opinion and American Democracy* (New York: Knopf, 1967), pp. 422-23.
[2] *Ibid.*, p. 411.

TABLE 12-1 PUBLIC OPINION AND PUBLIC POLICY IN THE STATES

	In States Where Majority Supports			In States Where Majority Opposes			Index of Agreement (States in Which Preference and Policies Coincide)	
	N	Have Statute	No Statute	N	Have Statute	No Statute	N	Percent
State Lotteries: Would you favor or oppose lotteries (or sweepstakes) in this state run by the state government to help pay the cost of government? (AIPO 672 and AIPO 688)	20	2	18	30	0	30	32	64
Capital Punishment: Are you in favor of the death penalty for persons convicted of murder? (AIPO 704 and AIPO 729)	21	18	3	29	22	7	25	50
Right-to-Work: Do you think a person should or should not be required to join a union if he works in a unionized factory or business? (AIPO 711, AIPO 717, AIPO 718, AIPO 723). An Affirmative "should," has been treated as a negative right-to-work legislation.	31	17	14	19	2	17	34	68
Public Accommodations: How would you feel about a law which would give all persons—Negroes as well as whites—the right to be served in public places such as hotels, restaurants, theaters, and similar establishments? Would you like to see Congress pass such a law or not? (AIPO 674, AIPO 676, AIPO 683)	34	32	2	16	2	14	46	92
Gun Controls: Would you favor or oppose a law which would require a person to obtain a police permit before he or she could buy a gun? (AIPO 681, AIPO 704, AIPO 717, AIPO 733)	50	8	42	0	0	0	8	16
TOTAL	56	77	79	94	26	68	145	58

Source: Data from Frank Munger, "Opinions, Elections, Parties, and Policies: A Cross-State Analysis," paper delivered at annual meeting of the American Political Science Association, New York, 1969.

opinion on public policy, we must have information on mass opinion and public policy in a significant number of political systems.

Let us begin by considering five state policies about which most people have opinions of some kind—legal lotteries, capital punishment, right-to-work laws, antidiscrimination laws, and gun controls. Professor Frank Munger converted national survey data about public opinion on these topics into estimates of opinion within the separate electorates.[3] He was able to designate the states in which a majority supported legislation on these topics and the states in which a majority opposed such legislation. Then he examined the laws of the states to ascertain the congruence between majority opinion and public policy. The results are shown in Table 12-1.

The really startling fact about public policy in these five issues is the general lack of congruence between public policy and public opinion. Munger concludes: "There are substantial discrepancies between electoral preferences and state policies; and there are great variations among the five policy areas in the closeness of fit between opinions and actions." The overall figure for policy-opinion congruence is only 58 percent; this means that the chances of a state's policy matching the preferences of its citizens are only a little better than the 50–50 ratio generated by chance! Of course, it is true that these five policy areas are by no means a representative sample of all public policy. And it is also interesting to note that in the area of civil rights—where many studies have suggested that public opinion is generally well defined and intense—state policy is in conformity with public opinion in the states. But on such seemingly important questions as lotteries, capital punishment, right-to-work laws, and gun controls, public opinion has little relationship to public policy. Certainly we have no evidence to support the assertion that public opinion is an *important* independent influence over public policy.

PUBLIC OPINION AND THE RESPONSIVENESS OF GOVERNMENTS

What are effects of differing political system characteristics on policy-opinion congruence? Is there greater policy-opinion congruence in states with more pluralistic politics? Given the surprisingly low overall level of policy-opinion congruence, is such congruence any greater in states with competitive parties, high voter turnout, and fair apportionment?

One can come up with all sorts of plausible-sounding theories about why increased competition and participation should result in greater congruence between popular preferences and public policy.

[3] Frank J. Munger, "Opinion, Elections, Parties, and Policies: A Cross-State Analysis," paper delivered at annual meeting of the American Political Science Association, New York, 1969.

TABLE 12-2 PLURALISM AND POLICY-OPINION CONGRUENCE IN THE AMERICAN STATES
Index of Policy-Opinion Agreement
(Percentage of States in which Policy Coincides with Majority Opinion)

	Interparty Competition			
	Least			*Most*
	I	*II*	*III*	*IV*
	(11 states)	*(13 states)*	*(13 states)*	*(13 states)*
State Lotteries	100%	54%	77%	31%
Capital Punishment	0	46	69	77
Right-to-Work	82	77	46	69
Public Accommodations	100	85	92	92
Gun Controls	9	15	15	23
Total	58%	55%	60%	58%

	Political Participation			
	Lowest			*Highest*
	I	*II*	*III*	*IV*
	(11 states)	*(13 states)*	*(13 states)*	*(13 states)*
State Lotteries	100%	46%	54%	62%
Capital Punishment	0	46	77	69
Right-to-Work	82	62	62	69
Public Accommodation	100	77	100	92
Gun Controls	9	23	23	8
Total	58%	51%	63%	60%

	Malapportionment			
	Maximum			*Minimum*
	I	*II*	*III*	*IV*
	(12 states)	*(13 states)*	*(13 states)*	*(12 states)*
State Lotteries	75%	85%	54%	42%
Capital Punishment	58	38	38	67
Right-to-Work	50	45	92	75
Public Accommodations	92	85	100	92
Gun Controls	0	23	15	25
Total	55%	57%	60%	60%

Source: Data from Munger, "Opinion, Elections, Parties, and Policies."

Advocates of responsible party government have consistently asserted that two-party competition facilitates majority rule. And it is not unreasonable to believe that highly competitive parties would seek popular approval by enacting policies supported by a majority of citizens. Likewise, it is not unreasonable to believe that public policy will be more likely to reflect popular preferences in states where voter participation is higher. Finally, one might reasonably expect the policies of well-apportioned states to be more congruent with majority opinion than the policies of malapportioned states. Yet despite the apparent logic of these propositions, they are *not* supported by the available empirical evidence.

At present, there is no empirical evidence to support the view that there is greater congruence between popular preferences and public policy in *pluralist* political systems than in nonpluralist political systems. Professor Frank Munger examined his data on policy-opinion congruence in lotteries, capital punishment, right-to-work, public accommodations, and gun controls, to see if such congruence was any greater in two-party, high-voter-turnout, well-apportioned states, than in one-party, low-voter-turnout, malapportioned states. The results are shown in Table 12-2.

On the whole, competitive two-party states are no more likely to have policies which conform to majority opinion than noncompetitive one-party states. There is no consistent increase in policy-opinion congruence as we move from the less competitive to the more competitive states. Likewise, there is no significant difference in the overall extent of policy-opinion congruence between high and low voter turnout states, or between states having well-apportioned and poorly apportioned legislatures. In short, there is no evidence that pluralism functions to bring public policy into conformity with majority opinion.

ELITE ATTITUDES AND PUBLIC POLICY

When V. O. Key wrestled with the same problem confronting us— namely, the determination of the impact of popular preferences on public policy—he concluded that "the Missing Piece of the Puzzle" was "that thin stratum of persons referred to variously as the political elite, the political activists, the leadership echelons, or the influentials."

> The longer one frets with the puzzle of how democratic regimes manage to function, the more plausible it appears that a substantial part of the explanation is to be found in the motives that activate the *leadership echelon*, the values that it holds, the rules of the political game to which it adheres, in the expectations which it entertains about its own status in society, and perhaps in some of the objective circumstances, both material and institutional, in which it functions.[4]

In view of our inability to find any direct links between public policy and popular preferences, it seems reasonable to ask whether the preferences of elites are more directly reflected in public policy than the preferences of masses. Do elite attitudes independently affect public policy? Or are elite attitudes so closely tied to environmental conditions that elites have relatively little flexibility in policy-making and therefore little independent influence over the content of public policy?

Elite preferences are more likely to be in accord with public policy than mass preferences. This finding is fairly well supported in the existing research literature. Of course this does not *prove* that policies are determined by elite preferences. It may be that government officials are acting nationally in response to events and conditions,

[4] V. O. Key, Jr., *Public Opinion and American Democracy*, p. 537.

and well-educated, informed elites understand the actions of government better than masses. Hence, it might be argued that elites support government policies because they have greater understanding of and confidence in government, and they are more likely to read about and comprehend the explanations of government officials. On the other hand, the correspondence between elite opinion and public policy may also indicate that elite opinion determines public policy.

Elite Opinion and the War in Vietnam

Let us consider, for example, the relationship between elite and mass opinion and the Vietnam War. Well-educated Americans gave greater support to the war during the Johnson Administration than less-educated Americans. The masses had greater doubts about the

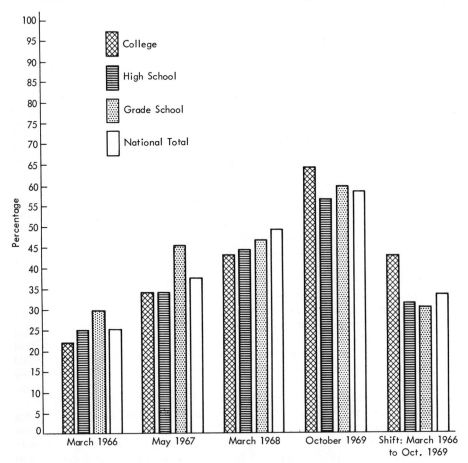

FIG. 12-1   AGREEMENT THAT U.S. INVOLVEMENT IN VIETNAM WAS A MISTAKE, BY
EDUCATION LEVELS

Source: Gallup Opinion Index (October 1969), p. 15.

advisability of the war than the elites. However, the Johnson Administration went ahead with a policy of escalation, increasing U.S. combat forces in Vietnam. By 1968 elite opinion was divided, and in the 1968 elections both Democratic and Republican Presidential candidates gave only guarded support for the policy of the Administration. By 1969, elite opinion had shifted dramatically; nearly two out of every three well-educated Americans had come to believe that U.S. involvement in Vietnam was a "mistake." Mass opposition to the war had also grown to a point where a majority now felt U.S. policy was a mistake. But mass opinion never shifted as dramatically as elite opinion. It was at this point that the policy of escalation was reversed, and President Nixon began his policy of gradual U.S. combat troop withdrawal and "Vietnamization" of the war.

Many other policy areas display the same elite-mass opinion linkages. It is usually the most highly educated, prestigeously employed, wealthy people who are highly supportive of government policies. Policy change more closely corresponds to changes in elite opinion than changes in mass opinion.

Elite Opinion and Desegregation

Another indication of the influence of elite opinion on policy is found in sociologist Robert Crain's important study, *The Politics of School Desegregation*.[5] Crain systematically measured and compared the desegregation policies of eight Northern cities, specifically in terms of their acquiescence to the demands of civil rights groups.

Perhaps the most interesting finding presented by Crain is that the ideological orientation of the school board members is the *most* important factor in determining how a community responds to demands for changes in racial patterns in the schools. Crain ranked his cities according to their acquiescence to civil rights demands and then searched for community factors which appeared to influence the degree of acquiescence.[6] Certainly the intensity of the demands of civil right activists did not lead to acquiescence; in fact the relationship was just the opposite; nonacquiescent cities were faced with the most militant civil rights activity.

While the cities with the largest Negro populations were most likely to have acquiescent school boards, the correlation was not as good as one would expect (r = .53). The potential Negro vote was *not* a very strong influence on school board policy making. Perhaps

[5] Robert Crain, *The Politics of School Desegregation* (Chicago: Aldine, 1968).
[6] Crain's acquiescence scale was as follows: (1) Pittsburgh: adoption of open enrollment after hearing parents' testimony; (2) Baltimore: decision by ad hoc committee to eliminate districting (June, 1963); (3) San Francisco: decision to close Central Junior High School (August, 1962); (4) Newark: adoption of open enrollment to settle suit (January, 1962); (5) St. Louis: receipt and adoption in general terms of Maher committee report (June, 1963); (6) Lawndale: refusal to change woodside boundaries (January, 1961); (7) Bay City: fruitless discussion of de facto segregation prior to the first boycott (June, 1963); (8) Buffalo: designation of Woodlawn school boundaries (March, 1963).

one reason why the percentage Negro does not correlate very well with acquiescence to Negro demands is that cities with the largest Negro populations have more anti-Negro sentiment among whites. But in an apparent paradox, it also turned out that the status characteristics of white populations, particularly high educational level, which might be expected to correlate with acquiescence to Negro demands, did not appear to influence board policy. Thus, Crain concludes that neither the characteristics of the community nor the activities of the civil rights movement (other than their initial presentation of the issue) had much influence on board policy.

The most important factor influencing desegregation policy was the civil rights attitude of school board members. Figure 12-2 plots the median civil rights liberalism (obtained by analyzing responses to questionnaires filled out by board members) against the acquiescence of the school board. The overall correlation (.65) is not very high. However, the pattern reveals an important difference between elected and appointed boards: the three cities which fall below the line of regression, being less acquiescent than we would expect from the liberalism score of the members, are all *elected* boards; the other five are all appointed boards. Apparently elected school board mem-

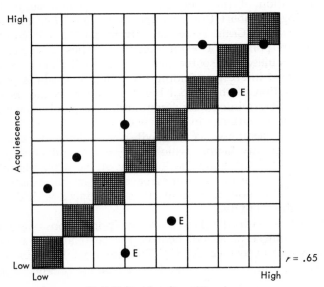

E indicates on elected board; *r* , among appointed
board = .97; *r* , among elected board = 1.00

FIG. 12-2   CIVIL RIGHTS LIBERALISM OF SCHOOL BOARDS AND ACQUIESCENCE IN DESEG-
REGATION IN NORTHERN CITIES

Source: Robert Crain, *The Politics of School Desegregation* (Chicago: Aldine Publishing Co., 1968). Copyright © 1968 by National Opinion Research Center. Reprinted by permission of Aldine-Atherton, Inc.

bers do not inject their own liberalism into board policy as much as appointed board members. Elected board members with the same liberalism scores as appointed board members are less acquiescent in the demands of civil rights groups.

Thus, public policy is more likely to conform to elite opinion than to mass opinion. (Additional evidence to support this conclusion is presented in Chapter 3, "Civil Rights: Elite Mass Interaction.") But elites themselves must be responsive to environmental forces; these forces generate demands for governmental activities and provide the necessary resources to support public policy. It is unlikely that elites can operate independently of environmental forces for very long. Decision makers are heavily constrained by the availability of resources, if nothing else. And they cannot long ignore pressing environmental problems. Virtually every public official and elected representative complains of the many specific demands and constraints placed upon him in decision making, demands and constraints which severely limit his policy choices. The question of how much *independent* effect elite opinion has on public policy remains unresolved.

PARTY INFLUENCE ON PUBLIC POLICY

Parties are important institutions in the American political system, but it would be a mistake to overestimate their impact on public policy. It makes relatively little difference in the major direction of public policy whether Democrats or Republicans dominate the political scene. American parties are largely "brokerage" organizations, devoid of ideology, and committed to winning public office rather than to advancing policy positions. Both the Democratic and Republican parties and their candidates tailor their policy positions to societal conditions. The result is that the parties do not have much independent impact on policy outcomes.

Both American parties subscribe to the same fundamental political ideology. Both share prevailing democratic consensus about the sanctity of private property, a free enterprise economy, individual liberty, limited government, majority rule, and due process of law. Moreover, since the 1930s both parties have supported the same mass-welfare domestic programs of social security, fair labor standards, unemployment compensation, and graduated income tax, a national highway program, a federally aided welfare system, countercyclical fiscal and monetary policies, and government regulation of public utilities. Finally, both parties have supported the basic outlines of American foreign and military policy since World War II—international involvement, anticommunism, the cold war, European recovery, NATO, military preparedness, selective service, and even the Korean and Vietnam wars. A change in party control of the Presidency or Congress has not resulted in any significant shifts in the course of American foreign or domestic policy.

Yet there are nuances of differences between the parties which can be observed in the policy-making process. Th social bases of the Democratic and Republican parties are slightly different. Both parties draw support from all social groups in America, but the Democrats draw disproportionately from labor, big-city residents, ethnic voters, Negroes, Jews, and Catholics; while Republicans draw disproportionately from rural, small town, and suburban Protestants, businessmen, and professionals. To the extent that the policy orientations of these two broad groups differ, the thrust of party ideology also differs. However, the magnitude of this difference is not very great.

Most votes in Congress and the state legislatures are *unanimous* ones. This suggests that consensus rather than division is the prevailing style of policy making. However, party divisions are still more persistent *than* any other kind of division. *Party* votes, those roll-call votes in which a majority of voting Democrats oppose a majority of voting Republicans, occur on about *half* of all of the nonunanimous roll-call votes taken in Congress. Roll-call voting follows party lines more often than it follows sectional, urban-rural, or any other divisions that have been studied. How much cohesion exists within the parties? Table 12–3 shows the number of party votes that have been taken in Congress in recent years and the average support Democratic and Republican congressmen have given to their parties. Democrats and Republicans appear equally cohesive, with members of both parties voting with their party majority more than two-thirds of the time. Party voting appears more frequent in the House than in the Senate.

Bipartisan votes, those roll calls in which divisions are not along party lines, occur most frequently in the areas of foreign policy and defense matters. Bipartisan agreement also appears on appropriation bills and roll calls where there is little dispute. Recently bipartisan voting has settled issues of federal aid to education, highway beautification, water pollution, voting rights, presidential continuity, and increases in federal employees' pay and veterans' benefits.

TABLE 12-3   PARTY VOTING IN CONGRESS

	Total Roll Calls	Party Vote Roll Calls	Percent of Total
1969			
Both Chambers	422	144	34%
Senate	245	89	36%
House	177	55	31%
1967			
Both Chambers	560	198	35%
Senate	315	109	35%
House	245	89	36%
1965			
Both Chambers	459	213	46%
Senate	258	108	42%
House	201	105	52%

Source: Congressional Quarterly, various issues, 1965-1970.

Conflict between parties occurs most frequently over issues involving social welfare programs, housing and urban development, medicare, antipoverty programs, and the regulation of business and labor. Party conflict is particularly apparent in the budget, the most important policy document of the national government. The budget is identified as the product of the President and carries the label of his party. On some issues, such as civil rights and appropriations, voting will follow party lines during roll calls on preliminary motions, amendments, and other preliminary matters, but swing to a bipartisan vote on passage of the final legislation. This means that the parties have disagreed on certain aspects of the bill, but compromised on its final passage.

What are the issues that cause conflict between the Democratic and Republican parties? In general, Democrats have favored lower tariffs; federal subsidies for agriculture; federal action to assist labor and low-income groups through social security, relief, housing, and wage-hour regulation; and generally a larger role for the federal government in launching new projects to remedy domestic problems. Republicans, on the other hand, have favored higher tariffs, free competition in agriculture, less government involvement in labor and welfare matters, and reliance on private action (see Table 12–4).

TABLE 12-4 PARTY DIVISION ON SELECTED KEY VOTES IN CONGRESS

| | House Votes | | | |
| | Republicans | | Democrats | |
	Yes	No	Yes	No
Medicare (1965)	65	73	248	42
Establish Department of Housing and Urban Development (1965)	9	118	208	66
Federal Aid to Education (1965)	35	96	228	57
Model Cities Programs (1966)	16	81	162	60
Rat control in cities (1967)	22	148	154	59
Anticrime grants to states (1967)	172	4	84	143
Turnover Poverty Program to states (1970)	103	63	60	168
Override Nixon's veto of Labor-Welfare funds (1970)	27	156	199	35

| | Senate Votes | | | |
| | Republicans | | Democrats | |
	Yes	No	Yes	No
Medicare (1965)	13	14	55	7
Repeal Taft-Hartley "right to work" provisions (1965)	5	26	40	21
Reduction in spending 5% across all items (1965)	26	5	17	41
Nomination of Abe Fortas to Supreme Court (1968)	10	24	35	19
Antiballistic missile (ABM) system (1970)	29	14	21	36

Source: Congressional Quarterly, various issues, 1965-1970.

Further, each party supports the president to a different degree. The president generally receives greater support from his own party than from the opposition party in Congress. The figures in Table 12–5 show that President Johnson received the support of 64 percent of all Senate Democrats and 74 percent of the House Democrats on the 274 roll calls in 1965 presenting clear-cut tests for support for his views. In contrast, the Republicans in both houses supported President Johnson on less than half of these presidential support votes. Democrats rarely opposed the President's program, while Republicans frequently did. However, Republicans were much more critical of the President's domestic programs than of his foreign policy programs.

TABLE 12-5 PARTY SUPPORT IN CONGRESS FOR PRESIDENTIAL RECOMMENDATIONS

	Nixon		Johnson	
	Democratic	*Republican*	*Democratic*	*Republican*
Overall				
Support				
Senate	47%	66%	55%	50%
House	48%	57%	66%	48%
Opposition				
Senate	39%	23%	24%	33%
House	38%	31%	18%	40%
Foreign Policy				
Support				
Senate	66%	72%	59%	57%
House	63%	51%	66%	44%
Opposition				
Senate	21%	16%	21%	24%
House	19%	33%	18%	43%
Domestic Policy				
Support				
Senate	40%	64%	53%	47%
House	46%	58%	67%	49%
Opposition				
Senate	45%	25%	25%	36%
House	41%	31%	18%	39%

Source: Congressional Quarterly Weekly Report (January 16, 1970), p. 147.

What then is the basis of party cohesion where it exists? Is party cohesion a product of effective party organization and discipline? Or is it really a result of similarities in the constituencies represented by each party? For example, is Democratic party cohesion a result of party organization pressures? Or is it the fact that Democrats typically are elected from metropolitan centers with strong labor groups, many Catholic voters, racial and ethnic minorities, and persons with few skills and poor education, and it is really constituency similarities that hold the Democratic legislators together? Could it be that Republican cohesion is a product of the fact that Republicans typically represent middle-class suburbs, small towns, and rural areas, and these types of constituencies have similar ideas about public policy?

PARTY, CONSTITUENCY, AND POLICY

It is unlikely that party organization and discipline alone is the cause of party voting, for organization and discipline can only be effective under certain conditions. The weight of evidence seems to support the hypothesis that *party influence is only effective where the parties represent separate and distinct socioeconomic coalitions.* Where the constituencies of a state are divided along social and economic lines, and where the party division coincides with these constituency divisions, only then will party program and discipline be effective in shaping policy in legislative chambers.

After investigating the correlations between party cohesion and constituency characteristics in twenty-six state senates, Le Blanc found that: (1) senators were more loyal to their party when their constituents voted heavily for their party in gubernatorial and presidential elections; (2) senators were more loyal to their party in partisan states where the Democratic party was heavily supported in constituencies of racial and ethnic minorities, low-income groups and the poorly educated; (3) senators were less loyal to their party in states where a more ambiguous relationship existed between the Democratic party and socioeconomic constituencies. He observed:

> It is understood, of course, that constituency influences on legislative voting are sometimes difficult to disentangle from party influences and the dictates of the legislator's own conscience or convictions. Often the several influences reinforce one another. Thus an individual of liberal convictions is politically involved in the Democratic party for that reason and, as the Democratic party's candidate for senator is victorious at the polls in a constituency conventionally associated with Democratic party success—perhaps a racially mixed, low income, urban constituency, heavily populated with industrial workers. In voting to increase workmen's compensation payments, the senator could be said to vote his convictions, his party's program, and his constituency.[7]

Pennsylvania is an excellent example of a state in which Republican and Democratic legislative districts are clearly differentiated by socioeconomic variables.[8] The parties are first divided along rural-urban lines, and within urban areas they are further divided along indices of socioeconomic status. Republicans dominate in rural areas and in the wealthier urban areas (upper middle-class suburbs and several "silk stocking" districts in Philadelphia and Pittsburgh). Democratic dis-

[7] Hugh L. LeBlanc, "Voting in State Senates: Party and Constituency Influences," *Midwest Journal of Political Science*, Vol. 13 (February 1969), 33-57.
[8] William J. Keefe, "Parties, Partisanship, and Public Policy in the Pennsylvania Legislature," *American Political Science Review*, Vol. 48 (1954), 450-64; Thomas R. Dye, "A Comparison of Constituency Influences in the Upper and Lower Chambers of a State Legislature," *Western Political Quarterly*, Vol. 14 (1961), 473-80.

tricts are found predominantly in the less wealthy, urban areas of the state. A similar pattern emerges if occupational, religious, or racial charactistics are considered. Republican districts within urban areas prove to be the districts with greater concentrations of professional, managerial, sales, and clerical jobs. Republican candidates fare badly among Negro voters. The Democrats dominate the southern and eastern European, Irish, Catholic districts which are frequently the big-city, mining, or mill districts. The Republicans draw heavily in the Anglo-Saxon northern and western European, Protestant districts of the state. This same sort of party division of legislative districts has been documented in Massachusetts and Michigan.[9] In short, the Democratic and Republican division of legislative constituencies in these states follows the socioeconomic divisions of national party politics.

It is this division of constituencies which is the basis of party cohesion and influence in the legislature. Evidence to support this view is provided if we examine the voting behavior of legislators elected from districts *atypical* of districts which usually elect members of their party. Since rural and high-income urban districts in Pennsylvania generally elect Republicans, and low-income urban districts generally elect Democrats, atypical districts are rural or wealthy urban districts which elect Democrats and low-income urban districts which elect Republicans. Studies in Pennsylvania, Massachusetts, and Michigan of the voting behavior of representatives from these atypical districts show that they tend to cross party lines much more frequently than representatives elected from districts typical of their party.[10] The threat to Democratic party cohesion in these states came from small bands of rural Democrats; insurgency within the Republican party originated from the urban Republican legislators. The fact that party cohesion breaks down among representatives elected by districts atypical of their party indicates that cohesion may really be a function of environmental forces rather than of party organization and discipline.

INTEREST GROUPS AND PUBLIC POLICY

Interest-group activity also provides a linkage between environmental forces and public policy. The interest group structure of a society clearly reflects its socioeconomic composition. Modern urban institutional societies spawn a multitude of diverse interest groups. The resulting multiplicity and diversity reduces the likelihood that any

[9] Duncan MacRae, "The Relations Between Roll Call Votes and Constituencies in the Massachusetts House of Representatives," *American Political Science Review*, Vol. 46 (1952), 1046-55; Robert W. Becker, *et al.*, "Correlates of Legislative Voting: Michigan," *Midwest Journal of Political Science*, Vol. 6 (1962), 384-96.

[10] Duncan MacRae, Robert W. Becker, Thomas R. Dye; see also Thomas A. Flinn, "Party Responsibility in the States: Some Causal Factors," *American Political Science Review*, Vol. 58 (1964), 60-71.

TABLE 12-6   RELATIONSHIPS BETWEEN ENVIRONMENT, INTEREST GROUP STRUCTURE, AND PARTY SYSTEM

Environment	Interest Groups	Parties	Interest Group Influence
Wealthy, urban, industrial	many, diverse	competitive, cohesive	indirect, moderate
Poor, rural, agricultural	fewer, consolidated	noncompetitive, faction-ridden	direct, strong

single interest group can determine policy working in all fields. In contrast, poor, rural, agricultural societies produce fewer interest groups, but the opportunity for these interest groups to dominate policy making in underdeveloped economies is greater.

Interest group activity is also linked to party competition, which in turn is related to economic development. Interest groups are more directly influential in policy making in societies where the party system is weak and undeveloped. In the absence of strong cohesive parties, interest groups play a direct role in legislative affairs, with little moderation of their influence by intervening party influences. In contrast, where parties are strong and cohesive, interest groups may be more numerous and active, but their influence must be filtered through, and moderated by, party affairs.

Union Protesters in Washington. Photo by Fletcher Drake

On what kinds of decisions are interest groups most likely to exercise influence? Party and constituency influence are most important on broad social and economic issues. But on narrower issues, parties are less likely to take a stand, and constituents are less likely to have either an interest or an opinion. The legislator is, therefore, freer to respond to the pleas of organized groups on highly specialized topics than he is on major issues of public interest. The absence of both party and constituency influence on certain types of issues contributes to the effectiveness of organized interests. Economic interests, seeking to use the law to improve their competitive position, are a major source of group pressure on these specialized topics. Of course, these arguments are phrased in terms of "the public interest." As Malcolm Jewell reports in Kentucky:

> Representatives of horse racing interests write that the introduction of dog racing would damage not only them but the state's way of life. The chiropractors are upset by a bill sponsored by the state medical association. Bank presidents wire to prevent a bill that would permit small loan companies to loan larger amounts. Florists and nurserymen want license laws to limit competition. Local dairies want legislation to guarantee orderly market practices and undercut methods used by chain stores.[11]

Particularly active in lobbying are the businesses subject to extensive government regulation. The truckers, railroads, and liquor interests are consistently found to be among the most highly organized and active lobbyists in state capitals. Organized pressure also comes from associations of governments and associations of government employees. State chapters of the National Education Association (NEA) are persistent in presenting the demands of educational administrators and occasionally the demands of the dues-paying teachers as well.

The actual policy impact of interest groups is difficult to measure. A majority of state legislators report that they have never been persuaded to *change* their views on a particular policy question because of lobbying activity.[12] Yet it is very likely that lobbying can be effective on issues on which legislators held no prior opinions. These are likely to be the specialized economic issues.

The only systematic study of the overall policy consequences of interest group activity is political scientist Lewis A. Froman's study of special advantages and privileges written into state constitutions.[13]

[11] Malcolm Jewell, *The State Legislature* (New York: Random House, 1962), p. 70.
[12] Harmon Zeigler and Michael Baer, *Lobbying: Influence and Interaction in American State Legislatures* (Belmont: Wadsworth, 1969).
[13] Lewis A. Froman. "Some Effects of Interest Group Strength in State Politics," *American Political Science Review*, Vol. 60 (December 1966), 952-62.

Professor Froman found that in states where interest groups are stronger, a larger number of special privileges and advantages will be granted by state constitutions. The stronger the interest groups in the state, the greater the length of the state constitution, the greater the number of proposed amendments, and the greater the number of amendments adopted. States with strong interest groups tend to have long constitutions, which deal directly with questions of public policy (labor practices, regulation of utilities, transportation problems, and so on). Typically interest groups press for constitutional provisions to protect their interests because they are unwilling to trust future legislatures in matters of public policy. Thus, strong interest group states are likely to have lengthy constitutions, which specify, among other things, public tariffs and charges, limit the taxing powers of the states and communities, place restrictions on state debt, specify the duties and powers of public service commissions and the regulation of utilities, set forth regulations on insurance companies, specify the hours and duties of local government officials, set the salaries of the state and local officeholders, exempt certain industries from taxation, regulate school systems, and so on. He concludes that constitutions are one of the means by which advantages and disadvantages are distributed in political systems, and that the strength of interest groups in gaining special constitutional advantages can be observed in the length of state constitutions and in amending activity.

BUREAUCRATIC, EXECUTIVE, LEGISLATIVE INTERACTION

The process approach to government devotes a great deal of attention to the formal and informal relationships between administrative agencies, chief executives, and legislative aides. Students of this approach concentrate their attention on the powers of chief executives over administrative agencies and over legislative proposals, and the powers of legislative aides over the actions of administrative agencies and chief executives. But the impact of patterns of administrative, executive, and legislative interaction on the *content of public policy* is largely unexplained.

One of the rare studies of the interaction between administrative agencies, governors, and legislatures, which focuses on the impact of this interaction on budgetary outcomes, is political scientist Ira Sharkansky's analysis of the budgetary process in nineteen states.[14] Professor Sharkansky examined the relationships between agency requests, gov-

---

[14] Ira Sharkansky, "Agency Requests, Gubernatorial Support and Budget Success in State Legislatures," *American Political Science Review*, Vol. 62 (December 1968), 1220-31.

ernors' recommendations regarding these requests, and legislative appropriations vis-à-vis agency requests and governors' recommendations. First he measured the "acquisitiveness" of executive agencies by the agency's request for the coming budget period as a percentage of current expenditures. Then he measured the "governors' support" of the agency's request by the governors' recommendation for each agency as a percentage of its requests. He measured the "governors' success" by legislative appropriations as a percent of the governors' recommendations. Finally, he measured "budgetary short-term success" in the legislature by legislative appropriations as a percent of agency requests, and "budgetary expansion" by legislative appropriations as a percentage of the agency's current expenditures. The results for nineteen states are shown in Table 12–6.

Several interesting ideas emerge from the analysis of this data:

1. More acquisitive agencies get their requests cut down more by governors and legislatures than less acquisitive agencies. However, the more acquisitive agencies end up with generally higher appropriations than the less acquisitive agencies.
2. The governors' support appears to be a critical ingredient in the success enjoyed by executive agencies in their budgetary requests to the legislature. Legislatures respond more to governors' recommendations than to agency requests. Agencies with the largest budget expansions were those that enjoyed the greatest gubernatorial support.
3. The governors which enjoyed the greatest budgetary success in the legislature tended to be governors who could be reelected. Governors with high tenure potential were better able to elicit legislative cooperation in funding requests than those who could not expect to remain in office because of constitutional limitations on their terms.

On the basis of these findings, Professor Sharkansky was able to explore three causal models of the linkages between administrative agencies, governors, and legislatures, in determining budgetary outcomes (see Figure 12–3). The first model suggests that agency actions affect governors' recommendations which in turn affect legislative appropriations, but agency actions do not directly influence legislative appropriations. The second model suggests that the agency actions are the key inputs in the budgetary process affecting both governors' recommendations and legislative appropriations, but governors' recommendations have no real independent effect on legislative appropriations. The third hybrid model suggests that agency actions affect governors' recommendations which in turn affect legislative appropriation, and agency actions affect legislative appropriations directly. The results of causal analysis support the inference that legislatures respond more often to governors' recommendations than directly to agency actions. In other words, Model 1 was the most frequent pattern of interaction in budgetary determination. However, there was evidence that in some states the legislature does respond to a combina-

TABLE 12-6 CHANGES IN THE BUDGETARY PROCESS BY STAGES FOR SELECTED STATES

State (with year of budget analyzed)	Agency Acquisitiveness: Agency Reports as Percentage of Current Expenditures	Governor's Support: Governor's Recommendation as Percentage of Agency Requests	Governor's Success: Appropriation as Percentage of Governor's Recommendation	Budget Short-term Success: Appropriation as Percentage of Agency Requests	Budget Expansion: Appropriation as Percentage of Agency Reports
Florida (1965-67)	120%	90%	93%	84%	109%
Georgia (1965-67)	153	86	100	87	139
Idaho (1967-69)	119	93	92	86	109
Illinois (1963-65)	118	83	102	85	108
Indiana (1965-67)	123	83	103	86	112
Kentucky (1966-68)	120	90	93	84	109
Louisiana (1966-67)	121	90	101	91	110
Maine (1965-67)	114	85	108	92	109
Nebraska (1965-67)	122	87	119	104	124
N. Carolina (1965-67)	120	84	105	87	112
North Dakota (1965-67)	124	74	111	82	111
S. Carolina (1966-67)	117	96	104	99	116
South Dakota (1967-68)	136	82	98	80	109
Texas (1965-67)	128	82	104	86	117
Vermont (1965-67)	121	87	106	91	115
Virginia (1966-68)	120	97	100	91	114
W. Virginia (1966-67)	125	88	97	81	101
Wisconsin (1965-67)	115	96	98	94	111
Wyoming (1967-69)	133	69	109	75	112

Source: Derived from Ira Sharkansky, "Agency Requests, Gubernatorial Support and Budget Success in State Legislatures," American Political Science Review, Vol. 62 (December 1968), 1220-31.

tion of gubernatorial recommendations and agency actions. Model 3 was the second most common pattern of interaction. Seldom do legislatures give greater weight to agency actions than gubernatorial recommendations, as suggested by Model 2.

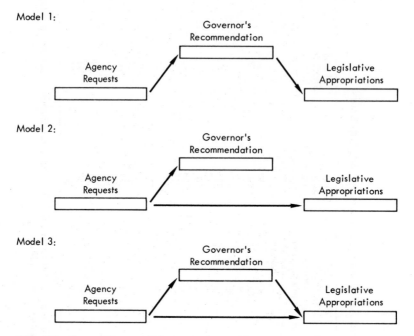

FIG. 12-3   Causal Models of Administrative, Executive, and Legislative Interaction in Budgetary Outcomes

Another study of the success of governors in passing their legislative programs in a number of states produced the following interesting conclusions: [15]

1. Governors appear more successful in competitive two-party states where they hold a *small* majority in the legislature, than in one-party states where their party holds an overwhelming majority in the legislature. We might think that the more seats the governor had to spare, the more successful he would be, but this is not the case. Apparently, the governor is better able to rally support within his own party when he has only a modest majority; when his party has a large majority, he has a more difficult time holding the support of various factions within his party.
2. A governor is more successful when he wins a large popular vote in a general election. Moreover, his success in the legislature is also closely related to his showing in the primary election. Apparently strong oppo-

[15] Sarah P. McCally, "The Governor and His Legislative Party," *American Political Science Review*, Vol. 60 (December 1966), 923-42.

sition in the party's primary indicates factionalism within the party and the resulting inability of the governor to secure the support of party members in the legislature.

SOME CONCLUSIONS ABOUT POLICY PROCESSES

Systems theory helps us to conceptualize the linkages between the environment, the political system, and public policy, but it does not really describe what goes on inside the "black box" labeled "political system." While political science traditionally concerned itself with describing political institutions, processes, and behaviors, seldom did it systematically examine the impact of these political variables on the *content* of public policy. Let us try to set forth some general propositions about the impact of political processes and behaviors on policy content:

1. It is difficult to assess the independent effect of public opinion on public policy. Public policy may accord with mass opinion but we can never be certain whether mass opinion shaped public policy or public policy shaped mass opinion.

2. There is no evidence that mass opinion is an *important independent* determinant of public policy. The masses have little knowledge of, or interest in, or opinion about, most policy questions. Research on state policy on lotteries, capital punishment, right-to-work laws, and gun control reveal very little congruence between mass opinion and public policy. Only in the field of state civil rights laws is policy congruent with opinion.

3. There is no evidence that pluralism contributes to opinion-policy congruence. There is no greater congruence between popular preferences and public policy in competitive, high voter-turnout states than in noncompetitive, low voter-turnout states.

4. Public policy is more likely to conform to elite opinion than mass opinion. Elite opinion has been particularly influential in the determination of civil rights policy. However, it is unlikely that elites can operate independently of environmental resources and demands for very long.

5. The Democratic and Republican parties have agreed on the basic outlines of American foreign and domestic policy since World War II. Thus, partisanship has not been a central influence on public policy. However, there have been some policy differences between the parties. Differences have occurred most frequently over questions of welfare,

housing and urban development, antipoverty efforts, health care, and the regulations of business and labor.

6. Most votes in Congress and state legislatures show the Democratic and Republican party majorities to be in agreement. However, when conflict occurs it is more likely to occur along party lines than any other kind of division.

7. Party influence is only effective where parties represent separate and distinct socioeconomic environments. Party voting on policy questions is more likely to occur when Democrats represent urban constituencies with strong labor groups, catholic voters, racial and ethnic minorities, and working-class groups; and Republicans represent middle-class suburbs, small towns, and rural areas. It is unlikely that party organization or ideology has much independent effect on public policy.

8. Interest groups have more independent influence on policy questions involving narrow economic interests. A rural, agricultural or non-diversified, single-industry environment is conducive to the emergence of powerful interest groups. But interest groups in urban, diversified economies also exercise great influence on specialized economic issues.

9. Acquisitive executive agencies have their budget requests cut down more by governors than less acquisitive agencies, but they end up with generally higher appropriations. The support of the chief executive is essential to budgetary requests. Legislatures respond more often to governors' recommendations than to agency requests. The most successful governors in legislative interaction are those who can run for reelection at the end of their term.

10. Governors are more successful in passing their legislative programs in competitive two-party states where their party holds a *small* majority in the legislature. Governors are more successful in policy affairs when they have little opposition in primary elections and win general elections by large margins.

BIBLIOGRAPHY

EDELMAN, MURRAY, *The Symbolic Uses of Politics.* Urbana, Ill.: University of Illinois Press, 1964.

KEY, JR., V. O., *Public Opinion and American Democracy.* New York: Knopf, 1967.

LIPSET, SEYMOUR MARTIN, *Political Man.* New York: Doubleday, 1963.

POMPER, GERALD, *Elections in America.* New York: Dodd, Mead, 1968.

SCHATTSCHNEIDER, E. E., *The Semi-Sovereign People.* New York: Holt, Rinehart & Winston, 1960.

ZEIGLER, HARMAN, *Interest Groups in American Society.* Englewood Cliffs, N.J.: Prentice-Hall, 1964.

POLICY IMPACT:
finding out what happens after a law is passed

CHAPTER 13

PROBLEMS IN ASSESSING THE IMPACT OF POLICY

Americans generally *assume that once we pass a law* and *spend money*, the purpose of the law and expenditure should be achieved in whole or in part. We assume that when Congress adopts a policy and appropriates money for it, and when the executive branch organizes a program, hires people, spends money, and carries out activities designed to implement the policy, the effects of the policy will be felt by society and the effects will be those intended by the policy. Unfortunately, these assumptions are not always warranted. The national experiences with the "war on poverty," public housing, urban renewal, public assistance, and many other public programs, indicates the need for careful appraisal of the real impact of public policy. There is a growing uneasiness among policy makers and the general public about the effectiveness and the costs of many public service and social action programs. America's problems cannot always be resolved by passing a law and throwing a few billion dollars in the general direction of the problem in the hope that it will go away.

We must distinguish between "policy output" and "policy impact." The impact of a policy is its *effect on real-world conditions.* The impact of a policy includes:

1. Its impact on the target situation or group.
2. Its impact on situations or groups other than the target ("spillover effects").
3. Its impact on future as well as immediate conditions.
4. Its direct costs, in terms of resources devoted to the program.
5. Its indirect costs, including loss of opportunities to do other things.

All of the benefits and costs, both immediate and future, must be measured in terms of both *symbolic* and *tangible* effects.

Identifying the target groups means defining the part of the population for whom the program is intended—e.g. the poor, the sick, the ill housed, etc. Then the desired effect of the program on the target group must be determined. Is it to change their physical or economic circumstances—for example, the "life chances" of blacks, the income of the poor, the housing conditions of ghetto residents? Or is it to change their knowledge, attitudes, awareness, interests or behavior? If multiple effects are intended, what are the priorities among different effects—for example, is a high payoff in terms of positive attitudes toward the political system more valuable than tangible progress toward the elimination of black-white life chances? What are the possible unintended effects ("side effects") on target groups—for example, does public housing achieve better physical environments for many urban blacks at the cost of increasing their segregation and alienation from the white community? What is the impact policy on the target group in proportion to total need? Accurate data describing the unmet needs of the nation are not generally available, but it is important to estimate the denominator of total need so that we know how adequate our programs are. Moreover, such an estimate may also help in estimating symbolic benefits or costs; a program which promises to meet a national need but actually meets only a small proportion of it may generate great praise at first but bitterness and frustration later when it becomes known how small its impact is relative to the need.

Policy impact is not the same as policy output. It is important *not* to measure benefits in terms of government activity. For example, the numbers of dollars operant per member of a target group (e.g., per pupil educational expenditures, per capita welfare expenditures, per capita health expenditures) is not really a measure of the *impact* of a policy on the group. It is merely a measure of government activity, that is to say, a measure of *policy output*. We cannot be content with measuring how many times a bird flaps its wings, we must assess how far the bird has flown. In *describing* public policy, or even in *explaining* its determinants, measures of policy output are important. But in assessing the *impact* of policy, we must find identity changes in the environment or the political system that are associated with measures of government activity.

All programs and policies have differential effects on various segments of the population. Identifying important nontarget groups for a policy is a difficult process. For example, what is the impact of the welfare reform on groups other than the poor—government bureaucrats, social workers, local political figures, working-class families who are not on welfare, taxpayers, others? Nontarget effects may be expressed as benefits as well as costs, such as the benefits to the construction industry of public housing projects. And these effects may be symbolic as well as tangible—for example, wealthy liberals enjoy a good feeling from participation in an antipoverty program, whether the program helps the poor or not.

When will the benefits or costs be felt? Is the program designed for short-term, emergency situations? Or is it a long-term, developmental effort? If it is short-term, what facts will prevent the processes of incrementalism and bureaucratization from turning it into a long-term program, even after the immediate need is met? Many impact studies show that new or innovative programs have short-term positive effects—for example, operation Head Start and other educational programs. However, the positive effects frequently disappear as the novelty and enthusiasm of new programs wear off. Other programs experience difficulties at first, as in the early days of Social Security and Medicare, but turn out to have "sleeper" effects, as in the widespread acceptance of the Social Security idea. Not all programs aim at the same degree of permanent or transient change.

Programs are frequently measured in terms of their direct costs. We generally know how many dollars go into program areas, and we can even calculate (as in Chapter 9) the proportion of total governmental dollars and the proportion of the gross national product devoted to various programs. Government agencies have developed various forms of cost-benefit analysis, such as Program, Planning, and Budgeting Systems (PPBS) and operations research, to identify the direct costs (usually, but not always, in dollars) of government programs. PPBS was originally developed in the Department of Defense under the direction of former Secretary Robert MacNamara to assist in making rational decisions about alternative weapons. President Lyndon Johnson was impressed with the results and ordered PPBS to be applied to all federal agencies. The purpose of PPBS is to calculate the unit costs of various programs, including as many indirect or "spillover" costs as can be identified, and then to calculate the unit benefits of these programs.[1] This is done by:

1. Defining the major objectives and programs in each policy area.
2. Defining the principal outputs of each program in a way that they can be subjected to precise measurement.
3. Identifying the inputs of each program in a way that they can be measured and summed.

[1] See Fremont J. Lyden and Ernest G. Miller, eds., *Planning Programming Budgeting: A Systems Approach to Management* (Chicago: Markham, 1967).

4. Computing the costs of each unit of output in a program, as well as the costs of a unit of output under alternative programs with different combinations of inputs and outputs.
5. Calculating the cost-benefit ratios associated with a program and alternative programs.

But it is very difficult to identify the indirect and symbolic costs of public programs. Rarely can all of these cost factors be included in a formal decision-making model. Often political intuition is the best guide available to the policy maker in these matters. What were the indirect symbolic costs for poor whites of the federal government's activities on behalf of blacks? What were the costs of public housing and urban renewal in the effects of relocation on the lives of slum dwellers? What are symbolic costs for the working poor of large numbers of welfare recipients? What were the costs of the Vietnam War in terms of American morale and internal division and strife?

TABLE 13-1 ASSESSING POLICY IMPACT

| | Benefits | | Costs | |
	Present	Future	Present	Future
Target Groups and Situations	Symbolic Tangible	Symbolic Tangible	Symbolic Tangible	Symbolic Tangible
Nontarget Groups and Situations (Spill-Over)	Symbolic Tangible	Symbolic Tangible	Symbolic Tangible	Symbolic Tangible
	Sum	Sum	Sum	Sum
	Present Benefits	Future Benefits	Present Costs	Future Costs

$$\text{Sum All Benefits} \quad - \quad \text{Sum All Costs}$$

$$\text{Net Policy Impact}$$

Moreover, it is very difficult to measure benefits in terms of general social well-being. Cost accounting techniques developed in business were designed around units of production—automobiles, airplanes, tons of steel, etc. But how do we identify and measure units of social well-being? In recent years, some social scientists have begun the effort to develop "social indicators"—measures of social well-being of American society.[2] This movement is just beginning; we are still a long way from assessing the impact of public policy on general social indicators or rationally evaluating alternative public policies by weighing their costs against gains in social indicators.

[2] See Department of Health, Education, and Welfare, *Toward a Social Report* (Washington: Government Printing Office, 1969); Bertram M. Gross, ed., *Social Intelligence for American's Future* (Boston: Allyn and Bacon, 1969).

All of these aspects of public policy are very difficult to identify, describe, and measure. Moreover, the task of calculating *net* impact of a public policy is truly awesome. The *net* impact would be all of the symbolic and tangible benefits, both immediate and long-range, minus all of the symbolic and tangible costs, both immediate and future. Even if all of the immediate and future, and symbolic and tangible costs and benefits are *known* (and everyone *agrees* on what is a "benefit" and what is a "cost"), it is still very difficult to come up with a net balance. Many of the items on both sides of the balance would defy comparison—for example, how do you subtract a tangible cost in terms of dollars from a symbolic reward in terms of the sense of well-being felt by individuals or groups?

THE SYMBOLIC IMPACT OF POLICY

The impact of a policy includes both its *symbolic* and *tangible* effects. Its symbolic impact deals with the perceptions that individuals have of government action and their attitudes toward it. Even if government policies do not succeed in reducing dependency, or eliminating poverty, or preventing crime, and so on, this may be a rather minor objection to them if the failure of government to *try* to do these things would lead to the view that society is "not worth saving." Individuals, groups, and whole societies frequently judge public policy in terms of its good intentions rather than its tangible accomplishments. Sociologist Edward Suchman distinguishes between policy "evaluation" and "evaluative research." Evaluation refers to the general popularity and public appraisal of a program. Evaluative research refers to systematic analysis of the real impact of a program in terms of desired results. The implication is that very popular programs may have little positive impact, and vice versa.

The policies of government may tell us more about the aspirations of a society and its leadership than about actual conditions. Policies do more than affect change in societal conditions; they also help hold men together and maintain an orderly state. For example, a government "war on poverty" may not have any significant impact on the poor, but it reassures moral men, the affluent as well as the poor, that government "cares" about poverty. Whatever the failures of the antipoverty program in tangible respects, its symbolic value may be more than redeeming. For example, whether the fair housing provisions of the Civil Rights Act of 1968 can be enforced or not, the fact that it is national policy to forbid discrimination in the sale or rental of housing reassures men of all races that their government does not condone such acts. There are many more examples of public policy serving as a symbol of what society aspires to be.

The subjective condition of the nation is clearly as important as the objective condition. For example, white prejudices about blacks in schools, in public accommodations, in housing may be declining over time. But this may not reduce racial tensions if blacks *believe* that racism is as prevalent as it ever was. Blacks may be narrowing the gap between black and white income, jobs, and housing through individual initiative and opportunity within the existing system. But if blacks *believe* that only massive government intervention in income employment and housing will assist them, this belief will become a critical factor in policy making.

Once upon a time "politics" was described as "who gets what, when, and how." Today it seems that politics centers about "who *feels* what, when, and how." The smoke-filled room where patronage and pork were dispensed has been replaced with the talk-filled room, where rhetoric and image are dispensed. What governments *say* is as important as what governments *do.* Television has made the image of public policy as important as the policy itself. Systematic policy analysis concentrates on what governments *do,* why they do it, and what difference it makes. It devotes less attention to what governments *say.* Perhaps this is a weakness in policy analysis. Our focus has been primarily upon activities of governments, rather than the rhetoric of governments.

WHY GOVERNMENTS DO NOT KNOW THE IMPACT OF THEIR POLICIES

Calculating the impact of public policy is a very difficult task at best. When this task is undertaken by government agencies it becomes impossible. Governments are very ill suited for studying the impact of their own activities. There are several reasons for this.

1. Governments pursue incompatible goals and policies at the same time. Overall policy planning or evaluation would reveal the inconsistencies of public policy and force consideration of fundamental societal goals. Since there is little agreement on these goals, such considerations would engender a great deal of political conflict. The conflict may be very bitter, because it would involve major "all or nothing" gains or losses for various groups. Government agencies would prefer to avoid such conflict, and perhaps it is best for the unity and stability of society that they do so.

2. Many programs and policies have primarily symbolic value. They do not actually change the conditions of target groups but merely make these groups feel that government "cares." A government agency does not welcome a study which reveals that its efforts have no tangible effects; such a revelation itself might reduce the symbolic value of the program by informing target groups of its uselessness.

3. Government agencies have a strong vested interest in "proving" that their programs have a positive impact. Administrators frequently

view attempts to evaluate the impact of their programs as attempts to limit or destroy their programs, or to question the competence of the administrators.

4. Government agencies usually have a heavy investment—organizational, financial, physical, psychological—in current programs and policies. They are predisposed against finding that these policies do not work.

5. Any serious study of policy impact undertaken by a government agency would involve some interference with ongoing program activities. The press of day-to-day business generally takes priority over study and evaluation in a governmental agency. More important, the conduct of an experiment may necessitate depriving individuals or groups (control groups) of services to which they are entitled under law; this may be difficult, if not impossible, to do.

6. Program evaluation requires funds, facilities, time, and personnel which government agencies do not like to sacrifice from ongoing programs. Policy impact studies, like any research, costs money. They cannot be done well as extra-curricular or part-time activities. Devoting resources to study may mean a sacrifice in program resources that administrators are unwilling to make.

7. There is generally wide disagreement about what the purposes of a government program really are. Is the object to serve as many people as possible? Or to bring about a great deal of change in the lives of fewer people? Or merely to make people happy—particularly Congressmen and other elected officials? Government administrators themselves frequently disagree about the purposes of the program.

Government administrators and program supporters are ingenious in devising reasons why negative findings about policy impact should be rejected. Even in the face of clear evidence that their favorite programs are useless or even counter productive, they will argue that:

a. The effects of the program are long-range and cannot be measured at the present time.
b. The effects of the program are diffuse and general in nature; no single criteria or index adequately measures what is being accomplished.
c. The effects of the program are subtle and cannot be identified by crude measures or statistics.
d. Experimental research cannot be carried out effectively because to withhold services from some persons to observe the impact of such withholding would be unfair to them.
e. The fact that no difference was found between persons receiving the services and those not receiving them means that the program is not sufficiently intensive and indicates the need to spend more resources on the program.
f. The failure to identify any positive effects of a program is attributable to inadequacy or bias in the research itself, not in the program.

THE LIMITS OF PUBLIC POLICY

Never have Americans expected so much of their government. Our confidence in what governments can do seems boundless. We have come to believe that governments can eliminate poverty, end racism, ensure peace, prevent crime, restore cities, clean the air and water, and so on, if only they would adopt the right policies.

Perhaps confidence in the potential effectiveness of public policy is desirable, particularly if it inspires us to continue to search for ways to resolve societal problems. But any serious study of public policy must also recognize the limitations of policy in affecting societal conditions. Let us summarize these limitations:

1. Some societal problems are incapable of solution because of the way in which the problems are defined. If problems are defined in *relative* rather than *absolute* terms, they may never be resolved by public policy. For example, if the poverty line is defined as the line which places one-fifth of the population below it, then poverty will always be with us regardless of how well off the "poor" may become. Relative disparities in society may never be eliminated. Even if income differences among classes were tiny, then tiny differences may come to have great symbolic importance, and the problem of inequality may remain.

2. Expectations may always outrace the capabilities of governments. Progress in any policy area may simply result in an upward movement in expectations about what policy should accomplish. Public education never faced a "dropout" problem until the 1960s when, for the first time, a majority of boys and girls were graduating from high school. At the turn of the century when high school graduation was rare, there was no mention of a drop-out problem. Graduate rates have been increasing every year, as has concern for the dropout problem.

3. Policies which solve the problems of one group in society may create "problems" for other groups. In a plural society one man's solution may be another man's problem. For example, solving the problem of inequality in society may mean redistributive tax and spending policies which take from persons of above average wealth to give to persons with below average wealth. The latter may view this as a solution, but the former may view this as creating serious problems. There are *no* policies which can simultaneously attain mutually exclusive ends.

4. It is quite possible that some societal forces cannot be harnessed by governments, even if it is desirable to do so. It may turn out that government cannot stop urban migration patterns of whites and blacks, even if it tries to do so. Whites and blacks may separate themselves regardless of government policies in support of integration. Some

children may not be able to learn much in public schools no matter what is done. Governments may be unable to forcibly remove children from disadvantaged environments because of family objections even if this proves to be the only way to ensure equality of opportunity, and so on. Governments may not be *able* to bring about some societal changes.

5. People adapt themselves to public policies frequently in ways which render the policies useless. For example, we may solve the problem of poverty by government guarantees of a high annual income, but by so doing governments may reduce incentives to work and thus swell the number of dependent families beyond the fiscal capacities of government to provide guarantees. Of course, we do not really *know* the impact of income guarantees on the work behavior of the poor, but the possibility exists that adaptive behavior may frustrate policy.

6. Societal problems may have multiple causes, and a specific policy may not be able to eradicate the problem. For example, job training may not affect the hard-core unemployed if their employability is also affected by chronic ill health.

7. The solution to some problems may require policies which are more costly than the problem. For example, it may turn out that certain levels of public disorder—including riots, civil disturbances, and occasional violence—cannot be eradicated without the adoption of very repressive policies—the forceable break-up of revolutionary parties, restrictions on the public appearances of demagogues, the suppression of hate literature, the addition of large numbers of security forces, and so on. But these repressive policies would prove too costly in terms of democratic values—freedom of speech and press, rights of assembly, freedom to form opposition parties. Thus, a certain level of disorder may be the price we pay for democracy. Doubtless there are other examples of societal problems that are simply too costly to solve.

8. The political system is not structured for completely rational decision making. The solution of societal problems generally implies a rational model, but government may not be capable of formulating policy in a rational fashion. Instead the political system may reflect group interests, elite preferences, environmental forces, or incremental change, more than rationalism. Presumably, a democratic system is structured to reflect mass influences, whether these are rational or not. Elected officials respond to the demands of their constituents, and this may inhibit completely rational approaches to public policy. Social science information does not exist to find policy solutions even if there are solutions. Moreover even where such information exists, it may not find its way into the political arena.

INDEX